Community as Church,
Church as Community

Community as Church, Church as Community

Michael Plekon

FOREWORD BY
Jason Byassee

CASCADE *Books* · Eugene, Oregon

COMMUNITY AS CHURCH, CHURCH AS COMMUNITY

Cascade Books
An Imprint of Wipf and Stock Publishers
199 W. 8th Ave., Suite 3
Eugene, OR 97401

www.wipfandstock.com

PAPERBACK ISBN: 978-1-7252-8753-2
HARDCOVER ISBN: 978-1-7252-8754-9
EBOOK ISBN: 978-1-7252-8755-6

Cataloguing-in-Publication data:

Names: Plekon, Michael, 1948–, author. | Byassee, Jason, foreword.

Title: Community as church, church as community / by Michael Plekon ; foreword by Jason Byassee.

Description: Eugene, OR : Cascade Books, 2021 | Includes bibliographical references.

Identifiers: ISBN 978-1-7252-8753-2 (paperback) | ISBN 978-1-7252-8754-9 (hardcover) | ISBN 978-1-7252-8755-6 (ebook)

Subjects: LCSH: Christian life. | Church. | Christianity. | Christianity and culture. | Christianity and culture—United States. | Christianity—United States—21st century.

Classification: BV4501.3 .P73 2021 (print) | BV4501.3 .P73 (ebook)

07/19/21

Contents

Foreword

EVERY TIME I READ Michael Plekon, I want to go to his church. He is an Orthodox priest, so he draws on all the traditions, sacraments, icons, and saints in that church's treasury. Yet he is neither blind nor deaf to the holiness God raises up outside his communion. He has no axe to grind against this or that outbreak of liberalism (or conservatism, for that matter). He looks hard at tangible realities, no matter how unpalatable to those of us who love the church: numbers are down, influence is down, the future looks bleak. Yet all he does is curate stories of resurrection. They will overwhelm you in this book: this or that outbreak of new life in some place where most of us would have long since written off any sort of future. God has this incurable habit of resurrection, and can't seem to help himself. Michael Plekon is paying attention. I beg you: read this book and pay attention along with him.

I worry about churches that *aren't* worried for their future. There are a few—where the numbers are flush enough and the money socked away and the programs amply subscribed. There are enough to make the rest of us jealous, at least. They can keep clicking on as if Jesus were not raised from the dead. Their future is secured. Most of the rest of us, however, are anxious about the future of the church. There is simply not enough of any of the things we think we need. Precisely here we need this book. Churches like these have no future on their own. Their only hope is in a God who raises the dead. These are the places for which I have immense hope. For the resurrection is the only thing the church has going for it in the first place.

The appeal of this book is simple: trust the local church. God is not through with it yet. In fact, that is where God does his best saving work (to echo Plekon's fellow New Yorker, Tim Keller). This book is chock-full of examples. The church will look dramatically different than its supposed halcyon days, whether those were in the 1700s or the 1950s or whenever (Plekon is plenty adept at puncturing those misremembered glories). It will be a death, a cross, an undoing of our hopes. "We had hoped he was the one to redeem Israel," the defeated disciples moaned, pouring out their misery to none other than the unrecognized risen Christ (Luke 24:21). Then there will be new life. The church will meet in a living room. Or around a dinner table. Or the church will feed its neighbors. Build affordable housing for them. Or the church will advocate for justice like never before. Raise awareness of an outrage the rest of the world missed. The church will welcome immigrants and refugees in an age bent on demonizing them. Such resurrection happening right under our noses, as we bewail our lack of future to the risen Christ, he keeps raising the dead despite our obliviousness. Plekon here has curated stories not of dozens of such seedlings, but of hundreds (one suspects he has thousands in his notes). The local church still has wisdom in its bones around how to innovate in a way that is a blessing to its non-members, resurrection to its defeated, unseeing disciples. For those bones have been breathed upon by the risen and resurrecting One.

Plekon also has wisdom for local pastors. You're failing. It's not your fault—the factors beyond our control are innumerable and insurmountable. Clergy are failures, he says, and if we will not admit this, we are liars. Strong words. They ring true. Our greatest danger is in thinking we can hustle our way out of this. Plekon also has legions of stories about seemingly "successful" churches that collapse like a house of cards. The pattern of the resurrection is unavoidable: if we carry a cross, and die with him, we will be raised into new life with him.

One of my favorite traits of Plekon's work is his willingness to name names, to list addresses. You can go and see these places. You can ring up these pastors, and marvel at the glow of new life shining in their faces. They have the surprised visage of someone who has been through death and new life and can witness this to others. The accounts are entirely falsifiable, if you can dig up evidence to the contrary. Just "come and see," as Jesus often invites us in the Gospels. The temptation in writing about the church is to stay abstract, to give general principles, to seek out timeless truths. Not here. These are actual places, specific street corners, locatable neighborhoods. The conclusion is clear: there is no reason it couldn't be yours. There is no how-to manual here. No simple steps to this or that outcome. All there is is a God of resurrection and a gathering of unlikely saints experiencing resurrection anew. My prayer is for more of this, Lord Jesus. Plekon's work gives us hope: more is indeed coming.

Jason Byassee

Feast of St. Augustine, 2020

Acknowledgments

As is always the case, there are more people to acknowledge and thank than I can adequately list here. I am thankful once again to those at Wipf and Stock Publishers who helped this book toward publication, Charlie Collier and Matt Wimer in particular. Jason Byassee was gracious in examining and then recommending the project and providing a foreword here. Tagor Vojnovic was of great assistance in suggesting Fr. Sieger Köder's work for the book cover. A number were willing to read the drafts and offer comments, criticisms, and suggestions for revision. I want to thank William Mills, Nick Tabor, John Jillions, Adam DeVille, John Hotrovich, Nicholas Denysenko, and Jeremy Ingpen, all gifted scholars, for taking the time to read the text and offer generous reactions.

A couple years ago, Cascade Books published a collection of reflections by laity and clergy on faith, ministry, and the parish in the twenty-first century. It was titled *The Church Has Left the Building,* and has led directly to the present volume. So I would like to again thank all those who contributed their experience in church and who helped bring that book into print.

I want to thank as well colleagues in ministry who shared their experience in faith, ministry, and church with me, some of it finding its way into these pages. Among these are H. Henry Maertens, Alexis Vinogradov, Seraphim Sigrist, Gary McCarthy, Christopher Savage, Stavros Winner, Rebecca Cown, Wongee Joh, David Frost, George Keith, Laura Brecht, Justin Mathews, Thomas Connolly, James Hess, Christopher Mietlowski, and John Frazier. Among those who read the text there are a number of fellow scholars. There are numerous others in the churches—Catholic, Lutheran, Orthodox, Episcopal, Methodist, Presbyterian, and more—both clergy and laity, who added to my understanding and practice of pastoral ministry. Too many to name. There are those who helped form me and have passed into the heavenly kingdom, teachers and confrères in the Carmelites like Albert

Daly and Vincent McDonald, and so many in the parishes in which I have served, also my teacher, Peter L. Berger.

Jeanne Berggreen Plekon, my beloved wife, a landscape artist of great skill, listens to my ideas and is generous in giving me time to think and work. Our children and their spouses also have listened patiently, carefully.

And to all the rest, some of whom I remember in prayer and thought, but others who I too easily have forgotten, many thanks.

Peace and all good.

Michael Plekon

The Dormition/Assumption of the Virgin Mary, 2020

Introduction:
Meal for Sinners

An Image of Communion,
Community, and Church

ON THE COVER OF this book is a painting completed by Fr. Sieger Köder. A priest and artist, he was born in Wasseralfingen in Swabia in 1925 and died in Ellwangen in 2015, having just turned ninety. During World War II, Fr. Köder was a prisoner of war. After the war, he took part in the Catholic renewal movement for Germany. His education was as a silversmith and painter, and he was also a high school teacher of the arts. Later in life he did seminary work, and in 1971 was ordained. He was a parish pastor alongside his painting and designs for stained glass, found in many churches, both in Germany and across Europe.

Fr. Köder was daring in his use of color and in the figures used for depicting scenes from Jesus' life. One can clearly see the influence of Marc Chagall and perhaps also Emil Nolde on his work, both in the boldness of depiction of persons of faith, as well as the powerful color. Köder's paintings are forceful proclamations of the word, bold imaginations of how Jesus lovingly but defiantly took the side of the marginalized, the outcasts of his society and tradition. In many of his works, the well-known scene turns into a challenge as well as a provocative confession of faith, the gospel in color. The painting on the cover of this book he did in 1973 for the Germanicum, the seminary for German students in Rome. Actually it was for the refectory of their house outside Rome, Villa San Pastore—or "the House of the Good Shepherd." The title is "Das Mahl der Sünder," the meal or supper of sinners.

It is the last supper, but instead of the twelve disciples usually depicted gathered with Jesus at table, here we have seven persons, three women and four men. We see the bread and cup of wine in the hands of the unseen host, Jesus, with other cups and pieces of bread in the hands of the guests and on the table. Jesus' hands are stretched out with the bread and cup, offering these to the guests, Jesus' friends, Jesus' community, Jesus' church. That is what this book is about.

From the marks of the nails in Jesus' hands we could take this to be the risen Lord but he is not reappearing to his confused, grieving disciples in first-century CE Jerusalem. Out the window to the right is the nearby town, Gallicano, the Villa San Pastore being located just outside the village. On the pathway up to the house are rocks, stones on which to stumble. The path is not smooth. What comes from being at this meal is not easy. This supper of the Lord is not yesterday in the distant past but right here and now. Jesus offers the bread and cup of himself in communion to these friends, but who are they?

Starting on the right is an African man, his arm bandaged, blood stains on what could be prisoners' clothing. Does he represent those oppressed in the developing countries, those who are the victims of racism and hatred, people caught in power struggles or condemned and tortured because they fought for justice?

Next is a well-dressed woman, likely upper class. Perhaps she has a country estate nearby. She is one who in looking round the table is shocked and maybe even frightened by her fellow guests. She has nothing in common with them in terms of income or dress or education or ethnicity. Yet there she is, invited to the feast, sitting along with them. The bread and cup are extended to her. She is a sister of them all.

On her right is an intense, bespectacled young man. Is he an artist, a writer, a political activist, a student, or a protestor? Is he one of those reviled today as "radical leftists," "thugs," one of those who only finds fault with and "hates" his country? Does he too wonder why he is here, since he is "done" with religion? As for church, he belongs to "none." Likely he too is bewildered at being invited to this group.

The clown appears in many of Köder's paintings. The clown is here too, in the classical sense of the one whose mask signals laughter but covers over tragedy and sadness. The clown is the one who can poke fun at the high and mighty, as in the song of Mary, the Magnificat. The clown reminds us that all the emblems of power and beauty are fleeting, temporary, incapable of bringing peace. Only compassion can do that and the clown does no harm to anyone.

Bent over, possibly trying to hear the words of the host about the bread and cup and what they are is an old woman, poor, likely handicapped in some way, and surely poor. She may not have a home except what she can find in the streets among other homeless folk. She has only what she can beg and scavenge, but here she is, invited to a feast, with the bread of life and cup of salvation, with more than enough to sustain her.

And her dining companion is the woman in red, made up, almost too pretty, like so many sex workers along the road out here in Rome and on the streets of every city. She offers sex for pay, her body the only commodity she has to sell in order to support herself and likely children or parents or siblings. She would never be invited to a wealthy person's home except for—her wares. But she is a welcome guest here. And her clutching her cup to her chest says she is deeply moved by what the host is saying and offering, boundless love.

Lastly we encounter a face full of longing, searching passion, even pain. Someone who has suffered for truth. Perhaps a rabbi or pastor, or a poet or writer, but most likely a seeker. He is the only one grasping his piece of bread and cup with intensity. He seems to know it is a meal that will sustain him, a new life.

We do not read only suffering and need in the faces. Somehow by being invited as guests, they are becoming a community, a household, the people of God. The host, Jesus, looks at them with forgiveness, not judgment. His face is reflected in their faces and perhaps a little in the cup of wine he extends to them. This is the house of love and service. All are sisters and brothers. Maybe we would not invite such people to our homes, but as in the parables of great feasts, Jesus tells us that this is what it looks like to follow after him. This is what church is—communion, community with Jesus and with each other. On the back wall of the room where the guests are seated are the outlines of another parable: the loving Father and the lost prodigal son. The parable confirms what the table is all about, community as church, church as community. And the force of Fr. Köder's image becomes even clearer when one knows where the painting, a massive one too, is located. It hangs in the dining room of a seminary where future priests and their teachers share the table beneath it.

There is a place for us at this table, as in the great icon of the Trinity by Andrei Rublev. But where will you sit? Where will I sit? Wherever that is, it will be in community, in church, with sisters and brothers and the Lord.[1]

---

1. For this reflection, I am indebted to the meditation on this painting of Fr. Köder by Fr. Pius Kirchengessner, https://www.pius-kirchgessner.de/07_Bildmeditationen/8_Neues-Testament/Mahl.htm.

CHAPTER 1

Community and Church, Church and Community

The church is the communion
of the whole world.[1]

First, Church

ONE HAS TO START with Jesus in talking about the church. This goes without saying. Or does it? I myself have heard others balk at being asked what Jesus might say about a particular church situation. "Don't bring him into it. This is about the chain of command, the rules, tradition."

I think Rowan Williams knows something about Jesus and the church. A priest for over forty years, almost thirty years a bishop, formerly archbishop of Canterbury and leader of the world Anglican Communion, a prolific writer and professor at both Oxford and Cambridge, one suspects he knows a bit about both Jesus and the church.

Williams has a striking description of how all we know and can say about Jesus comes into being. This is talk about Christ, "Christology" being the technical term. What we know of Jesus is by no means just the product and preserve of academic specialists—theologians, in their books, papers, and lectures. At the end of a challenging study about what we can know and say about Christ, Williams is suddenly clear and simple.

Forget all the schools of thought and doctrines of the past two thousand years. Williams places us right in the midst of a community on a Sunday morning. People are singing, praying, listening to the Scriptures being read; they are gathered around the bread and cup and then carrying what they receive into their homes, schools, workplaces, everywhere, in everyday life.

1. Augustine, *De Unitate Ecclesiae* II.3 (PG 43:434).

1

All that can be said about Jesus is embodied by the community who continue to follow after him:

> Christology, in short, is "done" by the Church; it is done in the practice of a community that understands itself to be the Body of Christ, a group of persons living and acting from the conviction that human community is most fully realized in the unconditional mutuality which is represented by the language of organic interdependence. Christology is done in the practice of lives that embrace their finitude and materiality without fear, lives that enact the divine self-identification with those who endure loss, pain, and contempt. Christology is done in a practice of prayer and worship that does not approach God as a distant and distinct individual with a will to which mine must conform—as if in a finite relation of slave to master—but acts out of the recognition of adoptive filiation and the intimacy that flows from this. It is done when we see that the doing of God's will "in earth as in Heaven" means that the eternal will of God is for the life of the world—that God is "satisfied" when our flourishing is secured.[2]

In other words, if you want to know who Jesus is, anything important about him, go listen to and go look at those who follow him. They will either tell you all you want to know—or send you running as far away from them (and Jesus) as you can get.

At a time when so many congregations are challenged by decline, shrinkage, and the difficulty of attracting and keeping members, is there a good reason for a book about church?

The point of all that follows here can be put very succinctly.

While church is many things—and community, likewise, includes a great deal—church is essentially the communal experience of God and each other and the area. Church is the household or family of faith: those who are the people of God. And then, the communication and actions of God and God's people.

Or, the church is best defined as community. Hence the title of this book. We know that church entails community, but I want to argue that church is best understood as a communal reality, as community.

---

2. Williams, *Christ the Heart of Creation*, 250.

The "Rediscovery" of Church

Religion has been defined as something an individual believes and practices. Accent individual. Alfred North Whitehead put it this way: "Religion is what an individual does with his solitariness."[3] "Belief," often described as adherence to various doctrines or teachings, is the very heart of religion. But such an individual focus ignores most of what passes for religion, what is visible, namely ritual, sacred texts, places, and feasts, not to mention rules and histories of important figures and events. In other words, religion is far from an individual pursuit but inherently communal, shared, touching every aspect of life from the economy and political order to food and family, marriage, sexuality, and of course birth and death.

It might seem peculiar that with "church" being such a common expression of public and group religiosity that somehow the communal core would have been eclipsed or forgotten. Yet many agree that there was a profound and transforming "rediscovery" of the church in the last century. The appearance of the ecumenical movement, early in the twentieth century, due to many clashes of churches in missionary efforts, is seen as a crucial impetus for reflecting on what divides and what unites Christians.

Looking back, it is clear that the ecumenical meetings held in Edinburgh in 1927 and Lausanne in 1937 and which led to the formation of the World Council of Churches (WCC) in 1948 were more than academic gatherings. In these meetings, there were powerful experiences of other Christians as sisters and brothers. Old stereotypes and divisions had obscured much of the faith that was still held in common. The sheer diversity of these gatherings, including for the first time many of the Eastern churches, was also a recognition of the global expanse of the gospel, moreover its inculturation in a stunning array of languages, music, liturgies, art, and customs. Instead of being divided Christians, disciples of Jesus began to experience that they were all one in the Lord and in the church.

In subsequent decades, the liturgical movement and the broader "return to the sources" (*ressourcement*) of the liturgy, Scriptures, early Christian writers, and saints was also part of the rediscovery of the church. This is not the church of canon law or the church of bishops or that even of dogma and doctrine. Rather it is the ancient, scriptural sense of church as "the people of God," as a communion or community rooted in baptism that does not simply wash away the sin of each individual but reveals all as sisters and brothers in the Lord. Nicholas Afanasiev described this as "eucharistic ecclesiology." Thus, "the eucharist makes the church and the

---

3. Whitehead, "*Religion in the Making,* 16–17.

church makes the eucharist," as Henri de Lubac put it. The church and eucharist are the gathering and action of all.[4]

Rediscovery of the Church in the Early Church

Nicholas Afanasiev (1893–1966) was a specialist in the church councils and the canons or rulings they issued. He also studied the liturgical rites and history of the church as well as the New Testament and early church writings of the apostolic and patristic periods. He was a renaissance scholar, an expert in so many areas. In his major study, he returned to the church of the first few centuries in order to establish the essential components of the Christian community. While even into the twentieth century, in both the Western and Eastern churches, the church was defined in terms of the councils, the canons, the bishops, and the church's organizational, that is, institutional structures, Afanasiev took a more basic approach. It was one that had been promoted by an ecumenical array of scholars from the late-nineteenth into the twentieth centuries, many of these being students of the liturgy, its origins, and development. Variously known as *nouvelle théologie* or the *ressourcement* movement, it included renowned figures such as Yves Congar, Henri de Lubac, Jean Daniélou, Louis Bouyer, and Hans Urs von Balthasar, to name a few.

Afanasiev, following the Acts of the Apostles, the apostolic letters, and the postapostolic writings, rediscovered the church as community. He saw the church not essentially in the great patriarchates and state-derived apparatus of dioceses and provinces but in the local assembly, the community of baptized believers. The gathering, the assembly of the people of God, defines and expresses what the church is. The people gathered around the table of the Lord. They were united in prayer, the reading and preaching of the Scriptures, in giving thanks, in the breaking of the bread and the sharing of it and the cup. This was not only a cultic gathering but a community which in turn spread their good news and engaged in the doing of works of lovingkindness.

Afanasiev stresses that by baptism there was a consecration of the faithful, the laity, to be prophets, priests, and kings. There was no original separation of priests and laity. The community identified leaders from their number, set them apart, and ordained them. These eventually became the ministries of bishop, presbyter, and deacon. The chosen and consecrated leaders remained members of the community and the relationships were

---

4. Lubac, *Splendor of the Church*, 133; Afanasiev, *Church of the Holy Spirit*; McPartlan, *Eucharist Makes the Church*.

ones of reciprocal love and service. At the conclusion of the first volume, *The Church of the Holy Spirit*, Afanasiev makes a forceful claim that the only power or rule in the church is that of love, not law (*vlast' lyubvi*). Later, law emerged as the framework of the church's structure and life. What had originally been a sacred community became divided into those with sacred characteristics due to ordination, the leaders of the church. Below them, inferior to them, subordinate as well to them, were the former "priesthood of the baptized," the laity (*laikoi*) Afanasiev describes. To be a lay person or *laic,* as Afanasiev puts it, is not merely to be nonordained. The laity are the general priesthood of the church, the bishops, presbyters, and deacons called out from among them and set apart for specific ministries. Every Christian has a ministry.

There were important local variations, and in these early centuries as yet neither a clerical caste nor the dominance of law was universal. Though convoked by imperial decree, the ultimate authority was the council, where bishops as well as clergy and lay people convened to make decisions for the church, both doctrine and practice. In time, both clericalism and law would reshape the churches. Afanasiev said he had only uncovered the original "eucharistic ecclesiology," the communal and sacramental pattern of the early church and the realization that the church was not its rules or law, not the hierarchy of its ordained leaders or the monastics, not even just the details of worship or the sacred texts or great witnesses, but persons of faith. The church was all of these, since it was a body, the body of Christ, a "communion" (*koinonia*), a community in communion with the Lord and with each other and the world. In New Testament terms, the only law in the church was that of the "new commandment," to love one another.

Toward the Church and the Parishes of Today

As we proceed here, I believe it will become clear that what Rowan Williams and Nicholas Afanasiev set before us are far from being just academic visions of the church. Already, their concentration on the communal nature of church, the concrete local church in the parish, the shared nature of worship, witness, and service—these are the essential elements of a congregation, the ways in which a community of faith gathers and then reaches out to the world around.

In reviewing Afanasiev's vision, we have the fundamental components of the life of every congregation, those in the early church as well as today. Diana Butler Bass noted the leading characteristics of vital parishes in a book based on a Lilly endowment project on Congregations of Intentional

Practice, conducted from 2002 to 2005. Looking for congregations that seemed to have found ways to renew themselves and speak to the world, she inventoried several ways in which this vitality was manifest.[5] Vital parishes and communities of faith showed hospitality not only to those visiting on Sunday who could be prospective members. They considered themselves to be part of the surrounding neighborhood and its people, part of the world they were to love and serve. Such parishes were places of healing, discernment, and diversity. They were supporters of justice in their larger areas, aware that their efforts in helping to feed, clothe, shelter, and protect those in need was the most powerful witness to Christ they could offer. Their sacred space and their worship were beautiful, able to sustain the transformation that is the life of the people of God. Parishes were doorways into the kingdom.

Another way of looking at these markers of renewal and faith was to say that a community is a fellowship of prayer, study, service, and connection to others—all the other detailed aspects being included. Contrary to critics who would fault him for concentrating on the eucharist, or on fellowship, or neglecting the distinctive place of the ordained, Afanasiev observes that in the early church, the local assembly incorporated all of the aspects just mentioned. The local church was not just a place of cult, like the temples in the Roman empire. There were living communities of women and men who continued to carry their faith into the neighborhoods in which they lived and worked. They reached out in charity to assist not only their members but others in need. They were not administered top-down, by the clergy, as in later centuries, but in a conciliar, communal manner.

I raise the salience of these basic characteristics of not just the ancient church but also the congregation now very deliberately. As we look at many examples of parishes that face the demographic and other changes of the twenty-first century in this book, it is striking how those that find a way to continue, no matter the form, to revive, resurrect, and reinvent themselves will have these elements as the components of their *koinonia*, their community, which is the heart of everything being looked at here. As the pastor of one of the parishes I know in-depth told me, there is no magic, no recipe, no tricks, no manual to follow, and it is surely not the accomplishment of the pastor alone—it is the resurrection of the life of the body of Christ, the people of God, the community of faith in a particular place.

Far from being a curious theological detour, Afanasiev's vision had already been seen and enacted at least in its documents by the reforming Moscow council of 1917–18. Like some early councils, it brought together

---

5. Bass, *Christianity for the Rest of Us.*

not just the bishops, but also the clergy, monastics, and laity. Hyacinthe Destivelle brilliantly describes how all sorts of traditional versus progressive impasses and clergy-laity conflicts were transcended by "conciliar" structure and procedure. Despite his reservations about some aspects of this council, I believe it was part of the impetus for Afanasiev's conviction, at the start of his scholarly life, that the church was essentially a community—something, of course, clearly there in the New Testament. His research while still at the university in Belgrade, under the supervision of Russian historian A. P. Dobroklonsky, rooted him in the communal nature of the church, whether at the level of the councils or that of the local church, the parish. Marianne Afanasiev, his wife, detailed the "genesis," as she calls it, of his vision of the church as a community, a eucharistic one, that is, shaped by both baptism and the gathering around the eucharistic table.[6] Much of this came from his own experience, as a parish priest in Bizerte, Tunisia, during WWII. He was known and loved as a pastor, a spiritual leader, and not just by his tiny Orthodox community but by other Christians and Muslims. His own pastoral experience connected him with the church of the first centuries, ecclesiology in action, incarnate. The other principal inspiration for Afanasiev's thinking was the greatest Orthodox theologian of the twentieth century, Fr. Sergius Bulgakov, dean of St. Sergius Institute. Bulgakov also rediscovered the eucharistic core of the church as well as the eschatological dimension, that is, the church as the experience of the kingdom here and now and a foretaste of the age to come.[7]

The local communities continued the patterns established by the apostles and earliest missionary disciples. Only much later did church and empire merge—the church of the Byzantine and the Roman courts becoming the "great churches" of East and West, and the churches of smaller local and national territories and peoples. It is not surprising that Afanasiev's work was the only piece of Eastern Orthodox scholarship cited in the study documents of Vatican II. That council's dogmatic constitution on the church, *Lumen gentium*, reflects the "eucharistic ecclesiology" Afanasiev revealed from the church's first four centuries. Later on, others would also emphasize such an ecclesiology. In the Western church, Tillard and others focused on a "communion of communions."[8] Zizioulas, while criticizing some of what he believed were Afanasiev's claims, also envisioned a eucharistic ecclesiology.[9] Despite

6. Afanasieff, "La genèse de 'L'Église du Saint-Esprit,'" 13–23; Afanasieff, "Nicholas Afanasieff (1893–1966) Essai de biographie," 99–111.

7. There is a considerable Bulgakov opus and secondary literature, but the major study of the Paris theologians is that of Arjakovsky, *Way*.

8. Tillard, *Church of Churches*; Tillard, *Flesh of Christ, Flesh of the Church*.

9. Zizioulas, *Being as Communion*; Zizioulas, *Eucharist, Bishop, Church*.

what some critics say, Afanasiev never reduced the church to the celebration of the eucharist. Neither did he neglect the importance of the assembly's consecrated leaders nor diminish the fundamental place of baptism—all of which are covered in *The Church of the Holy Spirit*.

More recently, Cyril Hovorun has presented a critical vision of how church structures have developed over the centuries, usually under state/political and social influence, not just theological impetus.[10] Hovorun brilliantly sketches the ever-developing institutional frameworks that called themselves "church." Rather, the perspectives church leaders showcase are often legitimations for political positions and state policies. He provides ample illustrations from the past as well as from the Russian Orthodox vision of a "Russian world" (*russkiy mir*) in our time. The large, amply funded church networks of today are far cries from the small, loosely organized churches that met in the houses of Andronicus and Junia, Aquila and Priscilla and Lydia, in the locales of Thessalonica, Corinth, Ephesus, Colossae, and Galatia.

All too often, we think we know what the "authentic" church was, the "primitive church" of the apostles and their immediate successors. Reformation church Christians in particular have believed that stripping away what seem to them to be the accretions, the merely "human traditions," of the past two thousand years, will bring us right back to the purity of the Acts of the Apostles and the communities planted by Paul and other apostolic wanderers. Even there, as Raymond Brown pointed out some time ago, "the churches the apostles left behind" were diverse in structure, self-understanding, and more often than not in conflict with their founders or with each other.[11] Hovorun and, in a more epic manner, Diarmaid MacCulloch force us to accept that the church has been just about whatever emperors or bishops, kings and mystics and theological intellects, not to mention fanatics as well as rank-and-file members wanted it to be.[12] Aidan Kavanagh created the famous "Mrs. Murphy" in his vision of liturgy as the first theology (*theologia prima*). She is the devout if not learned soul in the pew who knows what she believes and thus can tell truth from fraud in the liturgy, in the clergy, and in all that can be called "church."[13]

Even now, after the Reformation, the Renaissance, the Enlightenment, the Industrial Revolution, and the nuclear era, the question of how

---

10. Hovorun, *Scaffolds of the Church*; Hovorun, *Political Orthodoxies*; Hovorun, *Meta-Ecclesiology*.

11. Brown, *Churches the Apostles Left Behind*.

12. MacCulloch, *Christianity, the First Three Thousand Years*.

13. Kavanagh, *On Liturgical Theology*; Taft, "Mrs. Murphy Goes to Moscow."

the church is best defined and described continues to produce disagree-ment. A half century after Vatican II there is a strong and often vocal movement across some of the churches away from a communion or con-ciliar model to an essentially hierarchical one, a very top-down arrange-ment with bishops at the top, laity all the way down at the bottom—a pyramid often the best model. One also continues to see splintering of church bodies among the Anglicans, Lutherans, and Methodists, usually over conflict issues such as the status of LGBTQ people, their ability to be members or marry in religious services. But conflicts also have resulted in new divisions over the ordination of women as well as alleged deviations from historical church teaching on Christ, on the unique status of Chris-tianity. In other church bodies, political positions unify as well as divide: the evangelicals are currently experiencing conflict within themselves on where they stand in an America under Trump.

The church may insist it remains in an unbroken connection with Christ and the community of disciples who followed him, continuing his presence and work after his departure. Whether one leans on the "apostolic succession" of ordained ministers, whether they are called bishops, pres-byters/elders/priests and deacons or other names, or whether, as in recent ecumenical documents, one speaks of a broader tradition passed on—the "apostolic continuity" of ministers, Scriptures, baptism, eucharist, and other sacramental actions, church historians and students of liturgy recognize that just as now, so also in the first centuries, diversity accompanied unity. And, as will be seen within this book, older models of the local church or parish no longer are sustainable. New forms, reinventions, adaptations, and more have been discovered and implemented.

But looking too intensely at the church and its structures risks for-getting or minimizing the world in which it has always existed. Hovorun's efforts as well as those of others like MacCulloch constantly keep in focus the kind of state, economy, society in which churches live, and the symbiotic relations between church and world. In what follows here, the focus will move back and forth between church and world but will remain on com-munity, as a gathering that people both want and need.

But there will be a particular vantage point at work. This is the shrink-age, the decline in membership and thus in financial support and in activities of parishes of all church bodies here in America in the past decades. This trend seems to be continuing now and into the forseeable future. As will be noted, the reasons why parishes are changing dramatically are many and complex. The conviction that the shrinkage is due primarily to lack of belief could be argued from ongoing research that shows the number of nonpar-ticipating, also nonbelieving Americans, is growing, and not only among those under forty years of age. In the course of this book, there will be a look at the reasons. But the primary claim I want to make here is that for all the change, church is one of the increasingly rare locations for the experience of community, and community in a number of different ways.

Community

Community, it seems, is everywhere—and nowhere. There have never been more networks linking people together. But we often seem to be alone on our phones, or in our ever-longer workdays, or miles away from family. However, it would be an exaggeration to claim we are all lonely and yearning for togetherness. Some of us have more than enough of the "other," always "on call" by management or by our own devices. And the pressure to belong, to conform, to be constantly scrutinized—these are bits of the past we are happy to lack.

American philosopher Josiah Royce has been called the voice of connection and binding and even before Dr. Martin Luther King Jr. spoke of "the beloved community" crucial to our existence. Royce was singular among American writers of the nineteenth century in celebrating our nature as creatures who craved community because we were social beings.[14]

Robert Putnam, on the other hand, is but one of a number who see it differently.[15] He has argued that many of the ways in which we connected to neighbors and friends have disappeared or become much weaker. Bowling leagues and local teams are replaced by intense sports programs for our kids. The town and school networks that supported athletic teams and scholarships are not always there anymore. Many parents find fundraising is now the new normal for uniforms, transportation, and other parts of sports and band and the arts in their children's lives. The ability to travel and select where we spend free time has made neighborhood haunts like taverns and restaurants less likely to be where "our gang" regularly congregates.

However, his studies over the last two decades keep turning up examples where frayed, torn community is restored, made whole and vital again. There are no surprises about how this occurs. It is through coalitions for educational betterment, through unions, associations of healthcare professionals and librarians, and yes, even sometimes through local politicians. And omnipresent in the restoration and maintenance of community are churches, synagogues, masjids, and the communities within these and

14. Brooks, "Your Loyalties Are Your Life."
15. Putnam, *Bowling Alone*; Putnam, *Better Together*; Putnam, *Our Kids*.

across the lines of faith communities for local needs such as food, housing, legal aid, childcare, and better schools.

As we will see later, many observers and students of communities of faith note the profound demographic changes, also the economic and political shifts in our time that have left overwhelmingly negative impacts on membership and participation in congregations. Looking back at decades of data, Mark Chaves says one can only read the trends of the last fifty years for religious congregations as decline. And it is not surprising for American problem-solvers and their ingenuity that the number of efforts to reinvent one's community, to find different ways of being a parish, are many and diverse. Later chapters will look at a selection of these.[16]

But while many students of American religion see decline, others also detect persistence if not some vitality and growth. My teacher, Peter Berger, after years of watching Western societies become more secularized, and interpreting this in a larger theory of secularization, eventually changed his mind.[17] This was based on a number of countertrends and instances. A principal one was the work of scholars who show just such persistence and even expansion, not only among Muslims but among Christians and in all kinds of different locations internationally. One of these scholars, Nancy Ammerman, has, with her associates, tracked the dynamism of congregations and the presence of faith not just on Sunday and feast day services but in every activity.[18] Others, like Sally K. Gallagher, Nicholas Denysenko, and Ricky Manolo, have examined the tenacity of religious belonging in their observations of individual communities.[19] They have also shown that communities of faith, even when faced with decline, have been able to find ways to adapt and restructure themselves and survive, even as new and different entities.

As a sociologist of religion, I have long been a student of parishes and how they have changed. Raised in a church-going family and having been in ordained ministry for almost forty years, I also know congregational life from the inside, having served as a priest, alongside my academic work, in five different parishes. As a layperson and a pastor, I have worshiped and participated in Byzantine and Roman Catholic, Lutheran, Episcopal, Methodist, Presbyterian, and Eastern Orthodox churches.[20]

16. Chaves, "Sociologist Looks at the Church in America," 10–11; Chaves, *American Religion*.

17. Berger, *Desecularization of the World*; Berger, *Many Altars of Modernity*.

18. Ammerman, *Congregation and Community*; Ammerman, *Everyday Religion*; Ammerman, *Sacred Stories, Spiritual Tribes*.

19. Gallagher, *Getting to Church*; Denysenko, *People's Faith*; Manolo, *Liturgy of Life*.

20. Plekon, *World as Sacrament*.

While community has changed a great deal across the social landscape, perhaps nowhere have the changes been as profound and permanent as in congregations. Many ethnic-based parishes long ago lost their identity as the children and grandchildren of immigrants moved away and married out of their ethnic communities. Many congregations were historically located near factories, mills, mines, and other places of industrial employment. Those workplaces have disappeared, in many places, along with the jobs in them. Thus many have been left with little opportunity to work and support a family. This is true not only in "rust belt" manufacturing and mining areas but also in urban sectors where entire neighborhoods have undergone gentrification after earlier blight.

Probably the most significant manifestation of the demographic changes affecting parishes is the disappearance of multigenerational families, families whose roots and legacies spanned decades and provided an ongoing continuity of memory and identity in a community of faith. This disappearance is largely rooted in the general mobility in American society from the beginning of the twentieth century, but it finds expression, intense expression, in the life of a congregation. No longer does one find grandparents, their children, their grandchildren, and possibly great-grandchildren as the core of a community. Young adults continue to relocate for higher education and, whereas in earlier decades they would have returned to marry, set up homes, and have children, they have for decades now been going where the jobs are.

In addition to the disappearance of multigenerational families, there is the near disappearance of the forty and under cohorts, people in child-bearing and rearing years. Researchers and surveys, especially Pew, have been following the growth to over 30 percent of "religious Nones" among those forty and younger, a figure that grows with every new survey. These are individuals who, while they may believe in God and pray, do not belong to any congregation or participate in one regularly.

I have seen these two patterns of disappearance displayed most vividly in every parish in which I have served. At the parish where I worked for over twenty-five years, photos of those who were present at the liturgy on the feast of the patron saint are important records of demographic change. In one, taken not long after we arrived in 1995, sixty-seven children are present, a little less than half the total number of parish members in the group photo. Of those children, my own two now-adult children included, only eight still live near the church and of these, two are in some way active. A similar group photo today would show an even smaller number of adults, say seventy or so to the earlier 100. But there would be fewer than ten children in the photo.

Not long ago I came across yet another parish feast photo from this same congregation, but this from 1970, the first year the community was in its present church building. Of the fifty or so persons posing in the photo, more than half were younger children, with a few teenagers. Given the parish's founding just a few years earlier, in 1964, this is an especially important snapshot in the congregation's history. Of those twenty-five young people from 1970, none have remained in the parish. Only a handful, perhaps four or five of the adults in the photo, now all in their eighties and nineties, are alive and still in attendance at services and other parish activities. I have seen virtually the same disappearances of multigenerational families and of people under the age of forty, including children, at the first parish I served upon ordination thirty-eight years ago. That parish is now only a fifth the size it was in 1983.

Organizations that study religious behavior and collect data on it, in particular Pew, have come to call those who have no regular belonging or participation "Nones." For the population as a whole, the Nones are at 34 percent, and higher if one looks at those forty and under, around 23 percent for all age groups. And the numbers will continue to rise.[21]

The dwindling presence of younger adults, traditionally seen as the "future" of the parish and of the large church body, is a major demographic change. Not surprisingly, the other is the aging of membership. In one parish I know well, the pastor buried thirteen people in a year and their heavenly departure was accompanied by the relocation of another half dozen or so to assisted living, skilled nursing facilities, or simply to be closer to family as they became more frail. Such changes thus make one of the foundations of congregations in the past increasingly rare, namely multiple generations of a family present and active in parish life.

As the title of a collection of reflections I recently contributed to and helped edit puts it, riffing on an Elvis line, "the church has left the building."[22] This description bears a lot of different meanings, all the way from disappearing older as well as younger people to the increasingly unsustainable situation of large, almost cathedral-like sanctuaries, as well as educational and fellowship buildings and rectories. But as this volume will show, "leaving the building" as it was in the past does not necessarily mean the church is gone. Rather church, that is, God and the people of God, are able to move to many new houses, many different homes.

In the chapters that follow, the aim will be to explore further why communities of faith are shrinking or, in some cases, disappearing either in part

---

21. Riess, "Religious 'Nones' Are Gaining Ground in America."
22. Plekon et al., *Church Has Left the Building.*

or as a whole (ch. 2). The reality of course is not as secularization theory earlier framed it. Religion is not becoming extinct, no matter how much decline there consistently has been.

Thus, we look at several kinds of communities. We will examine ones that seem to have regained life, been revived. These are "destination" or niche communities that call into question the more dominant pattern of decline by their vitality (ch. 3). We will look at a number of parishes in the middle chapters of the book (chs. 4–6). Over against the grim, some would say pessimistic, consideration of why congregations are shrinking and declining, it is also necessary to look at parishes that are reviving, resurrecting themselves, repurposing not only their buildings but their communities to connect with the surrounding neighborhood, to serve different functions there, while at the same time being the body of Christ, the presence of God's kingdom in American cities, towns, suburbs, and rural areas. It is not too much to say that in some cases, these parishes have reinvented themselves, and in so doing moved to a new and different way of being a community of faith in the twenty-first century.

Every faith community is an organic fellowship, constantly changing even if it has a history of 200 years or more. Thus, the situation of most parishes remains tentative, fragile. The usual question of where a community sees itself in five or ten years no longer is one that can be answered with any certainty. Yet one does see signs of life even in buildings that may have but a fraction of their former membership. Survival, as one pastor keeps insisting in his preaching and conversation, is really not the appropriate goal or motivation for one's theology or Christian action. The largely prevalent denominational hopes of rebirth or revival are usually both in terms of bodies and bucks, that is, increased membership and giving. But reinvention and revival often do not include either. My gathering of examples of communities reviving, reinventing, or repurposing themselves must be seen as communities in process. Whatever we see of them is a kind of snapshot, a view at a given moment. Their stories develop in time. We are often preoccupied by the narratives of thriving communities, often very large congregations. For the most part, these are held up as success stories. The smaller, less spectacular efforts usually get little or no coverage. This is why in addition to some more typical success stories, a number of smaller efforts deserve a look and will receive it here.

Looking past the fear of demise of parishes, we will look at the many things such communities can do (ch. 4). The complicated, often less obvious, lives of these communities yield some surprising stories of persistence and strength. The question of the viability of small communities will be examined, parishes smaller even than the "pastoral" congregation of fifty to 150 members. The "family" parish of fifty or fewer active members is the kind of small church I am referring to here (ch. 5).

Lastly, I will address visions for parishes going forward in the twenty-first century. This is captured in Loren Mead's absolutely basic question: What is a parish, what is the local church for? Mead, Sam Wells, and Andrew Root, among others, have reflected on both what a parish is and what a parish does. And to ask what a parish is for necessarily entails asking the same question about pastors. While the whole of the book is a search for what community and ministry look like in practice today, in the end, there are questions, aspects of both, especially pastors, that are beyond the scope of the present volume. That, for me, often has meant another project. One thing leads to another. But we will give some attention to pastors, their formation and work.

Back to the parish. Rather than mirroring the social arrangements of a monarch or squire and the local subjects, the economic situation of an agricultural society in a bounded area, the parish of back then, of the last one thousand years, simply cannot be—in fact, is not—the parish of today. Further, rather than being a refuge for souls battered by difficult conditions in life and fearful of punishment after death, parishes are about what Jesus referred to as "abundant life." But I mean nothing disparaging here by saying "refuge." For indeed, parishes are refuges in the range of meanings this label can have. The church, as we'll see from St. Stephen's in Philadelphia, is one of the last remaining places where a soul can walk in, sit, or even lie down, be safe, at peace, reclaim quiet, be fed by the sacred images on the walls and in the windows, pick up a prayer book or Bible, talk to someone who will listen, and perhaps participate in a short service. Maybe even get a cup of coffee or a snack. I remember when I was a child that most churches were open on ordinary weekdays and we were encouraged to "visit" God in his house. The church was an oasis, a little taste of another world—the smell of the wax candles, the leftover aroma of incense, light streaming in through the stained glass. It was maybe the most beautiful and peaceful place in the neighborhood.

The parish church building from another era and outlook can stand as a witness to the transcendence of the gospel beyond political and cultural clashes, even beyond aging, sickness, and death. The parish, really the community of God's people, becomes one of the few places and ways in which we can be in communion with one another. It is more a bridge to our lives in the world than a "mighty fortress." As one colleague and pastor, David Frost, has put it, the dominant vision shaping the existence of many declining parishes is a "survival theology." Many strategies are employed to keep the roof and the heat on, to keep the building open, even if for a handful of members. If so, what kind of life does "survival," if only for a few more years, mean?

In reflecting about "community as church," then, the effort here is not to identify the most effective experiments in retooling or reinventing discovered by parishes across the country. This would be a return to some of the simplistic, not to mention spiritually empty, dreams of the "recipe" literature on the "church growth" movement of a decade or two past. It is not the intent here to tease out the best strategies to revive declining or dying parishes. Nor are we after the lingering elements of past parish life that need to be replaced. The Willow Creek megachurch experiment of the past twenty years comes to mind. The original aim there seemed to be removing everything people said they disliked about church. These were replaced by an imitation of suburban corporate headquarters for their sanctuary and other buildings. Willow Creek was cutting-edge in their reliance on marketing strategies for their efforts to attract those no longer much interested in church membership. Installing huge screens in historical church spaces has happened in the UK and elsewhere, for projecting words of hymns and scriptural lessons and worship leaders. Such moves are now in eclipse in many places. However, the actual attempts of laity and clergy to continue being the people of God, the body of Christ as a community in a locality— the wager here is that we can learn a great deal from them.

Some Things about This Book: Sources, Ongoing Lives, and More

As readers will quickly notice, the majority of references to congregations and what they have done to revive, redefine, replant, or repurpose themselves and their buildings are not published articles and books. Rather, they are links to serious pastoral and theological websites like *Faith & Leadership, Leadership Education at Duke Divinity, Religion News Service* (which gathers material from many other sources,) *Alban* (Institute) *at Duke Divinity School*, and to periodicals such as *Divinity* of Duke Divinity School, *The Christian Century, National Catholic Reporter, Commonweal, America, The Church Times* (UK), among others. Other links are to the websites and Facebook pages of congregations profiled. Research sources include the *Pew Research Center*, the *US Congregational Life Survey, National Congregations Survey, Faith Communities Today/American Congregation* studies, and a variety of websites specializing in the reporting of research on congregations and pastoral formation and ministry.

If the reasons for this are not immediately obvious, then here is some explanation.

The congregations examined here are works-in-progress. Even the linked reports on them are mere snapshots, views at the moment when the author of the article visited and interviewed members and observed parish activities, how space was being used, how worship and other community actions took place. As living communities, the body of Christ in place and time, the congregations will have changed by the time you read about them and what they have done to renew themselves. As I worked on the book, here and there I came upon a newer piece that updated what had transpired, things like transition of pastors, relocation, changes in how buildings were being used by neighborhood groups, and in some cases, the congregation ended its existence, moving to a new name and identity, new ways of being a community of faith.

One such case is Reconciliation Services (RS), originally based at St. Mary of Egypt Orthodox Church in Kansas City, Missouri. Justin Mathews, a former intern in my parish and friend, had succeeded the priest who founded the parish as its rector. Not long ago, Mathews stepped down in order to work full-time as RS executive director and as a liaison with other nonprofit groups as well as the local government and the private sector. In stepping down as pastor, Fr. Justin's "parish" expanded significantly, now encompassing not just the Troost Avenue neighborhood but all of Kansas City. Also within the past couple years, a major new project opened and is thriving at RS. Named for the founding pastor's deceased wife, who used to feed hungry people right in her own apartment, "Thelma's Kitchen" opened as a "pay what you can" eatery, with culinary chefs and students teaching culinary skills and preparing meals and with customers either paying what they could or exchanging other work and services for meals. This is the story of a parish becoming much larger and more connected to its community than anyone could have expected or planned.

In many of the congregations we will inspect, we'll hear the story of a journey and changes along the way to bring the congregation to where it was at the time of writing. Grace Episcopal Church in the Berkshires is just such a case. When two parishes in neighboring towns sold their buildings, prayer and study and conversation led to those members forming a new congregation, one which uses an events space for Sunday services and fellowship and maintains a small office and chapel in a local strip mall during the week. The merger not only joined two previous parishes and their histories but also enabled new outreach and work to come into being.

So a caveat. All the congregations you will read about are indeed on pilgrimage. What you will see of them is but a snapshot, not the ongoing record. They are communities in process or works-in-progress. This appears to be a remarkable feature of congregations in our era; namely, that they are in transition all the time and will continue to change. Of course, a historical perspective quickly reminds us that such was the case in the first fifty or 100 or, in some cases, the first 200 years of a community's existence. I take it as a given that some readers will either reject what they see in these congregations' efforts to reinvent, repurpose, and revive themselves. But I am sure still others will seize upon them as models for what needs to be done in their own parishes and elsewhere.

As natural as these reactions are, one thing is clear. None of the parishes surveyed are put forward as models of what to do. This is not a "recipe" book or "how to revive your congregation" manual. Far from it.

What I aim at here is reflection

1. on what "church" and "community" really are, hence the title;

2. on the complicated tangle of factors behind decline and shrinkage of congregations;

3. on how many congregations—those surveyed, as well as others—have revived themselves, that they are first and foremost communities and behave that way;

4. on what the church is *for*, both laity and pastors; that is, what are the reasons for being, for continuing as communities in the locations where they are based?

This may appear strange, given the millennia of Christian history and presence. But many of the political, cultural, social, and economic functions the church has served have vanished or are disappearing rapidly. The parish can no longer unquestioningly follow the model of a homogenous group of people, in either an urban or rural location, that remains there most of their lives. This is no longer an agricultural society of small, tightly knit communities composed of very similar people, ethnically and religiously. No longer is the mind and imagination of people completely open to the transcendent, the otherworldly, the sacred. Rather, as Charles Taylor argues, there is an "immanent frame" in which we seek answers only from science, only from reliable information, from empirical data. The self is "buffered" from the world of angels, demons, and saints.

Too often, those writing and speaking on the current state of congregations get stuck on secularism, or on the lack of faith or social reaction to the positions churches have taken, not to mention the abusive behavior of clergy. What we have come to in the secular age is irrevocable. Only sectarian, artificial efforts return one to a *status quo ante*, an imagined superior age of the church. Some of the harshest critics of Pope Francis give evidence of this in wanting to recreate a Catholic Church before Vatican II, complete with the Tridentine Latin liturgy as well as a culture that saw itself as the only church and had no meaningful connections with other churches, Protestant or Orthodox.

My own teacher, Peter L. Berger, as mentioned, famously "changed his mind,"[23] as *The Christian Century* series called it, on secularization. The Islamic world, Pentecostals in Latin American, and all kinds of Christians thriving in Africa and even in the Far East challenge the hypothesis of secularization. Except that across North America, and Western as well as Eastern Europe, even where churches are allegedly thriving, the participation of the overall population in them is very low, in the single digits. Russia is an important example, but there are many others.

How to make sense of apparently contradictory positions? Berger, Jose Casanova, David Martin, and Taylor have all attempted to do so. However, this is not the primary focus here. All that follows is based on the fundamental character of Christianity as communal. The well-known saying, often attributed to Tertullian, is relevant: *Unus christianus, nullus christianus*—"there can be no solitary Christian." While Andrew Root is right, along with Kaya Oakes and others, that those with no belonging and participation in religious communities often demonstrate significant faith, an authentic spiritual dimension, and that most acknowledge a reality or god greater than themselves and, most importantly, choose to do good, many also search for belonging, for community.

Not just from the Christian tradition and the Scriptures, not also just from the understanding of the Christian life as ecclesial, that is communal, but also from my perspective in the social sciences, I see the social, that is, communal, nature of a people as fundamental. Durkheim associated it with the very solidarity that enabled humans to live. He said that religion was indeed a social phenomenon, but what is more, society was a religious phenomenon. The history of Christianity, like that of Judaism and Islam and the rest of the world religious traditions, are the histories of communities, also histories of families, economies, and political relationships. So what is offered, echoing Durkheim, is an exploration of community as church, and church as community.[24]

23. Berger, *How My Mind Has Changed*.

24. Durkheim, *Elementary Forms of the Religious Life*.

CHAPTER 2

America's Changing Face(s)

Disappearing Communities, Why People
Don't Go to Church

Parishes and People: Data

SEVERAL YEARS AGO, THE US Census Bureau alarmed many by revealing that within the twenty-first century, certainly by 2060 if not considerably sooner, the United States would no longer be a predominantly white country.[1]

There is a parallel to this diversification of America in terms of religion. America will very soon no longer be predominantly Christian. A Public Religion Research Institute (PRRI) survey shows that.[2] What is more, recent Pew Research tells that Americans know very little about other faiths. But then, they also know little about their own tradition and community of faith.[3]

It well may be that the anti-globalism, anti-immigration, nationalist feelings of the Trump base as well as other American groups stem from the ever-deepening realization that this is a highly diverse society. Arlie Hochschild documented this in great detail in her study of a Louisiana "parish" or county. Accompanying this broader demographic research is the accumulating study on the shrinkage and decline of religious communities and religious belief and participation. Robert Wuthnow has been a prolific commentator on the surging resentment of rural Americans.[4]

---

1. Colby and Ortman, "Projections of the Size and Composition of the U.S. Population."

2. See Shimron, "Legacy Ministries to Dying Churches."

3. Banks, "Americans Have Limited Knowledge."

4. Hochschild, *Strangers in Their Own Land*; Wuthnow, *American Misfits and the Making of Middle-Class Respectability*; Wuthnow, *Small-Town America*; Wuthnow,

Mark Chaves, the leading interpreter of religion's trends in America, offers a sobering assessment. Looking back on numerous studies for over fifty years, Chaves argues that the data can only be read as documentation of continual decline. This decline is neither dramatic nor abrupt, rather it is steady and continual.[5] His principal source is The National Congregation Study (NCS), now up to its third wave of surveys, the last released in 2015. Data collection for the fourth wave started in 2018.[6]

While Landon Schnabel and Sheldon Bock feel that the most religiously committed and active Americans are persisting in their faith, Chaves and colleagues think otherwise. In an even more recent study with David Voas, Chaves does not diverge from this conclusion. While not as marked as the decline of religion in western Europe, the state of religion in America is nevertheless in steady decline too.[7]

These sociologists of religion look at the same indicators of intense religion—strong affiliation, regular attendance, how Scriptures are interpreted (intensity coupled here with literalism), ties with evangelical communities, and daily prayer (at various times). Chaves and Voas find decline in the first three of these indicators since 1973. Although the decline is not steep, it is within 3–4 percent. The decline appears to be generational and, as will be noted repeatedly here, the disappearance of multigenerational families in local congregations is a major indicator as well as cause of congregational decline.

We may still think of America as a religiously active country, but Gallup found in 2018 that only half of Americans belong to a church, synagogue, mosque, or other community. By 2020, it was only 47 percent. This may be the most solid indication that America no longer stands out as more religious from Europe. The decline has been cumulative but decisive. Membership in a church or other religious organization remained at 70 percent or so throughout the 1970s. However the last twenty years have seen a 20 percent decline.

What is the single biggest factor in the decline in church membership? Gallup researchers point to the ever-increasing number of "religious Nones," that is, those with no connection to a community of faith and

Remaking the Heartland; Wuthnow, *Left Behind*; Riess, "New Study of Millenials and GenZ Points to a 'Massive Realignment.'"

5. Grant, "Great Decline"; Chaves, "Decline of American Religion?"; Chaves, *American Religion*.

6. See Chaves, *Religious Congregations in 21st Century America*.

7. Voas and Chaves, "Even Intense Religiosity Is Declining in the United States"; Schnabel and Bock, "Persistent and Exceptional Intensity of American Religion"; Shimron, "Is American Religion Exceptional?"

who make no contribution to them of any sort. But even those with some identification with religion have withdrawn from membership in churches or other kinds of religious communities. The article uses a figure of 19 percent for American adults with no religious affiliation. More recent research has put that figure up to 23 percent. While a small figure, Gallup also found that, among Americans who express some religious affiliation, 9 percent do not belong to any church.

And, while there is decline across different population cohorts such as Traditionalists—those born prior to 1945—then Baby Boomers (born 1946–1964), Generation X (1965–1979), and Millennials (1980–2000), the youngest have far and away the lowest church membership. Millennials come in at 25 percent, Xers at 40 percent, Boomers at 57 percent, and Traditionalists at 68 percent.[8]

Different church bodies also have different membership numbers. Catholics show higher rates of decline, from 76 percent twenty years ago to 63 percent now. Protestant decline is from 73 percent to 67 percent. The drift away from established denominations to nondenominational churches produces the answer "Christian" rather than "Baptist," "Lutheran," or "Methodist," but Gallup found such nondenominationals less likely to belong to a congregation than those who identified with a particular church body.

Overall, the picture Gallup presents is essentially what we will see sketched here. While some religious leaders and even a few researchers continue to argue for a distinctive, robust situation for religion and religious communities here, Chaves and most other researchers challenge such a view. No matter the age group, the area of the country, the political affiliations, income or education levels, the trend is one of decline in religious affiliation and membership. Jeffrey M. Jones, in reporting on the Gallup numbers, concludes that a significant pervading factor is the eroding confidence in religious organizations and their leaders. The continuing revelations of clerical sexual abuse and financial malfeasance only heighten the distrust and outright repulsion felt by the population.[9]

The findings of the three waves are what we have seen already. Congregations are aging, particularly predominantly white ones. The number of nondenominational parishes is increasing, likely indicating decreasing "brand loyalty" to the church body in which one was raised. The average congregation shrank again, according to the last wave of surveys, to an average of seventy members and an annual budget of $85,000. Just over half

8. See "In U.S., Decline of Christianity Continues."
9. Jones, "U.S. Church Membership Down."

(61 percent) of all congregations are led by a full-time pastor/leader, but the number of part-time clergy who also work at other professions continues to climb, as do the numbers of lay people who share church leadership and parish work with a member of the clergy. Greater diversity in the patterns of pastoral ministry are evident despite 61 percent of all congregations having a single pastor. Where part-time clergy service a parish there is much greater lay participation in the leadership and work of the parish. Later on, we will see a number of intriguing examples of congregations in which members have taken on their baptismal "ordination" as priests, prophets, and queens/kings of the kingdom. Whether there is a part-time pastor—one with a "day job," that is, or full-time employment alongside ministry—women and men no longer see themselves as merely followers but leaders in pastoral care, worship, administration, and outreach. And while there are still relatively few parishes able to financially support one or more assistant or associate pastors or other professionals in music and education, these larger congregations are now accounting for ever-growing numbers of all members of congregations. The largest congregations amount to only 7 percent of all parishes but account for over half of all membership.

About 10 percent of congregations have multiple sites, but the number is growing. The most frequent form of congregational social outreach (52 percent) is food assistance: food banks, pantries, soup kitchens, collections of food for community center distribution, etc. The issues on which congregations are most likely to lobby political leaders or engage in protest or activism are poverty, abortion, and LGBTQ rights. And from one wave of surveys to the next, greater acceptance of LGBTQ rights is evident.

So, even touching on just the most salient findings of ongoing NCS research, clearly there is a great deal of change that is, from any standpoint, positive and constructive. The important study by Putnam and Campbell underscored the growing tolerance in many directions—gender, sexual identity, race, and ethnicity—as perhaps the most constructive and attractive element of change in American religious communities, along with growing ethnic diversity and compassion for those in need.[10]

But the same study also noted political use of religion and divisions along political, class, and racial and ethnic lines as what continues to drive people from membership and activity in congregations. Since this study, however, other researchers we cite here point to increasing economic inequality, partisan media reporting, and political manipulation of information as deepening division in American society, as well as congregations. Numerous

---

10. Putnam and Campbell, *American Grace.*

commentators see in this the cause of further estrangement from communities of faith on the part of Americans, particularly those forty and under.

Why Do They Leave? Why Don't They Come?
Looking at the Numbers

I realize that whether one employs graphs or numbers, some readers will want to flip through this chapter as quickly as they can or just move on. Numbers are not as fascinating as the stories of congregations we will hear soon. But while numbers cannot capture some aspects of the changes taking place for congregations, they do make clear just how profound, how serious, and how real these changes are.

When attempts are made to explain why congregations are shrinking, why there are so few people under the age of forty in them, as well as what happened to multigenerational families, the effort to make sense can head in numerous directions. It was only a decade or so ago when the Pew Research surveys shocked us by pointing out the rising number of religious "Nones." Originally somewhere close to 20 percent, the number has steadily climbed to around 34 percent for younger Millennials and 36 percent for older. And this is no longer, as it was at first, a trend among Millennials. It is to be found across all age cohorts in the US. Overall, for the entire population, the number of the religiously unaffiliated Nones, those for whom religious identity is atheist, agnostic, or "nothing in particular," has risen to 26 percent, this being a jump from 17 percent in 2009.[11]

When Pew started reporting on religious Nones a decade or so ago, there was a response bordering on shock and disbelief when the number of those with no membership in a congregation, no active participation in services or financial support, and no particular belonging to a church tradition or denomination was reported. One could read reactions to this as a wake-up call, but also as the empirical verification of unbelief, secularism, or even the decline of values or morality. None of which, as it turns out, is at all accurate. Kaya Oakes is but one of many who listened carefully and respectfully to the Nones, hearing their own stories of religious disillusion and how they distanced themsevles from extreme religious positions, and even escaped abuse. It is not possible to write off the Nones as being without any spiritual roots. Most survey research shows they do believe in God, pray, and have strong moral positions. However, as in many other aspects of life, they are not big joiners. The reasons why Nones do not

11. See "In U.S., Decline of Christianity Continues."

identify with or attend churches are varied. The same is the case for those who once were members of a congregation or church body but now no longer are—religious "Dones."

A conference at Fordham brought together authors referenced here such as Oakes, Ryan Burge, and Tara Isabella Burton, author of a recent study on alternative religion and spirituality among the Nones, and also Pew Research scholar Alan Cooperman. The conference focused on the steady rise of religious Nones and the inability of churches to come to grips with this.[12] Cooperman echoed Pew findings presented in the chapter, but noted that 35 percent of Millennials and 29 percent of Xers identify as nonaffiliated, with the last ten years seeing an increase of 30 million not connected to any religious community. As with Robert Putnam, he and Burge both felt the connection of religion to conservative politics was a factor in driving more progressive younger people from churches. Possibly the decrease in marriage rates are also a factor, as well as the waning effects of needing to pass religion on to one's children or returning to it in later life, with aging and loss looming.

Kaya Oakes was most perceptive in her contributions at the conference, as she was in her study. Having trained in spiritual direction at Berkeley with the Jesuits, she has had to turn away Millennials who want spiritual accompaniment in their lives. She also noted that would-be evangelizers of the Nones, such as Catholic Bishop Robert Barron, show little understanding of or experience with younger adults. Barron rather sounds as though the Nones were to blame for their distance from the church. In my work as a parish priest, I have watched young adults, including my own children, disappear from church. The majority of those who grew up in the parish where I have served for the last twenty-five years have relocated for education and work. The few who still live in the area do not come. Major holidays, of course, bring young adults "home," both to parents' houses and to their old parish, as do "rites of passage" such as baptisms, weddings, and funerals. And I have heard quite a few horror stories of young adults trying to join another parish, only to find an ethnic enclave or a tightly enclosed clique or a legalistic pastor who presented obstacles. Thus in my other life as a professor teaching undergraduates, I often found a deep sense of a spiritual life and commitment to doing good. So I flinch when I hear clergy appeal to Millennials to return to church to see all they have been missing!

The Fordham conference underlined, among other realities, what Oakes and other researchers have consistently found; namely, that being unaffiliated with a congregation and not identifying with a particular church

12. Manson, "As US Nones Increase"; "In U.S., Decline of Christianity Continues."

body or tradition is not equivalent to atheism, lack of a spiritual sensibility, or animus towards all things religious.

A look at belief on the part of the Nones indicates that about 19 percent have their own ideas about God or a higher power, the majority subscribing to a more traditional, biblical God.[13] Religious Nones, according to Ryan Burge of Eastern Illinois University, in the General Social Survey (GSS) released early in 2019, now make up 23.2 percent of the population, an increase from 21 percent three years ago. What is significant is that the Nones are now the same size as the Catholics in America (23 percent) and the evangelicals (22.5 percent)—actually, a little larger. As evidenced in other studies, the mainline Protestant churches have seen the biggest decline in numbers.

But this new finding suggests that down the line, the political clout of evangelicals may be waning. Well into the Trump administration, a number of evangelicals have parted ways with him and the Republican party. The editor-in-chief of *Christianity Today*, Mark Galli, published an editorial calling for the president to be removed from office.[14] Nones are typically center-to-progressive regarding social, cultural, and political perspectives. However, in 2016, 26 percent of the electorate were evangelicals. Burge attributes this turnout, one that is higher than their share of American churchgoers, to their age and race—predominantly white.[15]

More recently, Burge has pushed his inquiry further. He looked at data from the GSS and found more to support what we are seeing here.[16] While in the 1970s, 38 percent of Americans attended church weekly or more (another third never or rarely, and the remainder occasionally), already by the 1990s, this pattern was starting to change and the percentage of those attending began to decline, a trend that only accelerated the closer we came to the present. But what really was provocative to Burge was the life and writings of the late Rachel Held Evans.[17]

She documented her upbringing in a rigorous evangelical church where questions and doubts were not allowed. Religion brought, or at least it should bring, certainty. Evans describes her painful exodus with her husband from this absolutist Christianity and the rupture in family relations it caused them. Noting the growth of the Nones, Burge sees in the GSS data that half of these still believe in God in some way. So, echoing

13. Oakes, *Nones Are Alright*; Oakes, "When Americans Say They Believe in God."
14. Galli, "Trump Should Be Removed From Office."
15. Jenkins, "Nones Now as Big as Evangelicals and Catholics in the US."
16. Burge, "Age of Nones May Favor Churches Who Welcome Doubters."
17. Evans, *Searching for Sunday*.

Evans, he wonders what kind of churches would still be even remotely possible locations for those who are None or Done due to the overwhelming pressure to be certain. Clearly, it is churches that are open enough to allow doubt and questions.

Yet, as Burge knows, across the churches, not just in evangelical ones but now among many mainline ones—Catholic, Methodist, Presbyterian, Lutheran, Eastern Orthodox—a wave of neotraditionalism has emerged, a desire not just to assert unchanging doctrine but also to attack divergence from and questioning of beliefs. The decision of the United Methodist Church (UMC) in January 2020 to split over unresolvable differences regarding the status of LGBTQ people in the church and ministry is one example.[18] This split, due to the Covid-19 pandemic, has been postponed at least until 2022.

The recent Pew Research only confirms the pattern described here.[19] The report says 65 percent of Americans identify as Christian, this a decrease from 77 percent ten years ago, while the percentage of religious Nones is up to 26 percent. There are now more Americans who say they attend services just a few times a year or fewer (54 percent), which is more than those who go once or twice a month (45 percent). Of those identifying as Christian, the percentage attending once or more a month is the same as a decade ago (62 percent). While 84 percent of seniors, the "Silent Generation," identify as Christian, only 49 percent of Millennials, those born between 1981 and 1996, do. Thus, the pews in houses of worship are less populated by the disappearing elders and are not being filled by the next generation or the one after that. These and other findings, such as that a third of Democrats are Nones as opposed to 16 percent of Republicans, come from Pew's yearly political survey work. Even among those who identify themselves as Christian, the decline progresses.

Belief in God characterizes 80 percent of those surveyed as opposed to 19 percent who say they do not believe. Those who believe in God as described in the Bible are 56 percent of those surveyed. Another 23 percent say they believe in some kind of power or spiritual force, but not the God described in the Bible. Of those who say they do not believe in God, 9 percent still believe in some kind of higher power or spiritual force. The numbers remain high when it comes to those who try to communicate with God (75 percent), though 47 percent admit God does not reply. Seventy-seven percent of Americans, again, according to Pew Research, believe

18. Hodges, "Diverse Leaders' Group Offers Separation Plan"; Gilbert, "Panel Offers Peek behind Scenes of Separation Plan."

19. Shimron, "Pew Report."

God has protected them. Sixty-seven percent feel God has rewarded them, and 61 percent feel God will judge people's actions. Many surveys find a high level of personal belief in God, also of reaching out to God in some manner. This is individual behavior. Yet religion is a highly communal reality, despite the still-widespread notion of its intensely personal character.

But why are people distancing themselves from church? Other Pew Research suggests that up to half (49 percent) are distanced from participation in church because they don't believe, while another fifth (20 percent) simply dislike organized religion and nearly another fifth (18 percent) are unsure of what they believe or what churches profess.[20] Sixty percent of those who don't have anything to do with organized religion say it is because they question religious teachings. Not surprisingly, 49 percent are opposed to the stances religious groups take on social and political issues. Forty-one percent simply do not like religious organizations, while 37 percent don't believe in God and 36 percent find religion irrelevant.[21]

What of those who continue to go to church? Of those who go to church once a month or more, 81 percent say it is in order to be closer to God. When further queried, they say that they experience this in religious services in various ways. Sixty-nine percent of regular worshippers indicate they attend for their children's moral and religious education, while 68 percent say it has helped them be better people. Sixty-six percent worship for comfort in times of trouble or sorrow. One would be hard pressed to find anything startling in these findings. On the other hand, for those who do not attend on any regular basis or rarely, almost four in ten (37 percent) say they practice their faith in other ways, outside of churches and services. Twenty-eight percent say they don't attend because they no longer believe in God, and 23 percent have yet to find a house of worship they like.[22]

Jean Hopfensperger, whose articles on religion in Minnesota and the heartland we will continue to hear from in later chapters, notes that younger Catholics who have drifted away from the church have done so for the same reasons as the Pew surveys found for the general population. These include losing belief in God, disagreement with church teachings on social and political matters, and disillusionment with the organizational church and its leaders. John Vitek of Saint Mary's Press in Winona, Minnesota, a major publisher of Catholic texts, commissioned a study from the Center for Applied Research in the Apostolate (CARA) at Georgetown

20. See "Why America's 'Nones' Left Religion Behind"; "Broad-based Declines in Share of Americans Who Say They Are Christian."

21. Alper, "Why America's 'Nones' Don't Identify With a Religion."

22. See "Why Americans Go (and Don't Go) to Religious Services."

University of Catholics ages fifteen to twenty-five. Just over 200 subjects were included in a random sample survey with fifteen personal interviews. The disagreements with church teachings had to do with same-sex marriage, contraception, and abortion, among other issues, and half said they were searching for spiritual homes and practice more in harmony with their outlooks.[23]

Even if one looks beyond Pew and the other major research centers on religion in America, the picture of the decline is the same. Allen Downey of Olin College looked at the General Social Survey and found that the increasing trends of religious Nones would most likely continue and the percentages grow larger in future decades, the growth in distancing from religious organizations having increased significantly from the 1980s to the present.[24]

There appears to be a spectrum of decreasing comfort with religion across birth cohorts. It would seem the younger the population, the less experience they have with traditional faith and community, and more likely they are to be igorant and suspicious of these as well. Yet once more, one cannot simply dismiss these young people as without any spiritual sensibility.

At Forbes, Zara Stone works off the Barna Group's reporting of 59 percent of Millennial Christians leaving church within a decade of turning twenty-one. In the HBO series *Silicon Valley*, a web developer who is gay is inadvertently outed—as a Christian! But while one could say that Bay Area people have "church PTSD," with over 60 percent not having anything to do with church or services, there is a whole other dimension, one that now has become almost a caricature.

The Persistence of Things Spiritual

While institutional religion is in serious decline, this is not so with all things spiritual. Enter entrepreneur Tara-Nicholle Nelson, who is developing *Soul-Tour*, a hybrid social network app and offline community for the spiritually hungry who are turned off by traditional religion. Mainline churches and other religious organizations have been seeking very similar doctrine-light but ritual-rich spirituality projects for some time. These range all the way from a Gregorian chant celebration of the office of Compline in cathedrals and large urban churches to retreat centers that offer open, eclectic programs for meditation, yoga, silence, and walking labyrinths. Pilgrimages, with the

---

23. McCarthy and Vitek, *Going, Going, Gone*; Hopfensperger, "Study Shows Why Young Catholics Leave the Church."

24. Johnson, "US Is Losing Its Religion Faster than You Think."

Camino de Compostella as the basic model, and nondenominational quiet days can be found from Rhinebeck, New York's *Omega Institute,* to numerous Ayurveda centers. Monasteries have also opened their retreat facilities, making sure that membership in a church body or adherence to doctrines are not necessary for experiencing monastic practices such as corporate prayer, meditation, meals in silence, and spiritual "companioning"—a kind of ancient spiritual "coaching."[25]

Along with malls, small-town stores are closing in the face of big-box outlets, and small-town school districts are shrinking and further amalgamating. It seems as though the same trend of contraction and disappearance is also facing churches. This kind of economic change is now occurring rapidly enough that we are often momentarily stunned to see photos of abandoned and deteriorating shopping malls, with their food courts and multiplex cinemas, hair and nail salons and endless strings of national brand stores. Of course, this is not the case everywhere, but where malls could not match new shopping locations, especially grouped around Costco, Home Depot, Best Buy, Whole Foods, and the like, the older structures soon lose tenants and start to appear dated and dilapidated. The same, of course, has happened with the veritable temple-like edifices on old main streets that once were our libraries, post offices, and banks. Recently I was struck when in a new version of a shopping center near Los Angeles, one store was a "vintage" grocery store that resembled the mom-and-pop delis and tiny A&Ps of my childhood.

Nostalgia works for many Baby Boomers who are attracted to diners and candy stores with soda fountains that hearken back to the 1950s. But this does not happen so often with historical brick-and-mortar houses of worship. On a trip to an arts festival in upstate New York with my wife, a *plein air* painter, I had an opportunity to observe this process of urban change and decay closely. Cortland, New York is a county seat that, despite the presence of a State University of New York campus, has many empty storefronts and shabby multiunit dwellings, all advertising for student housing.

Once the major town in a predominantly agricultural county, it retains all the noble public buildings and grand mansions that were built with its prosperity in the late-nineteenth and early-twentieth centuries. The rural areas surrounding Cortland had dairy farms. Other farms produced feed crops. The town itself became a center of manufacturing, home to Brockway Motor Company and Wickwire Brothers Mill, a leading producer of window screens. There was Durkee's, a large bakery that supplied much of Central

25. Stone, "How a Spirituality Startup Is Solving Silicon Valley's Religious Apathy"; Brinius, "Why These Americans Are 'Done' with Church, But Not with God."

New York State, and Smith-Corona typewriters, the last big manufacturer to close. What was remarkable to me, as I walked around the downtown area, where the banks, post office, country administration buildings, and shops were located, was the array of magnificent stone churches from every denomination imaginable—Presbyterian, Methodist, Episcopal, Baptist, Roman Catholic, Unitarian. These are spacious, beautiful structures, some from the nineteenth, others from the twentieth, century, with sprawling educational and social buildings. Several had important historical connections with the Underground Railroad and the Women's Suffrage and Abolitionist movements. But as I toured them, I was struck by how many were sitting completely closed, one or two boarded up, with others now joined to other congregations. This is a pattern visible across the country, from major urban centers to small towns. Many factors, as we are seeing, contribute to these changes, of which the closing of churches is but one.[26]

It is possible to put a better construction on the shrinkage of congregations, as Ryan Stewart does, echoing Ed Stetzer of *Christianity Today*, Union Seminary president Serene Jones, and writer Held Evans, among many other observers of American religion today. Shrinkage is surely what we are seeing, but may it not also be a dying in order to rise new and more authentic? Could it be that the imposing church buildings of Cortland or Seattle or Minneapolis—all locations we will visit—are not just expressions of fervent faith? I believe that like the many cathedrals across Europe and the innumerable small parish churches that are lovingly photographed on the Facebook page *Churchcrawling,* these are holy places, sanctified by centuries of prayer, preaching, baptism, eucharist, marriages, and funerals. But as the nineteenth-century Danish hymnwriter, reformer, and bishop N. S. F. Grundtvig puts it, each one is, at root, an "earthly dwelling place for a heavenly guest," echoing King Solomon's prayer when he consecrated the first Jerusalem temple.[27]

The empty pews that can be seen in every church building and the closed churches all across the country signal more complicated trends, more complex changes. The "culture wars" that have raged for decades now have not just evoked fierce stances from adherents on opposing sides. As Peter Beinhart observes, a surprising diversity and number of Americans are "done," finished with religion. These are people who pride themselves on their conservative values, who oppose big government, despise political elites, and are repulsed now by universities and learning. One could argue

26. Marty, "Malls, Small-Town Stores Are Closing."

27. 2 Chr 6:3–21. Allchin, *N. S. F. Grundtvig*; Stewart, "Is It Good or Bad When Churches Shrink?"

that their resentment is principally due to their economic displacement and decline, to their abandonment by corporations as far as employment and pensions go, by banks, and, of course, the government, at every level, for ignoring their troubles. Thus it is easy to target immigrants and people of color for their impact on jobs, values, stability, and to idolize political figures who claim to be "swamp drainers" and anti-politicians, Trump a principal example. But as various observers from Arlie Hochschild to Charles Murray and J. D. Vance note, many of these white, less-educated, and resentful citizens have little to do with church. They experience broken marriages and families, suffer from addictions, and are just as messed up as any of those they suspect and dislike. As John Judis points out, appeals of populism and nationalism antedate the Trump administration. Recall the rhetoric as well as the perspectives of the Tea Party and Freedom Caucus and, further back, of Pat Buchanan and Newt Gingrich.[28]

Beinhart also recognizes that the secularizing effect reaches across traditional and progressive boundaries. Black Lives Matter employed none of the black church symbols or language in their protest. Ta-Nehisi Coates likewise explicitly describes his alienation from the black church and its vision, so fundamental to African-American culture and community.[29] The thoroughly secular campaign of Bernie Sanders is yet another example, along with the delicacy with which religion was treated both by Barack Obama and Hillary Clinton, though both were churchgoers who did not shy away from drawing on biblical sources. I have been struck by the pervasive secular character of many fellow Boomers I encounter, especially in the desert town I live in for half the year. These are politically progressive folks, well educated, many having been professionals in the medical, educational, information, and engineering fields. The number of those others is impressive. Some are committed to outreach to the community in ESL tutoring, volunteering as teaching consultants in the arts in math and the local schools. Still others are practicing artists, as my wife is. Others staff the local food banks and chamber of commerce. There was a sizable turnout for a women's march the day of Trump's inauguration and there have been regular gatherings at the traffic circle in protest of Trump's policies. Some indeed were raised in church and synagogue. Few now belong to any or attend any congregations, except for the Christmas concert and for the "rites of passage." For them, religion needs neither house of worship nor doctrine. Rather, their spiritual lives are expressed in serving the neighbor in need,

28. Judis, *Populist Explosion*; Judis, *Nationalist Revival*.
29. Coates, *Between the World and Me*; Coates, *We Were Eight Years in Power*.

acting to protect the environment, being politically active, and remaining informed. Communities of faith serve no purpose for them.[30]

To take one more look at people leaving church and why they are leaving, a brief glance at Stephen Bullivant's study of Catholic disaffiliates and disaffiliation since Vatican Council II is useful.[31] Bullivant's work is a thorough inspection of the data of those who have stopped attending services, those who no longer belong to parishes and in some cases do not engage in spiritual activities. Vatican II is seen as not just a watershed event in church history. In the eyes of many commentators, Bullivant as well, the Council's many changes to the place of the laity, its promotion of the ecumenical outlook of the church toward other churches and faith traditions, and in particular, the changes instituted to liturgy appear to have resulted in mass exodus of members rather than an *aggiornaménto*: an update or renewal of faith and life.

However, as one of the most influential expert theologians at the Council, Dominican Yves Congar, argued that the secularization process and the drift away from the church—not just the Catholic Church—preceded the Council and was in evidence even in the 1930s, if not earlier.[32] If one considers the patterns of decline and shrinkage being examined in this book, these patterns are to be found almost everywhere, in all churches, whether Catholic, Orthodox, or Protestant (namely those of the various Reformations of the sixteenth century). While it can be claimed that some of the liturgical changes promulgated for the Catholic Church by Vatican II found analogous changes in other church bodies, for example the Anglican, Lutheran, Methodist, and Presbyterian churches, it is difficult indeed to credit those changes of more accessible language and more emphasis on Scripture and communion and participation of the worshipping assembly to the massive fall off in attendance and belonging and belief. Priest and sociologist Andrew Greely, likewise with Congar, felt the decline and shrinkage was tied up with larger social, cultural, and political factors.

And while Bullivant approvingly cites Dean Kelly's claim that only conservative churches were retaining members and growing, this in the 1970s, research by Pew and the Congregations study, as well as the findings of Mark Chavez, Nancy Ammerman, Charles Taylor, and Peter Berger, do not see all the change in religious behavior and belief as so powerfully rooted in the texts, outlook, and renewal implemented by one ecclesial event such as Vatican II. John O'Malley and Massimo Faggioli also argue

30. Beinhart, "Breaking Faith."
31. Bullivant, *Mass Exodus*.
32. Congar, *True and False Reform in the Church*; Émile, *Faithful to the Future*.

this.[33] A closer look at who's gone, no longer in the pews, and why is a reminder that the decline of religion is no simple rejection of doctrine or ritual, and what is more, is not restricted to categories of age, education, political preference, or region.

A New Religious Typology from Pew

Is there a new and different way of looking at religious belonging in America? Recently, researchers at the Pew Research Center have created a new typology or method of categorizing the different relationships Americans have with religion and congregations.[34] It is based on "cluster analysis," the grouping of people by how they answer sixteen key questions. Other questions help further refine the character and beliefs of the groups. As is the case with typologies, there is a continuum or range of individuals, highly religious to extremely secular or nonreligious, and a healthy spectrum in-between.

Pew calls the most active and most involved in their communities "Sunday stalwarts," noting that while there are other holy days, the majority of those surveyed were Sunday worshippers. Eighty percent of these attend services weekly, and they also surpass all others in reading Scripture and praying privately (40 percent do so every day). Particularly for our focus, what distinguished this subgroup from all the highly religious is not so much their traditional beliefs or devotions but their membership in a community of faith. For them, as for the other two highly religious groups, religion is much more than an identity or label but an everyday reality, a way of life and vision of the world. Stalwarts put their money where their mouths are, or better, their engagement where their faith leads them. They are more involved in the outreach and volunteer organizations in their communities. Their rooting in the faith community is reflected in other local involvements.

Also among the highly religious are "God-and-Country Believers." These fuse their very conservative political views with their religion. They are quite a bit less likely to say religion affects all aspects of their daily life, and they are clearly on the side of many of the positions of the present chief executive and his party (who at the time of this writing is Trump), as well as the Religious Right and those opposed to immigration and protections for people of color and other nonwhite ethnics in America. Stalwarts, by the way, also trend toward the same set of positions in terms of values and the "culture

33. O'Malley, *What Happened at Vatican II*; Faggioli, *Vatican II*; Faggioli, *Council for the Global Church*.

34. See "Religious Typology."

wars," half expressing such orientations. Like the Diversely Devout and God-and-Country Believers, they are certain that belief in God makes for morality and that religion and communities of faith are crucial to this.

The Diversely Devout differ mostly in terms of their openness to new age beliefs, astrology, psychics, and like alternative spiritual resources. While strong on some kind of belief and religiosity, the Diverse are far more liberal in social and political matters, more likely to support LGBTQ persons and legal protections again racial, gender, and other types of discrimination. The Diversely Devout are themselves not as white as the other two highly religious groups, more than half coming from nonwhite backgrounds, this making them the only typology group that is not majority white. They are also from decidedly lower incomes than the other two highly religious groups, and more likely to be receiving social entitlements as well.

The other end of the continuum are the nonreligious, labeled by Pew the "Religion Resisters" and the "Solidly Secular." These tags are perhaps more accurate descriptions of the people in these groups. They are never at services except for a wedding or funeral, do not pray or read sacred texts, mostly do not believe in God, and they actually view religion as toxic and destructive. As might be expected, they are overwhelmingly more liberal and tolerant than their highly religious counterparts, a reality that gives some credence to their criticisms of religion as narrow and judgmental and divisive. God is simply not part of their outlook or vocabulary, and the Solidly Secularly would not even want to claim they are "spiritual" rather than "religious." Both groups are better educated, have higher incomes than the highly religious, and, as noted, are more open and progressive politically and socially.

This leaves us with the "somewhat religious," who are called the "Relaxed Religious" and the "Spiritually Awake." The majority of this group (85 percent) feel there is a higher power or God and some sort of afterlife or other realm. In their view, the Bible should not be taken literally but is inspirational material. Of all the groups, the Spiritually Awake are open and positive toward alternative spiritual movements and individuals, including new age practices and beliefs like psychics, astrology, and reincarnation. For the awake, spiritual practices are very important, doing a great deal to guide and shape life.

Most Christians in the US, not surprisingly, fall into the highly or somewhat religious groups. But beyond that it is not possible to match a particular church body or denomination with any specific group within the highly and somewhat religious. My sense is that many of the somewhat religious were either raised or later on in life belonged to churches, but after their children were finished with religious education or confirmed, they drifted away. This would bear out the classic theory that, as far as religious participation goes, church was at least in the past, after WWII, a social necessity and an important component of childrearing. So, most Catholics, Protestants, and, I would think, Eastern Orthodox churches are represented all over the spectrum, but largely in the highly and somewhat religious categories. Jews and Muslims likewise are dispersed across the spectrum.

The full report also explores some details of religious and nonreligious behavior. There is exploration of social and political positions, as has been noted. The more intense the religious commitment, the higher likelihood of conservative perspectives. Another is the extent to which people are open to new age beliefs and practices, also to other perspectives such as astrology and reincarnation and the work of psychics. As one moves away from very active, engaged believers, the diversity of sources of religious and spiritual belief and practice increase, though toward the more secular end of the typology, even spiritual sources fade. Just as the classic, biblical vision of an almighty, all-powerful, all-knowing God dominates the "Sunday Stalwarts" and "God-and-Country Believers," there is simply no sight of such a deity at the other end of the spectrum. And predictably, the perceived value and efficacy of communities of faith, belief, and religious practices such as services, study, and prayer go from very important to nonexistent as one moves from highly religious to nonreligious. Really, none of these findings are surprising, but rather are so predictable as to be thought of as common-sense knowledge about religion.

It is not surprising that while the highly and somewhat religious groups describe affiliation with a religious community, albeit in varying degrees, the nonreligious are essentially unaffiliated. The study makes it clear that the nonreligious, the Nones, are not the only ones at some distance from religious community belonging. With the exception of the Sunday Stalwarts, there is very little attendance at services and likewise little participation in other aspects of the life of a religious community among all the other religious groups. This corroborates the many other research projects and their data referred to earlier, showing the continual shrinkage of congregations in America.

The profile of Americans' affiliation with and engagement in religion the Pew Research brings us adds substance to the other studies earlier cited on the size and vitality of congregations. It deepens our understanding of a fundamental reality we have been tracking and will continue to explore here, namely, the decline but also the persistence of communities of faith in America.

In a probing ongoing series of articles, *Minneapolis Star-Tribune* reporter Jean Hopfensperger tracked the dwindling number of members in

Catholic, Lutheran, and other church parishes in what many still consider a religiously solid Midwestern location, that of Minnesota. She found that the fastest-growing "religion" appears to be "no religion," or at least, no religion in traditional terms. Once again, it is the appearance of Nones far beyond the forty-and-under cohorts that populates the landscape of America, one that used to be characterized by widespread membership in congregations of all kinds and adherence to their traditions of faith, regular participation in services, and financial support of these communities as well.

Americans do not appear to categorically reject religion. As Pew Research and the Hartford Institute and other studies show, it is more complicated. As the individuals profiled in this *Star-Tribune* article make clear, they have had problems with the clash of religion versus science, also with churches slow to welcome LGBTQ folk and women and others in the growing demographic diversity of the country. Hopfensberger allowed Greg Pratt, Stacy McClendon, Maria Arriola, and Curt Weinrich to share their stories. They are indeed spiritual people, finding joy, clarity, and inspiration in meditation, yoga, learning, the struggle for social justice, and the ordinary beauty of farming and the raising of domestic animals. All profess faith in an everyday wholeness and holiness. While short on doctrine, such a vision nevertheless celebrates the goodness of creation and the sacred nature of every person. As Pew Research findings tell us, there are several widely shared reasons for people leaving religious traditions and communities. These Minnesotans Hopfensberger interviewed are diverse, and while their explanations vary, they clearly have not abandoned spiritual life. They have found their former communities and faiths lacking, and have sought out new paths.[35]

More on Why They Are Leaving: Listening to David Gushee and Others

Having taken a data-rich look, it is worthwhile to come in closer and more personally, so we will listen to a few voices within the church on the shrinkage and decline. David Gushee has long been a public Christian intellectual with decades of writing for *Religion News Service* and other outlets. He has authored numerous articles and books. Gushee's recent memoir tracks his upbringing in, and then drifting away from, the Catholic Church to evangelical Christianity and subsequent training and ordination as a pastor in a Baptist church. But he is more than a parish pastor. His education in church-related

---

35. Hopfensperger, "Fastest Growing Religion is None."

schools such as Southern Seminary culminated in a doctorate, under Larry Rasmussen, at Union Theological Seminary in New York City. Glenn Stassen was also an important mentor, as was social-justice evangelical Ron Sider. His academic career has taken him from schools in which he was pressured to political maneuvers deemed appropriate for the evangelical project.

He eventually ended up at the McAfee School of Theology at Mercer University. Even with his evangelical credentials, Gushee has taken risks. He made public his serious changes of perspective, not only on LGBTQ people and their relationship to the church and the law, but also on a range of other issues dear to the Christian Right. In two volumes, Gushee puts forward in a clear and provocative way several reasons why he believes people of all ages and backgrounds are leaving Christianity in particular, and religion in general.[36] Gushee is well aware that none of the factors he identifies are original discoveries on his part. The narrative of these reasons for the decline derive from his personal settling up with faith and his vocations as a scholar, teacher, and pastor.

Not surprisingly, the decline is rooted both in the church and in those who seek to believe and practice their faith. Gushee notes the increasingly extreme social and political positions, the excesses and rigidities of conservative religious leaders. Pastor and writer John Pavlovitz is more blunt in his assessment of why people are leaving in his open letter to the church.[37] He argues that at root it is the churches' fear of controversy keeping them silent about the atrocities being perpetrated in this country and around the world—and the list is very long! It is a lack of commitment to the teaching and life of Jesus and distraction detours into being trendy or being nostalgically traditional. Whether it is the migrants, especially the children, Muslims, immigrants as a whole, Jews, people of color, LGBTQ folk, women, low-income, addicted, chronically ill or challenged souls—the church largely ignores the suffering, makes feeble attempt to give assistance, and hides from the bold witness that would evoke anger and attack from those who like the present climate of division, suspicion, and hate. Pavolvitz's hard words ring true across the churches. And this is not to mention the churches' own internal abuses and bickering.

Washington Post columnist and journalist E. J. Dionne Jr., a practicing Catholic, echoes much the same view as Gushee on why so many Americans, especially those under forty (40 percent) are distancing themselves from organized religion.[38] It has become the opposite of what they

---

36. See Gushee, *Letter to My Anxious Christian Friends*; Gushee, *Still Christian*.

37. Pavlovitz, "Dear Church, Here's Why People Are Leaving."

38. Dionne, "No Wonder There's an Exodus from Religion."

are—intolerant, politically partisan, legalistic, exclusive. This was the finding of Putnam and Campbell in their study, *American Grace*. They found
that when religion became intensely politicized, when it fostered suspicion,
fear, division, even hate among Americans, there would be retreat from
membership and participation. Dionne notes the glaring contradictions
between Donald Trump's actions and words and the faith he alleges to be
supporting, protecting, even restoring in America.

If we move to the other end of the spectrum, we will find conviction but
obduracy too. Rod Dreher has been a voice for conservatives who feel they
have been betrayed not only by the liberalism and secularism of intellectuals
and universities but also by what they perceive as a growing domination
of government by liberals and progressives. Much of the trouble seems to
center around sexual-identity and gender-definition issues. With the Supreme Court recognition of the legality of same-sex marriage (Obergefell
v. Hodges, 2015) and further legal protections for transgender individuals
and the tyranny of liberalism in the classroom, there is a growing feeling of
victimization, of the oppression of those with conservative religious beliefs.
Their dissent is no longer legally protected. Thus the emergence of statutes
protecting "sincerely held religious beliefs."[39] In a Supreme Court case, a
Denver baker was allowed to refuse to serve customers because of their
sexual preference, though the actual question of discrimination because of
sincerely held religious beliefs was not addressed.[40]

The hardening of perspectives is seen in Dreher's claim that refusal
of dialogue with those in disagreement is both a way of protecting and affirming unchangeable positions. Rejecting conversation prevents those in
disagreement from establishing "beach-heads" from which their liberal opposition could grow and challenge traditional beliefs.[41] Of course, he had
in mind the movement for rights of LGBTQ people, but then, why not the
civil rights and women's movements and those for gun control? Dreher's
"Benedict option," a withdrawal from connection with the culture and anyone other than like-minded conservatives, thus appears as a retreat, a very
different motivation for being "none" and "done."[42]

Even more questionable stances on Dreher's part—adherence to a European culture superiority, along with an anti-immigration stance and dubious views on race—all raise even more flags about his promulgating a return

---

39. Notice OLP Docket No. 165, 82 Fed. Reg. 49668 (October 26, 2017).

40. Liptak, "In Narrow Decision, Supreme Court Decides with Baker Who Turned
Away Gay Couple."

41. Dreher, "Fundamentalism and 'Dialogue.'"

42. Dreher, *Benedict Option*.

to an introverted Christianity. Staying with conservative trends, there is the recent work of Tara Isabella Burton. She claims that the attraction of very conservative forms of liturgy and doctrine for disenchanted people may be more than the search for older aesthetics, certainty, and a preference for the politics and racial standards of another time.[43] Admittedly, though, the attraction to what Burton terms "weird religion" is a niche phenomenon, engaging but a sliver of the young. There are many reasons why so many Americans, not just younger people, have become Nones and Dones. The resurgence of the Religious Right ranks high in this trend, not just during the Trump administration, but before it.[44]

Premodern claims of religious traditions also have become untenable in the face of science but also with respect to the growing diversity of ethnic and religious traditions around us. Peter Berger argued that pluralism—the availability of alternative worldviews, ways of thinking, and acting—inevitably challenged traditions that formerly had enjoyed privileged positions in a state or nation.[45] The conflicts between faith and science, between what one's tradition said and did in another historical period too, cannot be simply resolved by appeals to the authority of God and a text, or for that matter what one's parents or grandparents believed. The intellectual coherence and ethical credibility of Christian doctrine have been profoundly shaken, not just by science but by the apparent hypocrisy of leaders and the lack of meaningful connection of beliefs to complex issues of today.

Closely related, for Gushee, is the appalling quality of authentic leaders in the churches—those who could both articulate the faith and point out how it could be enacted. In their place we find lobbyists for certain political parties who are deemed supportive of significant issues whether pro-life or the clash of LGBTQ legal protections with alleged "religious freedom" to discriminate. The deafness of many, though not all, evangelicals to Donald Trump's personal life and divisive talk have cast doubt on their ethical integrity—likewise, their support of even his June 1, 2020 photo-op, standing before St. John's Episcopal Church, Lafayette Square (actually in front of the parish house), holding a Bible in the midst of protests over the killing of George Floyd. Some evangelicals have taken their distance from him, to be sure. However, the political efforts of evangelicals predate the Trump era, as Rebecca Sager has shown.[46] More recently, Mark Noll and others have taken

---

43. Comacho, "Racial Aesthetics of Burton's 'Weird Christians.'" See also Burton, "Christianity Gets Weird," and Burton, *Strange Rites*.

44. Robert Putnam and David Campbell found this in their study, *American Grace*.

45. Berger, "Good of Religious Pluralism"; Berger, *Many Altars of Modernity*.

46. Sager, *Faith, Politics and Power*.

a longer look at evangelicals' growth and ascent to influence in politics.[47] Gushee also notes that the ecclesial fall from grace, namely the specter of clerical sexual-abuse cases, have made it very difficult for people to grant the leaders the obedience and deference they formerly enjoyed.

Perhaps because he has roots in the more conservative churches, Gushee does not shy away from noting factors that some might not seriously consider in their distance from traditional faith. While recognizing the difficulty, and sometimes the inability, of parents to share and then pass on their faith to their children and grandchildren, Gushee sees this as part of a far more widespread phenomenon. Evangelism or its disappearance is the conventional description. But there is more to it than the passing of the old school door-to-door method to inquire about one's faith and church membership. It is also not just the infrequency of old-time revivals, missions, and preaching tours like those of Billy Graham and those before him like Sankey and Spurgeon. There are of course numerous "big box" churches with charismatic leaders and professional musicians and actors—Willow Creek comes to mind—where every Sunday service is a kind of revival. Or is it?

Religion of this large-church size has become minutely scripted, every detail maximized for marketing effect. Gushee also believes it has become privatized, with a targeted market of consumers. The truly communal character is gone. That is, religion is no longer public and it has become an historical oddity that appears when presidents or their wives die and the funeral services are broadcast on national TV. The historic church buildings stand proudly on major urban streets but more often they are known for concerts or lectures. Few enter for a service, whether Sunday or otherwise.

Gushee does not take aim at liberals, secular elites, and the media as so often religious conservatives do. He does not charge the culture with relentlessly attacking religion, thus necessitating new legislation to protect "religious beliefs" from LGBTQ people or agnostics intent on defining separation of church and state. As a Baptist pastor and theologian, he sees the decline coming primarily, as we have seen, from within the community of faith itself.[48] Specifically, scandals of sexual abuse, misappropriation of contributed funds, and poor leadership that is mainly defensive and adversarial rather than compassionate and inspiring. For a brief moment, the preaching of Episcopal presiding bishop Michael B. Curry at Windsor Castle for the marriage of Prince William and Meghan Markle showed what a Christian leader could do with words, and in about thirteen minutes.[49]

47. Noll et al., *Evangelicals*.

48. Gushee, "Why Is Christianity Declining?"; Gushee, "Seven Follow-Ups."

49. Curry, "Video & Text."

The church's difficulty in speaking to a world that no longer operates with premodern views of science, and which has little understanding of anything beyond the empirical, has long plagued religious writers and church leaders. The traditional temptation is to keep on reciting the same formulas, whether from the Authorized King James Version of the Bible or other versions, and to insist on the literal truth of each event therein (the miracles quite importantly)—all of this clashes with a world full of conflict but also a world in which continuing medical advances heal previously incurable illnesses and give years of life to those who would have been dead much earlier in their lives. But how do religious leaders and the faithful explain that such medical care cannot be made accessible to all, regardless of ability to pay? More recently, in the pandemic, some pastors have defied local government directives to hold services in packed church spaces with singing, claiming biblical authority trumps that of the state. Some believers have argued that following the advice of medical experts, listening to science, is insubordination to God. Such disconnect with the world of most Americans struggling to survive the coronavirus and to survive financially drives many away. Internal church corruption, misstatements, and hypocrisy have also been factors in the exodus from the churches.

There are other factors, such as the inability of believers to explain why they believe what they believe and how their beliefs would make for a better world. I think the overarching factor is the disconnection between faith and our life. Increasingly, faith seems to be a kind of escape into delusion, faith appearing to take people away from the difficulties of contemporary life with no engagement in working for the good. I find it striking that an extreme conservative commentator like Russ Douthat can only interpret Pope Francis's emphasis on mercy and pastoral discernment as signs of the weakening of absolute doctrines, thus the tottering of the foundations of the faith.[50]

But the churches have maintained a commitment to the works of mercy. We will see numerous examples of this here in chapters to come. Churches have been able to find in the Scriptures warrant for a just economy, for needed social change, for adaptation to new conditions, for mercy to people seeking reconciliation with the church. Churches have signaled that not only their doors but their communities and the eucharist are open to all the children of God. The seeming intransigence of religious leaders and intolerance passing as "sincerely held religious beliefs" have driven people of discernment and compassion away. One simply does not have to remain in an oppressive institution to believe in God, pray, and do good in

---

50. See, for example, Douthat, *To Change the Church*.

one's life. They are "done" with religion that is intolerant and judgmental. Some simply opt out—Kaya Oakes found this in her careful listening to religious Nones. Others "shopped around" until they found more progressive churches that were open to women, diverse people, LGBTQ folk, and others who often find no welcome in church.[51]

Linda Mercadante, author of a study like Kaya Oakes's, finds that there is substantial common ground between Christians and Nones. Contrary to often-made caricatures, people who identify as "spiritual but not religious" (SBNR) have a range of considered reasons for not remaining within communities and traditions of faith in which they may have grown and spent years of their lives. Despite their distancing themselves from traditional understandings of God, community, and ritual, SBNR folk do not reject everything outright. They do refuse to revere a judgmental, distant God who is essentially a lawmaker and judge. Likewise they want inclusivity and toleration, not a community turned in on itself. Other forms of intolerance passing as fidelity to faith are also dismissed, and here the list is well known, from same-sex marriage and LGBTQ people to wanting to keep church and state, doctrine and civil society separate.

Within the Christian tradition, she says, there are numerous resources for meeting and listening between members of churches and SBNRs. Where does one begin? The very belief that each human being is a child of God, that each face is another face of God, that God is always creating and nurturing us into new life and forgiving. This sense of growing into God, what the Eastern church calls *theosis*, and the intense identification of the human and divine predicated upon the incarnation—God's becoming one of us, one with us— these would be just a few of the tools in the box, as it were.[52]

Nones and Dones have also been the interest of Angie Thurston, who is part of the Ministry Innovation Project at Harvard Divinity School.[53] With her co-author, Casper ter Kuile, she has studied numerous organizations that have become spiritual communities and ways for "spiritual but not religious" (SBNR) people to find belonging where they can put their values into expression and action. One report, "How We Gather," has explored just such alternative forms of community such as CrossFit, Soul-Cycle, and other spiritual wellness groups such as The Sanctuaries and Juniper Path and advocacy groups like Ctznwell, also the Dinner Party—a gathering for those experiencing loss and grief and how we become our aspirational selves in some surprising and diverse venues such as SCUL:

51. Oakes, "Unlikely Alliance."

52. Mercadante, *Belief without Borders*; Mercadante, "Start by Listening."

53. See "Angie Thurston."

Subversive Choppers Urban Legion, a mutant bicycle gang, Comic-Con, and Burning Man, among others.

Thurston and ter Kuile, as the list of their groups and venues suggests, have looked well beyond the boundaries of even the most experimental church gatherings. That said, they acknowledge there is a massive legacy of traditional wisdom, ritual, and texts that conventional churches possess and are more often than not quite willing to share. It is worth noting that neither Thurston nor ter Kuile have any suspicion or antipathy toward traditional communities of faith. Their participation in the Harvard Divinity project attests to that. And they are emphatic about how welcoming and how hospitable churches can be to those seeking a sense of belonging and spiritual deepening. Thus they are happy to share what they have learned and note that openness and the willingness to accept those with both issues and doubts are important gifts, attitudes that go a long way in offering Nones and Dones points of contact and opportunities for interaction with congregations. We will see several other examples of parishes in transition, in the process of reinvention and repurposing, that exhibit just such holy hospitality. These include Dave Barnhart's St. Junia house churches in the Birmingham, Alabama area, Reconciliation Services in Kansas City, and Redeemer Lutheran in North Minneapolis.

Criticism from Within

One has to add to what has been described here several changes already mentioned. The disappearance of multigenerational families in congregations, the mobility that takes people away from hometown and parish to university, marriage outside of one's community—these are elements of the fading of cultural religion, though not necessarily of personal faith. As noted, the sheer diversity of ethnic and religious backgrounds in America have exploded the older enclaves—some would call them "ghettos"—of language and faith. Here and there, among some ethnic communities, there is still formidable social and psychological pressure to stay within the group. The most recent immigrant and refugee groups—Middle Eastern Christians, Latinos, and Asian communities—remain solid. Yet the recent history of Eastern European countries in the post-Soviet years gives evidence that striking resurgence in church attendance and vocations to religious life and the ministry are not indefinite. Poland, for example, has witnessed decline in religious participation since the resurgence in the early 1990s. In Russia, the lifting of state oppression and restrictions on religious participation seemingly have had little effect on revival. Despite the return of hundreds of churches, monasteries, and schools, the percentage of Russians who attend services is low. About 7 percent attend weekly, 30 percent yearly, and only 11 percent report sending children to religious instruction.[54]

One of the most important takeaways I retain from years as a Kierkegaard scholar is the power of his attack on clergy, not from outside the church, but precisely from one who defiantly remained within, even if engaging in ecclesial and sacramental protest.[55] The most penetrating criticism comes from within the household. So, Gushee's is a voice to which we should listen, one speaking from within the community of faith as are others like James Martin, Jim Wallis, Brian MacLaren, Richard Rohr, Sister Simone Campbell, and most notably Pope Francis.

However, things are not always what they seem. Barna Institute researchers found that those who had drifted from regular church attendance and membership were not all atheists or agnostics. Some had more diverse and diffuse spiritual interests, but were just not connected to organized communities. But still others revered "Jesus, not church."[56] The Barna researchers found this group had grown to comprise 10 percent of Americans. While some leaders such as Pope Francis have said one cannot love Jesus and not be in some way associated with the others who love him, namely the church, this remains a neuralgic issue. At the risk of repeating things already said here, clearly there are many things the institutional church has done to dissuade those who love Jesus from having anything to do with the organization calling itself the church. Ghandi was famous on the contradiction between the words and actions of Jesus, on the one hand, and those of his organized followers on the other. The modern ecumenical movement was largely born in the very early twentieth century out of horror at the behavior of competing church bodies in mission work in non-Christian lands.

What the church is today and has been historically remain obstacles to some people inspired more directly and without church influence by Jesus. The Barna Institute found that respondents in its survey who "loved Jesus but not the church" were just as likely as their church-belonging counterparts to pray daily or meditate, but they were less committed to reading Scripture. The Barna researchers point out what we learned earlier, namely, that it is not primarily disgust or dislike of the church that feeds those who reject church but hold on to Jesus. Rather, these nonchurch believers find they do not need what church offers, both what they reject in terms of narrowness and legalism but also the other neutral, important

54. See "Religious Belief and National Belonging in Central and Eastern Europe."
55. Plekon, "Kierkegaard at the End," 68–86; Plekon, "Before the Storm," 45–64.
56. Shellnut, "Just Give Me Jesus."

functions such as corporate worship and ritual, preaching and learning opportunities, and ways of doing outreach and service. Most all of these church activities can be satisfied in other ways, from meditation, yoga, and retreats, to study groups and volunteering at soup kitchens, food and clothes pantries, shelters, and the like. This distinction, between those remaining in the church and those who have never belonged or who have moved away, shows up in quite a bit of research about religion today. It is by no means the case that not belonging to a church, attending services, or supporting a congregation—the definition of Nones—also implies lack of any belief or spiritual life and practice whatsoever.

One other aspect of historical religiosity in America is conversion. Lincoln Mullen has charted how conversion is a distinctive feature of religious belonging and revival in this country. Other research suggests that many Americans will migrate several times, and not only within their traditions either. Pew Research says one-third of Americans currently identify with or belong to a tradition different than the one in which they were raised. Depending on how religious traditions are defined, say, as various denominations or church bodies within the Christian tradition, then the percentage grows much higher. Changing affiliations is a feature of American religious life in which believers are very much consumers and for which churches have for most of the modern era employed marketing strategies.[57]

From the great revivals of the eighteenth and nineteenth centuries to the celebrity preachers of the recent past—Billy Graham being one of the most notable—religious communities have used advertising, music, and more accommodating venues to draw converts. Willow Creek Church's founding pastor, Bill Hybels, famously used survey results to craft a worship experience and campus setting based on avoiding what people found undesirable about the churches they formerly attended. While claiming to adhere to the essentials, the fundamentals of Christian faith, all else was negotiable. Thus no cross, candles, or sacred images; no vestments, prayer-books, or hymnbooks; no altar, font, or pulpit, but a stage in which a kind of entertainment worship unfolded, with paid professional musicians and singers, minidramas, and very brief messages. No collection, no asking guests to stand or wear name tags. Giving was completely voluntary. But if you asked about joining, you then entered a network of small groups in which there was intense fellowship, contact through study, worship, and service work during the week. These smaller "churches" were not at all like the laid-back, low-key variety show performances on Sundays. Over time much of this changed at Willow Creek.

57. Mullen, *Chance of Salvation*; also see Green, "Convert Nation."

A few megachurches, often clustered around high-profile pastors like Joel Osteen or T. D. Jakes or pastor and best-selling author of *The Purpose Driven Life*, Rick Warren, have flourished. But they are anomalies when placed against the background of most congregations in America. As we will see in subsequent chapters, the desire to continue to be the body of Christ in a particular place looks different from one parish to another. There are innumerable variations on this effort to continue, to reinvent, to recreate, to revive, and to redefine a community when the former conditions no longer exist, when the old model has become unsustainable.

Location and Population

The real estate mantra of "location, location, location" is amazingly accurate when it comes to something quite different from the decline and shrinkage we have examined—and will continue to consider. Austin, Texas seems to be exactly counter to the patterns of congregational decline that appear to be the new normal throughout the country. Perhaps it is the state capitol status and maybe also the setting within the "Bible Belt" of the South, but the demographic growth of Austin has resulted in mainline Protestant congregations working hard to accommodate growth seen almost nowhere else in the country. Covenant Presbyterian in central Austin has four services, all of them well-attended. One is contemporary, the others traditional. This congregation has attracted 500 new members in just the past five years. Newcomer classes jam into a room in the church basement. In Campbell Elementary School on the other side of the city, The Well church meets for services each Sunday with the now-customary praise band. The space is filled for the two contemporary services offered there weekly. Austin has grown from about 850,000 thirty years ago to over 2 million today, making it the fastest-growing large city in the US, according to WalletHub.[58] We will also visit Austin again in chapters to follow to see resurrection at Servant UMC, First UMC, and Austin New Church.

Seattle is also growing, as well as Denver and Portland, Oregon, but these cities have not seen the crunch on churches by newcomers seeking a congregation. Dallas and Nashville, on the other hand, have seen an upturn in congregational life for established as well as new ones. There will be examples looked at here of congregations that have refashioned themselves so that a casual observer might wonder whether these are churches at all. But likewise, there are those parishes that have retained historic liturgy, hymns, vestments, and icons and are alive as well as attracting new members.

58. Flynn, "In Booming Austin TX, Churches Struggle to Keep Pace."

Mark Chaves suggests that what appears to be significant congregational growth is rather the effect of population expansion in that area.[59] Actual attendance may be simply the same, but the expansion makes it look like parishes are growing. Austin's Covenant Presbyterian is part of the Presbyterian Church in the USA (PCUSA), a mainline denomination. Yet it is also very much a spin on the traditional congregational model, with space in their buildings of 6,000 square feet. Really, it is a "big box" church. They have a much larger staff than most congregations and numerous programs. They offer use of their space for community activities such as AA, ESL classes, and projects assisting immigrants and asylum seekers. As a "big box" congregation, Covenant's sheer size and numbers make it attractive—nothing succeeds like success. But the reality has been, and still remains in the US, that the average congregation is by any comparison smaller, now around seventy members, without multiple pastors and support staff and numerous programs.

Still in Austin, The Well is an outgrowth of Hill Country Bible Church, a multicampus church that has established numerous other smaller congregational starts in Texas. It has an overwhelmingly young membership, age selection being a quality of contemporary congregations in the megachurch model. One salient feature of larger churches is the effort to create a network of small groups, often centered in neighborhoods so that members can interact all week long. One pastor, Karen Thompson, of Metropolitan Community Church (MCC) in Austin, suggested that the wisdom in churches today is that in growing bigger you also need to get smaller. With roots in the MCC tradition of a church for LGBTQ Christians of all backgrounds, the progressive spirit and openness of MCC in Austin appears to have attracted members in light of the growth of hate crimes, racism, anti-immigrant sentiment, and the otherwise divisive climate since Trump's election. It is worth noting that MCC does not present itself as a gay church but as a welcoming, hospitable one. So it has a hospitality in common with many other mainline churches, among them the Episcopal, Lutheran, Methodist, United Church of Christ, and Presbyterian churches, as well as some Catholic parishes.

As Chaves implies, what sometimes looks like a boom may be a demographic phenomenon. One reason for seeking out a church after possibly years of being religiously inactive is the question of the spiritual upbringing of children. When asked, new members at several of the Austin congregations noted mentioned this as determinative in their seeking and finding a church home. Students of religious life and church have long assumed that "a little child shall lead them" (Isa 11:6). Peter Berger, along with Dennison

---

59. Chaves, *American Religion*.

Nash, explored this decades ago.[60] Experienced parish pastors are also quick to underscore the return of inactive people to church in light of the "rites of passage." At least one pastor Eileen Flynn interviewed, Jonathan Dodson of City Life Church, admits the market angles he employs: a really good band will bring in more members, as will attractive facilities and, yes, big turnouts. Nothing succeeds like success, something Mark Chaves observes. And as noted, the high memberships of the larger congregations have an effect on data on congregations, suggesting that more people belong to big churches. In reality, most belong to the proverbially average "small" church, since there are far more of these.

Areas of significant population growth like Austin also see a great deal of population turnover, not just moves out of town after a few years, due to new job locations, but also relocations to parts of the city or suburbs with more affordable housing and better schools, commerce, and entertainment. This has an impact on any church that plants itself imagining it can remain and simply grow in place, as Pastor Tom Goodman of Southern Baptist Hillcrest Church found, along with Pastor Dodson of City Life Church. Especially young families may have started, before children, in more stylish downtown areas. However, with expanding families, the need for more space and better schools and less traffic takes them away to spots that make commuting back to a church base less convenient. Big churches that do multiple congregation plantings learned this pattern and responded to it by increasing the number of venues and communities.

Such apparent marketing success in ever-expanding big churches raises a question; namely, that of the long run. One of the solid patterns of congregations in the past, as we saw, was longevity—parishes in which multigenerational families were the norm and the backbone of the community. Mobility, marriage out of ethnic and church traditions, and other demographic shifts have done away with such long-term stability in local communities of faith. The case of Austin is a confirmation in a subtle way. While population growth in a short period soars, apparently so does the size of some congregations (and not others, it must be noted). How long will these members remain? What will City Life, Hillcrest, The Well, and Covenant look like five years from now, or ten?[61]

When Willow Creek was yet a new, amazing phenomenon of unprecedented growth in congregational life, even establishing groups of consultants to advise other parishes on their modes of growth, some students of

60. Nash, "'Little Child Shall Lead Them,'" 239–40; Nash and Berger, "Church Commitment in an American Suburb," 105–20.

61. McCann, "Fastest Growing Cities."

parish life, myself included, had questions. These were not just about actual membership data, but it was almost impossible to find exit data on those who came and then left. The scandals of abuse by the founding pastor of Willow Creek, Bill Hybels, raised questions about accountability and oversight in large congregations. At Willow Creek, there was dysfunction and the congregation board was unable to effectively oversee and deal with his behavior. It also took too long for them to admit this. Hard questions remain about such megachurches. There are often no checks or balances both within or from without, as they might have in a denomination or church body. Tish Harrison Warren has wondered about what the Willow Creek disaster means in precisely this vein. Hybels is also just the best known of a number of other charismatic pastors and entrepreneur founders who have been forced out in the wake of financial and personal improprieties. Andy Savage at Highpoint Church in Memphis, Dean Curry of Tacoma's Center Assembly of God Church, James MacDonald of Chicago's Harvest Bible Chapel, and John Ortberg of Menlo Church are additional cases.[62]

The Past Disappears, Now the New Normal

My own experience as a priest has taught me that much of the parish culture and groups I knew at the start of ministry have disappeared or changed dramatically. Even the ways in which one defines "regular" members, regular church participation—in services, support, study, fellowship, outreach, and service—have had to be recalibrated. Weekly Sunday attendance is now the pattern for fewer and fewer people, possibly less than 20 percent of a parish. The new normal would be varying frequencies of attendance with different levels of further involvement in parish support and activities. These are added by the use of different clergy, due either to using "supply" pastors or a ministry team covering several congregations. In a parish I know well, more than half the community are seasonal members: coming to the desert for late fall, winter, and spring, then returning "home" for summer. While this may be a variation peculiar to vacation and retirement areas in the southwest and southeast, what would amount to part-time patterns of membership and attendance may be elements of the new normal for parishes.[63]

62. Warren, "Willow Creek's Crash Shows Why Denominations Still Matter"; Shellnut, "#ChurchToo"; Robinson, "Megachurch Meeting Reveals that Fired Pastor Faced Two Separate Investigations for Sexual Misconduct"; Shellnut, "James MacDonald Fired from Harvest."

63. Kirkpatrick, "Adjusting to the New Normal."

We will see a variety of strategies employed for confronting and dealing with this "new normal." In many Catholic dioceses, the strategy has been to carefully study parishes as well as invite their own self-studies. The outcome has been, in many places, the merging of geographically proximate parishes and the closing of ones that no longer serve the ethnic community or a neighborhood no longer in existence. Decreasing numbers of parishioners attending Sunday Mass are coupled with the decline in the number of clergy. Many retirements and deaths are not replaced. Like moves in the Boston Catholic archdiocese, often with little input from the parishes, resulted in protests and occupations of to-be-closed parish buildings, in some cases for several years. The same process, in the New York Catholic archdiocese, also appeared to be very top-down, with the input of the parishes often being dismissed in the aim of fiscal responsibility. In Pittsburgh, Bishop David Zubik recently announced a program in which close to 200 parishes would become just sixty merged ones, a reorganization plan that covers six counties. How many of those almost 200 congregations would close is not yet known.[64]

Other instances in dioceses are often painful, such as the inability of the Catholic archdiocese of Hartford to find a priest for St. Joan of Arc Church. Clergy shortage, not financial problems or dramatic decrease in attendance, was the sole reason for its closure and merger with a neighboring congregation. However, it was just part of a larger reorganization in that diocese, with more than 140 parishes being consolidated into sixty 60 new ones, and 26 buildings closed. This is a 40 percent reduction in the number of parishes in that diocese, leaving it with 127 parishes. And like reorganizations are ongoing across the country in Roman Catholic dioceses, as well as other mainstream church bodies such as the Methodist, Lutheran, Episcopal, and Presbyterian churches, all of which will appear as we move further in this book. This includes the largest of American Catholic dioceses, such as New York and Chicago. The demographic changes we have described, including mobility and relocation, marriage out of ethnic groups and churches of origin, as well as increasing drift-away from organized religion (i.e., the Nones)—all are factors. For Catholics in particular, the continuing and severe clergy shortage is a cause for concern.[65] Sometimes selling the building and relocating and regrouping is the way. The Episcopal Church of the Advent in Chicago, after dwindling to twenty members, decided to put the

64. Smith, "Bishop Zubik Unveils Parish Reorganization Plans for Pittsburgh Diocese."

65. Schenk, "Parish Is the Body of Christ."

building up for sale, with the approval of the diocese. It is now luxury housing apartments renting for up to $4,000 a month.[66]

Death and Resurrection

There are plenty of other outcomes like this one, a radical repurposing of a church, taking it completely out of the sphere of either spirituality or service. But we will see enough examples in other directions to counter any thought that the trajectory of the church is simply down and out. But it is not just the decline and closing of parishes that is reported. After all, Christianity is rooted in resurrection. And so there are numerous accounts of death and then rebirth. I think this is the major pattern we will see in the many and different congregations we will visit in this book, in the next four chapters in particular.

Even before the Gospels were redacted and appeared in written form, Paul was describing the central action of Christian faith as the baptismal descent into death and rising to new life with Christ. But the paschal or Easter experience of baptism is to be repeated over and over again in the life of the community of faith. They gathered to hear the Scriptures and preaching, to pray and then give thanks, to break the bread of Christ's body and share the cup of his blood. Death and resurrection are inherent in the eucharist. We will perhaps at first be discouraged to encounter what seems an unstoppable decline, the inevitable shrinkage of members and deaths of congregations unable to continue in worship. But from even the closures of beloved churches, from the termination of formerly active, growing congregations, we will indeed see new life spring up and in ways we might not be able to imagine. It is my hope here that this central movement of cross and empty tomb will convince us that as the angel told the women who came to the tomb, "He is not here, he has been raised from the dead and indeed he is going ahead of you to Galilee; there you will see him. This is my message for you" (Matt 28:6–8). Now, let us see resurrection at work in communities that are the body of Christ.

Carr UMC in East Durham, North Carolina had a long, thriving existence. Yet it eventually started shrinking to the point that there appeared to be no future. Is there a way for a community of faith to have a "good death?" It would seem that coming to terms with the good done and other possibilities in the future can make even this unlikely event possible, in the view of Carr's last pastor, Cheryl Lawrence.[67] In the buildings that

66. Bloom, "Historic Logan Square Church Now Luxury Housing Complex."

67. Lawrence, "Good Death."

once housed Carr UMC in Durham, an entirely new community came to birth: Shepherd's House Methodist Church. Nonprofit groups from the community use the educational space, one a county public health class on food prep and nutrition—for kids.

Founded in 1886, the Carr UMC parish targeted cotton mill workers in a (then) newly established factory. For a couple years, Carr UMC and Shepherd's House shared the complex of buildings that was once Carr's. Shepherd's House continued to grow, with more Zimbabaweans gathering into the congregation. Carr kept shrinking as aging members relocated or died. There were shared fellowship meals, a Christmas Eve communion service with carols and prayer both in English and Shona. But when a conflict-resolution specialist came in to meet with Carr's dwindling membership, the fearful inevitability became something not fearful at all. Good Friday does not complete or end Jesus's story. Easter and resurrection do.

So after the "funeral" of that parish in January 2008 under Pastor Cheryl Lawrence, a new community received the property as a gift and started worshipping, learning, enjoying fellowship, and reaching out to invite the community to use the rooms and facilities during the week. Only recently did Pastor Johannes Gumbo start to do the sermon and much of the Sunday service in English, Shona having been the previous liturgical language. Why? Because the resurrected community of faith here in Durham was Zimbabewean, the dream of refugees who had arrived in 2002 in North Carolina's Research Triangle area. So a double wonder of death and resurrection, of Good Friday and Easter in the community, resulted: the death of one parish became the birth of a new parish and for a new, more diverse people too.[68]

Throughout the country, many UMC parishes were founded in the eighteenth and nineteenth centuries, when transportation was large horse and buggy and when populations remained in the same village, whether farming or manufacturing, for generation after generation. In time, these formerly vibrant, small congregations were faced with inevitable shrinkage and decline. I know just such a collection of Methodist parishes well, for they surround the hamlet in which I have lived for over forty years in the Hudson valley, in Dutchess County, New York. One of them, founded in 1766, is within walking distance of my house. A good friend, a UMC pastor, has been involved for almost a decade in an association or co-op of six of these parishes, all within as little as ten minutes' drive, a half hour at the most, from each other. As of July 2020, this association will be closed, with two relatively healthy parishes remaining.

68. Shimron, "Church Reborn."

In another North Carolina town, there was a different story, rebirth coming in a passing on of a legacy. In Richfield, North Carolina, the local textile mill closed years ago, along with those in nearby Albemarle. Thus began the migration of residents away from the area to where they could find work and education, or where marriage led them. Richfield UMC parish saw its membership dwindle for years.

The United Methodist Church promotes a program called Church Legacy Initiative. In it, there is a period of reflection, consultation with other local congregations, as well as national church and conference pastors and other staff, about the future. There are pathways towards revitalization, but these require a congregational decision to change, to start worshipping, studying, meeting, and doing service work with other neighboring parishes. It means getting out of the comfortable place and space that some members have enjoyed all their lives. Parishes might have to choose a site that would continue serving as a congregation and then be willing to leave their old building and be part of a merged parish, perhaps merged with yet another congregation or two. The legacies of a number of congregations would then be brought together—first and foremost the people of God, their members, but also the property that they had built up and used for God's worship and work for many years. In the cases of the congregations that would close, these spaces could be put to use in numerous ways. So, in either path, the legacy of a historic congregation would be celebrated and be used for continuing work. This became the case for the Richfield parish legacy. The parsonage was turned over to Pfeiffer University, a UMC-related school, for dormitory space for early childhood education students doing internships and student-teaching stints at local schools. The sanctuary and educational annex would become a kitchen and storehouse for a local food kitchen, food being stored and prepped there and meals being served daily to the hungry.[69]

Not surprisingly, since the decline and shrinkage of parishes is a universal, ecumenical reality, Methodists have both lessons to teach others (for example, Catholics) about struggling parishes in urban areas. It is crucial to note that like all denominations, Methodists and Catholics close parishes. However, most church bodies, unlike the Catholics, because of their history and their more communal patterns of action, do not just close parishes, but tell members to go to St. X's Church nearby, and then put the building up on the real estate market. This can happen, but due to the Methodist Church Legacy Initiative, there are other possibilities for both the congregation left

---

69. Shimron, "Legacy Ministries to Dying Churches Give Congregations a Way to End Well."

behind as well as their buildings, as we have just seen from Carr UMC and the new Shepherd's House UMC.

The UMC, because of its distinctive tradition historically of itinerant pastors traveling from one community another, have 32,000 parishes throughout the country. As one church leader describes the Methodists, they have pretty much the saturation level of the USPS. Catholic heritage is built on successive waves of immigrants, so unlike many small worship centers for an itinerant pastor to ride to, the Catholics established new ethnic/language-specific parishes for new groups migrating. As with the multiple Methodist parishes in relatively small areas, so too, multiple Catholic parishes are often within blocks of one another in urban areas—one Italian, another Polish, still more German, Irish, Slovak, and more recently, Latino, Filipino, Vietnamese, Caribbean, and so on. Whatever theological and historical differences Methodists and Catholics may have, they are in the same situation, along with Eastern Orthodox, Episcopalians, Presbyterians, Lutherans, and others when it comes to the complex, multilayered demographic changes affecting all communities of faith in America today.[70]

But we are not in some kind of particular challenge in this country. It is much the same in Canada, in Mexico, and the lower Americas, and in western Europe. A clergy study group has been pursuing the issues of parishes all over the UK, most of which are historic buildings, some now declared redundant and in different states of abandonment or preservation. The parishes that remain open, whether rural and small-town or urban, face the same situations as just described for Catholic and Methodist and other church body parishes here. The supply of clergy and parishes that can actually support a pastor do not match each other. So in many cases, a pastor has not just one small congregation and set of buildings, but often two or three or more. Some of the clergy who serve multiple parishes have shared their experiences at a number of conferences, calling themselves the Littlemore group, for the village in which John Henry Newman served as a Church of England rector.[71]

What Is the Church's Heart? Community

In a conference on the situation of parishes in the UK, there were some important things to remember.[72] The bishop of Kensington, Graham Tom-

---

70. Feuerhard, "Methodist Experiences in Closing Congregations Offers Lessons to Catholics."

71. Martin and Coakley, *For God's Sake*; Wells and Coakley, *Praying for England*.

72. Thornton, "What Future Does the Parish Have in the 21st Century?"

lin, noted that after two major catastrophes in the greater London area, the Grenfell Tower fire and the Parsons Green Tube bomb, "if the parish system did not exist, 'you'd sure as heck want to invent it.'"[73] Much as with St. Paul's Chapel and St. Joseph's church near Ground Zero after 9/11, the nearby parishes of St. Clement's and Parsons Green immediately opened their doors to the first responders and victims and families, becoming oases not only for comfort and counsel but also for food, drink, and contact. All across the UK, there are parish churches everywhere, some no longer functioning and most of them still having services with communities gathered. Until a disaster, many take these venerable buildings for granted, regarding them more as historic venues to visit. But in a moment of great terror and need, there they were, the churches, irreplaceable not only as historic sites but as places of encounter and gathering.

Biblical scholars emphasize that the earliest communities were very small and very local. They were absolutely tied to a place and life, work, and all else that went on there. This century and the one preceding have seen technology explode every meaning of place, community, and work. We no longer work where our company is located. We no longer live where our grandparents and parents lived. Who knows where our own children and their children will live. Our neighbors are as likely to be in the same situation. And while we may all speak the same language, there may be innumerable other differences among us. We are an increasingly diverse country now—something that we see has provoked fear, suspicion, and, tragically, hate among many. But unlike a generation or two past, our churches are no longer as psychologically and theologically distant from each other as they once were. We have married outside our ethnic and religious communities of origin. And, as we have seen, many have no regular experience of belonging to a local community of faith, a local congregation.

All this said, however, a church is often one of the few places where we experience the gathering and sustaining of community—this is the central claim of the entire book. Community is not easily found anymore in our landscapes. And yet, as we also have seen, parishes of every church background are shrinking in membership, some simply dying, though members may join up elsewhere and the buildings used to good purposes. One researcher participating in the British conference, Nick Spencer, put it bluntly:

> The parish, as we know it, was designed for an agricultural, pre-mobile, geographically defined society. We live in a post-industrial, highly mobile, and socially defined society. At the moment, it is paid scant attention to by very many people. Two

---

73. Thornton, "What Future Does the Parish Have in the 21st Century?," para. 1.

percent of the population will attend an Anglican church on
a Sunday morning, and those that do cross parish boundaries
willy-nilly.[74]

Spencer noted that, sadly, fear of doing anything new, anything that
would disturb or anger the dwindling membership, paralyzed parishes,
almost certainly condemning them to eventual demise. The Methodist
Church Legacy Initiative in the US recognizes exactly this possibility and
tries to confront it constructively, in the hope that seeing the legacy of
one's beloved parish living on somehow, somewhere, will soften resistant
members' opposition to any change. In England, the minster system, going all the way back to missionary days and the Benedictine monastic
missionaries, might offer a possible model for going forward: the larger,
healthier of the churches would be mission bases and offer resources for
the smaller, more radically declining congregations.

Andrew Rumsey, Team Rector in the Oxted Team Ministry in the
Church of England Southwark diocese and author of a major study, was
perhaps the most direct in his description of many a parish in the UK, saying that

> the structure is ailing and . . . is broken in many places. So
> I've got colleagues in the West Country who've got 15 parishes,
> 15 Grade-I listed buildings, 15 congregations with a dozen
> people, 15 PCCs[Parochial Church Council]. It's ridiculous,
> and utterly unsustainable . . . However, we therefore have to
> find ways of changing the structure, but without abandoning
> the parish principle.[75]

Another church historian, Alison Milbank, warned against fantasizing
about a past in which it seemed all the parishes were flourishing, church-
going being a social necessity and pious obligation. One wanted to avoid
being sent to hell! And church is where one saw all one's neighbors. The
Grantchester series from the UK on PBS portrays the local parish mostly as
where the village gathers not just on Christmas and Easter or for funerals
and baptisms and weddings, but regularly on Sundays. The vicar or pastor
knows everyone and is entwined in village life.

Closer examination of earlier historical periods simply does not bear out
such rosy views, which are often employed to castigate the godless, secular
character of society today. There is often more romanticizing of the past, even

74. Thornton, "What Future Does the Parish Have in the 21st Century?," paras.
12–13.

75. Rumsey, *Parish*, quoted in Thornton, "What Future Does the Parish Have in the
21st Century?," paras. 20–21.

the recent past, than there is any accurate depiction of behavior then. From my own work on the church in Kierkegaard's time, the first half of the nineteenth century in Denmark, as well as the churches in late-nineteenth and early twentieth-century Eastern Europe, it is difficult to find "golden" periods of flourishing, and even acknowledged times of renaissance or revival usually are limited and not typical of populations as a whole.

One of the aims of the present volume is to come to terms with profound and irrevocable change. These changes have produced both the world and society of the twenty-first century. Sometimes internal church body programs and consultants speak and act as though these changes were simple bumps in the road, merely the latest challenges to spreading the kingdom, capable of being dealt with by "fresh expressions," as the Church of England calls them. The Brompton Holy Trinity Alpha Program is a significantly updated version of revivalism. These approaches, despite modifications, amount to using strategies that have been employed since the emergence of Pietism and the revivals of the seventeenth century, down to our own time. Rousing songs and emotional music, charismatic preaching, stress on the terrors of hell, the costs of sinful behavior, and reminders of the awesome judgment of God and eternal punishment or the unfathomable abyss of God's mercy—these are tools used by notables such as Jonathan Edwards, George Whitefield, and Francis Asbury, down to Billy Graham in our time. Heavy on the emotions, and often using small-group intensity as pressure, this approach wants to create a new mini-community whose fervor transcends the pull of the culture outside it. I am not attacking the "Fresh Expressions" project or Alpha Program of the Anglicans specifically, only noting that the revivalist reliance on small-group dynamics and the need for belonging exert pressure on neophytes.

We have seen, though, that the UMC Church Legacy Initiative envisions different ways of facing parish decline. Some paths are radical, such as allowing a congregation to grieve its passing and then be part of a new one starting in its old worship, fellowship, and educational space. Other examples of this are forthcoming in a subsequent chapter. There is also the ending, celebration of, and giving thanks for a parish's life and grieving. But there is then property transitioning to other service functions such as education, feeding the hungry, and directly providing important services from community resource centers. There are of course still other ways of proceeding, a common one being opening up a congregation to other community activities while it continues to function as a worshipping community. And there is the entirely new mission start, the planting of a community of faith in a more promising location, where there was no church before. Add to these the combining of congregations to form new, merged parishes, redundant building passing to other uses or possibly to other congregations. There are similar agencies that national church bodies have created to consult with and assist congregations in finding ways to re-invent themselves, replant, and reconnect with the neighborhoods around them and to repurpose the property they have used for decades.

The churches need to come to terms with the profound, irreversible changes, many of them demographic, that are shrinking parishes. The UK conference referenced above was a healthy instance of this, as was the work of the clergy study group from the Church of England and the UMC Church Legacy Initiative. There are numerous diocesan and other local efforts to hon-estly confront these changes and their consequences for parishes. One of the UMC leaders associated with the Church Legacy Initiative speculated that in the next decade, possibly a third of the almost 32,000 UMC congregations in the US would close or merge with another parish. In the Evangelical Lutheran Church in America (ELCA), a local bishop admitted not long ago that about the same number of parishes in the greater New York City area would either merge or close or pass over to other church bodies. An ELCA parish in the Bronx was essentially gifted to the community of the Ethiopian Orthodox Church in New York City to serve as their parish church after they spent many years using space at Union Theological Seminary.

We will look at a number of different efforts to resurrect parishes in the chapters that follow, efforts to replant, reinvent, redefine themselves and reconnect with their neighborhoods while remaining communities of faith, the body of Christ in a particular place.

CHAPTER 3

Community Death and Resurrection

Repurposed, Reinvented, Replanted

Repurposing Churches

THE MOTIF OF DEATH and resurrection is at the core of Jesus's life. Death and resurrection are the culmination of his ministry, the heart of the gospel. Death and resurrection define the community that follows Jesus. Community as church is the focus of this book, and death and resurrection lie at the heart of the community of faith. When we call this community "the body of Christ," as Paul does, death and resurrection both are implied, for the body of Christ is always at once crucified, dying and raised, a new life (1 Cor 12:12–27; Rom 12:5; Col 1:18, 24).

In the previous chapter, we looked at some of the factors at work in the decline and shrinkage of many congregations throughout the country. We listened to several trying to make sense of these trends and their consequences, such as David Gushee's account of why churches are in decline. We also began to review examples of parishes that attempted to address the reality of their failing situation—some through allowing the good death of the historic congregation to be celebrated and grieved. But we saw, as well, new congregations emerge from the passing of the former ones. We looked at the work of the UMC Legacy Initiative with several parishes, just one of numerous programs church bodies have developed to help congregations face decline and both death and possible revival.

In this chapter, we will examine the death and resurrection of communities of faith. Death and resurrection are part of the regular, ordinary lives of congregations. New Christians are made by water and spirit at the font. Christians of all races, genders, ethnicities, and social and political stripes share the bread and cup at the Lord's table. They are joined in marriage in the church, celebrate all the anniversaries, sorrows, and joys there.

They share food and drink and friendships, sometimes over a lifetime, sometimes for just months. And the people of God are sent on their transition to the kingdom of heaven from the church. Church, community in Christ, are about life, death, and resurrection.

But we see death and resurrection in parishes' shrinkage, closure, or transition to a new congregation. Here we will follow this, but also parishes' efforts to reinvent, repurpose, and restructure themselves. There is no way this can be exhaustive, not only for economy's sake here, but simply because these experiments are in process and new ones appear all the time, some succeeding, others being abandoned after valiant effort. Looking further at them will help show the diversity of assessing what happened over time to a parish and then what steps to take in addressing the future.

We will only look briefly at the fascinating repurposing of church buildings that has turned them into performance and events spaces, restaurants and clubs, commercial sites for clothing, food, or galleries for art or historical objects. Nevertheless, it is necessary to see that such a repurposing remains one of the most common paths of a congregation when it decides it can no longer continue its life and work in a building or in a neighborhood. One notable case is the deconsecration of Holy Communion Episcopal Church in the Chelsea neighborhood in New York City and its transformation into Limelight, a club that soon became notorious, then into a commercial marketplace, a gym, and most recently an upscale Chinese restaurant. Such completely secular, market-driven repurposing has evoked extreme reactions, from outrage and indignation to admiration for discerning entreprenurial experiments.

Congregations in Canada

Canada has seen a more decisive secularization and more pronounced turn of people away from church membership and attendance than the US. In Montreal, the church of Notre-Dame-du-Perpétuel-Secours has become Théatre Paradoxe, a multipurpose event space for cover bands, Zumba classes, fetish parties, and talk shows—among them, a celebrity confession show that uses the old confessional booths, "Y'a du monde à messe," or "Everyone's at Mass." But the same former church offers training in theater and events planning and entertainment industry skills to school dropouts, those in recovery, and ex-cons. The director of the Paradoxe sees important connections between church as a place of liturgy and now as a place of performance and learning. The former chapel of the Grey Nuns motherhouse is now a library and reading room for Concordia University, as well as space for student residence. Whereas 95 percent of Quebec attended Mass on Sundays in the 1950s, 5 percent do today, and over 500 churches in the province have been closed as parishes and many repurposed as described. Still others have been turned into restaurants, such as the church of Saint-Mathias-Apôtre, which offers low-cost quality meals to low-income area residents, including many artists and students. Sainte-Élizabeth-de-Warwick is now an artisan cheese shop—La Fromagerie du Presbytère—where a space is retained as a chapel for Sunday Mass. St. Jude Church is a gym and spa. The uses of former sacred space are numerous, many here in the US becoming upscale housing and commercial venues.[1]

The repurposings in Montreal are intriguing. Some may evoke criticism since they appear to be commercial, not at all connected to the building's former use. Others are more in the spirit of what the former sacred spaces were about, such as learning, community, and service. Artisan cheese and fetish parties maybe not so much. Bonnie Allen reports that almost 9,000 churches across Canada are set to close and will be either repurposed or demolished. This has become a concern for the National Trust for Canada regeneration project. Its head, Robert Pajot, says that virtually every community will experience the closing of houses of worship going forward. This will not be only the loss of beautiful, historic sacred spaces. Along with it will be, as we are seeing over and over here, the loss of a community and its life and outreach into the larger neighborhood.

All the demographic factors noted earlier here are in play. Successive generations of families relocate for education and work, leaving congregations without the continuity of multiple-generations of families. People marry out of both ethnic and religious communities. Then there are those who have stopped or never started connections with religious organizations, the Nones and the Dones. Aging congregations have less ability to financially sustain what are often aging physical structures that demand intensive maintenance or restoration and renovation. It sounds repetitious, but the variables at work are the same everywhere, no matter which church body or religious tradition or country.

In parts of Canada, the figures are startling. In some Catholic dioceses, close to half the churches will close in the near future. And in Canada, as elsewhere, the decline and shrinkage and closing, as well as repurposing, of churches is truly ecumenical—all churches experience these changes. One example of the effort to reinvent and repurpose is seen in St. Luke's Anglican, located west of downtown Ottawa. The rector, Victoria Scott,

---

1. Bilefsky, "Where Churches Have Become Temples of Cheese, Fitness and Eroticism"; Allen, "From Sacred to Secular."

listed the measures taken in the parish in the last years. These included demolishing a hall and putting up affordable housing, setting up a soup kitchen, a daycare, and a parking garage. The sanctuary itself was made more flexible for multipurpose use as well as rental. So not only was there an eye to economy and revenue, but also real service and outreach to the surrounding neighborhood.

Another Anglican priest, Graham Singh, is organizing the transition of a hundred Quebec church buildings into community centers with a variety of services and programs ongoing. In St. Jax (formerly St. James the Apostle) Anglican church in Montreal, space is devoted to various performance artists, a notable one being Le Monastère, a circus troupe.[2] The patterns vary. At St. Jax, there is a Sunday service preceded by coffee and the famous Montreal bagels. There are also other congregational activities such as talks, church school, and a course called "date night," which is both for marriage preparation and enrichment of life for married couples. Graham Singh came out of the well-known Holy Trinity Brampton Alpha Course from the UK, mentioned elsewhere here, that sought to revive parishes as well as reopen closed churches and replant communities in them. Thus the Alpha Course is an essential ingredient in the reinvention of St. Jax. It has at the base an introduction to the fundamentals of the Christian faith with no presumption whatsoever of previous familiarity. In Montreal, just such people abound, as well as others long absent from church participation, some with painful experience and memories as well. So St. Jax is a case study in death and resurrection, the resurrection of a parish that ended its existence and then came to life once more as a very different kind of community of faith, one with both strong evangelical character and evangelism as a primary goal. Only time will reveal whether the replanting works.

Allen chronicles a number of other efforts in Hamilton and Peterborough, Ontario, in Edmonton, Alberta, where venerable church buildings well over a century old were found to be in such states of deterioration that restoration was either impossibly expensive or impossible from architectural and engineering standpoints. As in other cases reviewed here, these sanctuaries were demolished and in their place went affordable housing and multipurpose spaces for a diversity of community programs and services. This was just one of the ways in which the "death" of houses of worship gave way to the "resurrection" of places and spaces for continued service and care for those in need. One can see that resurrection need not mean only the replanting of a parish or the repurposing for specifically religious activities.

---

2. McKenna, "Montreal Church Partners with Circus Company to Help Pay the Bills."

If the point of the good news of death and resurrection is new life, there are many forms this can take.

Congregations Repurposing in Harlem, New York City

In Harlem's ongoing development boom, historic black congregations are having a hard time resisting the urge to simply sell off their properties and relocate. With the shift of so much African-American population out of and away from Harlem and the existence of so many churches, from tiny store-front operations to massive spaces in former theaters or stone edifices, there is really a crisis going on there. Some, like St. Martin's, have been shut by higher-level authorities such as the Episcopal diocese of New York. With a forty-bell carillon and bell tower no longer structurally safe, and a dwindling congregation, there were few alternatives, though some members resisted the move of the congregation to a building on the grounds of the Cathedral of St. John the Divine not far away.

Nearby Metropolitan Community UMC is in the same situation, with the ceiling of the main sanctuary having collapsed. There, the decision to sell off the property and construct a much smaller church on a lot was the path forward, though as with St. Martin's, there was opposition. For New Covenant Temple, housed in the spacious former Washington Theater, with almost 1,500 seats, the dilemma is virtually identical. Over seventy years old, the congregation has declined to a handful and the roof is leaking. In the past fifteen years, 20 percent of Harlem's black population has relocated, despite overall population growth from 109,000 to 143,500 in 2016. A walk down the main street, 125th Street, is telling. African-American vendors dot the sidewalk, there remain take-out shops, restaurants, clothing stores, furniture stores, and even a few big-box ones. But the people on 125th Street are from everywhere, Asian, Latino, African—in other words, the extreme diversity now characteristic of much of New York City.

The black churches were the real pillars of the Harlem community running from 110th to 155th Streets. Everything was rooted in the church-es—education, employment, meeting people with whom to do business or marry. And several major churches like Abyssinian Baptist are still thriving, with busloads of tourists coming to hear gospel music and fiery preaching. The Church of the Master, a Presbyterian congregation at West 122nd Street, took down the crumbling 1893 sanctuary, then renovated a building next door. The site of the former church was leased to a devel-oper, bringing in the income necessary to renovate and continue ministry next door. Leasing was a more solid procedure, enabling a congregation to continue to receive income, avoiding the failure of developers who purchase property outright and then fail, their bankruptcy ruining the congregation that sold to them. Peter Green describes many church-to-developer deals that went bad, leaving the parish with neither property nor income. New Covenant Temple, a former theater that is not landmarked and too costly to restore or renovate, hopes to go the lease route so that their ministry can continue in another location.[3]

Here again we see that the challenges facing congregations are not restricted to the drift away from faith and membership in communities of faith. Rather, there are several interwoven social and economic variables at play in Harlem and in numerous other urban locations. Gentrification is the rebirth, the revival of neighborhoods—not only their historic housing stock but new residential starts as well. And making this possible is investment in new businesses, stores, restaurants, and bars. Whole Foods and Target have opened stores in Harlem. Harlem is having yet another renaissance, though not like the black one rooted in the arts decades ago. The are many new eateries in addition to the historic Sylvia's, like Red Rooster, due to the investment of Chef Marcus Samuelsson and the location of his group on Lenox Avenue. However, gentrification is also the displacement of the former population and businesses and neighborhood institutions like churches. There is also the drift of residents away from Harlem to other areas of the city. The African-American community has not completely left Harlem, but the political and social base in now in Brooklyn.

In its heyday in the late 1940s and early 1950s, St. Martin's had 3,000 members, and its founder, Fr. John Howard Johnson, was leading boycotts against Harlem merchants who discriminated against blacks. Abyssinian had the famous Adam Clayton Powells Sr. and Jr. as its pastors, and the present pastor, Calvin Butts III, has been a powerful voice in New York politics. Many of Harlem's smaller congregations face the same demographic and economic challenges that all parishes in America confront now.

The pace of developers pouncing on soon-to-be-former churches to turn them into very high-end residences has accelerated in New York City, as *New York Times* reporter C. J. Hughes documents.[4] While some arrangements with developers recognize congregations' desire that the property they vacate and transfer will somehow continue the good work of their church, much of the time it is the market that controls the future of their building or the land on which it stands. In rapidly gentrifying parts of New

---

3. Barron, "Bells of St. Martin's Fall Silent as Churches in Harlem Struggle"; Green, "Houses of Worship Grappling with Harlem's Development Boom."

4. See Hughes, "Church Turned Club Is Now a Market."

York City, churches are those rare properties with space. It is a complex, often tangled situation when congregations that are closing start transacting with developers. Often, once the papers have been signed, there is no ability to influence the developers' plans. Hughes points to several examples of churches and parish houses or rectories that have turned into high-end residential structures, for example, Brooklyn's Episcopal Church of the Redeemer becoming 561 Pacific, or Madison Avenue Baptist's parish house becoming 30E31, Lagree Baptist on West 125th Street becoming 11 Hancock, and others. Over three dozen houses of worship in the city are in some form of transition such as this. Smaller ones are usually less desirable but still of interest and space capable of redevelopment.

There are unfortunate tales of unexplained and unjustified delays such as Azimuth Development Group's failing to finish the new sanctuary space that was a part of its contract to build a new apartment building where St. Luke Baptist was on West 123rd Street. A few congregations, to avoid just such problems, contracted to be co-developers. This was the case for Second Canaan Church, which now has space on the ground floor of 10 Lenox, with almost thirty units just a block from Central Park. The Church of Jesus Christ of Latter-Day Saints vacated its property in the Murray Hill section of Queens for a larger parcel and bigger building not far away in Linden Hill. Rong Xin Realty purchased the Murray Hill building in 2018 for almost 30 million and is putting up Flushing Garden Condominiums. This will be over 130 units at market rate, about $1,000 a square foot. The congregation was able to finance its new building, and housing stock in Queens will be enhanced.

Hughes points to the alarming fact that developers are actively hunting for troubled congregations, ones that have shrunk or have postponed building maintenance and need funds to deal with their situations. Despite so many stories of church properties turning into residential buildings affordable to very few, there are also a few tales of outcomes more in line with congregations' visions of doing good. There will be more of these in this and other chapters. Judson Memorial Church in the Village now has five congregations using its space, sustaining their existence without the property burdens they formerly had. First Presbyterian Church of Jamaica was able to enter into a partnership with the Bluestone Organization toward a twelve-story, 174-unit affordable housing structure on their old parking lot. The building will be called Tree of Life and it will have space, though limited, even for low-income residents. The Jamaica Church, vibrant with 500 members and an array of outreach ministries, including health and recovery services and a soup kitchen, is one example of a congregation able to buck the trend toward selling and seeing no footprint of their beliefs and good work left behind. Its pastor, Patrick O'Connor, emphasizes that affordable housing is one of the most difficult realities in the greater New York City area now. Congregations can have some impact on efforts to grow affordable housing when it becomes time to negotiate on their property's future.[5]

Some congregations that are still open, healthy, and desirous of making an impact on the surrounding community have made impressive moves in offering their real estate for affordable housing. St. Paul's Episcopal in Walnut Creek, California and Clairemont Lutheran in San Diego are offering just such housing possibilities in areas where affordable housing has become a major social problem.[6] In counterpoint to the usual NIMBY, congregation members answer YIGBY—"Yes in God's backyard"—when it comes to space for people of modest means or low income, people not wanted in many neighborhoods. Clairemont is awaiting a change in a San Diego area ordinance that requires so many parking spaces for a house of worship. If this is obtained, about half their parking lot can be developed for affordable housing along with space in a former fellowship hall. The San Diego county tax collector, Dan McAllister, found that over 1,000 houses of worship had real estate that could be used for purposes like affordable housing. The challenge now is to get building codes and environmental requirements to be synchronized with plans to create such housing. It is notable that income from those inhabiting such housing should cover the construction costs in time. Some creative financing seems to be necessary going forward. St. Paul's Commons, as the parish is calling their development, is a mixed-use space that have services and a place for the homeless but forty-five units of affordable housing as well. These efforts stand in stark contrast to the sale of property to developers who then use former church real estate for upscale housing, despite congregation efforts to get them to include at least a few affordable units.

The communities of closing congregations face real challenges. Developers can consider the adaptation of architecture designed to make the spirit soar, large spaces that on their own have very few practical uses save being event spaces, restaurants, and the like. Yet there then is the issue of the reaction of the community and greater public to large-scale desacralization of sacred spaces. Should stained-glass windows and frescoes depicting biblical events and holy people be left in a space designed for dance and banqueting? Likewise, altars, crosses, statues, and other sacred symbols

5. Hughes, "For Churches, a Temptation to Sell"; De La Cruz, "Light to the City."
6. Molina, "'Yes in God's Backyard' to Use Church Land for Affordable Housing."

linked to sacred rites once celebrated in the now-empty churches—should these remain or be removed?

The already-mentioned transformation of the Church of the Holy Communion in Gramercy in Manhattan into the Limelight Club stands as a case study that should inform present-day developers. With its beautiful stained-glass windows now much more visible than in Limelight days, the space of the former 1844 Episcopal Church of the Holy Communion, designed by the noted Richard Upjohn, architect of Trinity Wall Street, is lighter and brighter. Now a kind of indoor market, there are sixty spaces for vendors—the Limelight Marketplace.[7] Previously, the market hosted David Barton Gym and Jan Lue Club.[8] As Hughes and others note, market considerations often win out.

Resurrection: Bethesda at Haw Creek Commons and Other Repurposings and Replants

Church consultants have been able to suggest other noncommercial, primarily service- and community-oriented uses for closed and functioning parishes and their buildings. Jonathan Merritt, writing in *The Atlantic*, notes the creative repurposing of two Methodist parishes, White Rock UMC in Dallas, Texas, and Bethesda UMC near Asheville, North Carolina, in Haw Creek.[9]

Larry Duggins and Elaine Heath run Missional Wisdom Foundation, a source of innovative thinking about the use of former parish properties. Heath was professor of evangelism at Southern Methodist University, where Duggins also studied after a career in investment banking. Both are retools themselves. With 60,000 square feet of space, White Rock UMC had lots of possibilities, and the team started in the 15,000-square-foot bottom section of the building. What ensued was a series of spaces for local craftspeople, a yoga studio, and a dance studio, along with an economic empowerment center, where English as a Second Language and other employment skills were made available for recent immigrants and all others interested.

With such a new economic base in their basement, the congregation has been able to regroup and continue, engaging with the surrounding community in new ways while able to financially continue service. The

---

7. Hughes, "Church Turned Club Is Now a Market"; Krishna, "From House of Worship to House of Sin."

8. Kurutz, "Many Lives of Limelight."

9. Merritt, "America's Epidemic of Empty Churches."

same happened through the Missional Wisdom Foundation's consultation at Haw Creek, as we will see. It is clear that despite the numerous challenges to shrinking and even closed congregations, there are real possibilities for meaningful repurposing of space and the providing of space for needed and important commercial and service-oriented activities in the local community. These, as we will see in many other accounts of parishes reinventing themselves, are really different ways of living out the gospel, of celebrating the Sunday liturgy all through the week in a liturgy of presence and service in the local community.

Bethesda UMC in Haw Creek, North Carolina has been a parish since 1844. However, in recent years the congregation has looked as if its days were numbered. A small, battered parking lot and weathered sign offered little welcome to anyone beyond its dwindling membership. Enter the Western North Carolina Conference of the UMC and Missional Wisdom Foundation staff. It took three years, but it is now Bethesda at Haw Creek Commons. The Bethesda congregation is still in residence there, worshipping in the sanctuary on Sundays. The rest of Bethesda's buildings are now home to programs that connect the parish to the surrounding community. A community development organization uses the sanctuary as a community meeting place. The former education rooms have become a collection of spaces for a commercial kitchen, for woodworking, ceramics, and textile work. Other space goes for meetings: yoga, dance, exercise, and larger performances. The parsonage is now a retreat house. External space on campus includes a community garden for participants and the food pantry, also bee hives and a playground.

Bethesda parish continues now, but it is no longer the owner and operator but a guest in the Commons. It is led by Pastor Ben Schaeffer and a family pastor, Amy Leachman. Bethesda's community has grown as a result of the outreach of the Commons to greater Asheville. There is centering and Celtic prayer and Scripture study, church school, and other social events.

Much in the manner of other congregations in decline, Bethesda followed the counsel of the Missional Wisdom Foundation advisers. It need not be an end-of-the-congregation ultimatum. Many of the congregations we will see here rejected the choice to dissolve and simply join another parish. Bethesda chose to continue to be the body of Christ in their location. What appeared to be death was in time the resurrection of the congregation. The way to do that was to repurpose their physical plant facilities and accept the possibility of being a small yet vital church.[10]

10. Heath, "Breathe."

Houses of worship that close need not be mourned as signs of a lack of faith, emblems of defeat. There are numerous examples of where they take on new lives of serving those in need and acting as places to gather. One path is for rehab of the building and the planting of a new congregation, such as at Temple Beth-El in Hackensack, New Jersey. There the existing community teamed up with the Orthodox Chabad-Lubavitch to establish a new congregation. Chabad is an Orthodox movement, so Beth-El is actually returning to its roots from over a hundred years ago. Such a shift to a new congregation is one of the more frequent paths that aging, sometimes dying congregations take to find new life.

Chabad, part of the Lubavitch Orthodox movement, with the late Rebbe Menachem M. Schneerson as its spiritual head, is a youth-dominated and growing religious organization. Hackensack is but one of a number of locations on the East Coast where Chabad came in to assume leadership of a declining congregation. Chabad is, of all the Orthodox groups, the most open and welcoming, also the one with the most intense sense of, and structures for, community in their local congregations. So whether in Hackensack or Swapscott, Massachusetts, those remaining from the earlier congregation are welcomed, as are all Jews. No judgments or exclusions. It is but one of numerous living examples we will encounter here where strong relationships, vibrant community, is at the heart of the revival and repurposing of a congregation.

Likewise, in Kansas City, the Wornall Road Baptist Church had dwindled to less than twenty members. It welcomed a new mission plant by the Southern Baptist Convention and now houses a growing community. Unlike the Hackensack temple, whose building had deteriorated due to long-deferred maintenance, Wornall Road Baptist's sanctuary and other buildings were in good shape, but the community was so small that no future other than closing seemed possible. The more mission-oriented, outreach-focused congregation that the Southern Baptist Mission Board planted started making ties to the surrounding neighborhood, schools, and residents real. Athletes from the high school were hosted for a Friday supper. There was a reaching out to the nearby elementary school. Memorials were held for victims of violence in the area. In short, the parish once more became part of the neighborhood, a neighbor to other neighbors.[11]

Jonathan Merritt began *The Atlantic* story on the emptying of churches and other houses of worship with a startling description of a deteriorating, now-closed Catholic Church in his Brooklyn neighborhood. Nationwide, nearly 10,000 congregations close each year. The bottom line

---

11. Kellner, "Shuttered Houses of Worship Get a Reboot and Find New Life."

for parish survival is financial feasibility, which means maintaining or increasing membership. Growth is the ideal, stability is what many parishes dream of, but shrinkage is increasingly the reality.[12] Merritt thus sees hope in the work of Larry Duggins and Elaine Heath in the Bethesda at Haw Creek Commons story.

David Frost, as noted, accurately describes the vision that often takes over in struggling congregations as "survival" theology. It's myopic outlook ends up turning a community in upon itself rather than outward, toward their neighborhood, the rest of the world, and other churches. Finances become an obsession. There is paranoia about anything said in preaching, classes, or meetings that might offend, since the loss of even one member is crucial. There is no vision of the future, of how to move forward. Nostalgia for the "good old days" grows, for a time when people were coming out in numbers—at least in this romantic memory of the past, when there was little change from one year to another.

Yet a quick survey of the last 100 years makes a lie of this supposed calm and order. What of the explosion of technology, of the car changing how people lived, of the toll of WWI, then the Great Depression, then WWII, what of the years of the Red Scare and Cold War and the nuclear arms race that followed, and Vietnam, the Civil Rights, womens, and eventually LGBTQ movements? So much for a legacy of calm and changelessness. The lives of the last three to four generations have been ones of constant change and challenge. Despite the pull of memory, the church of beloved past has long since ceased to exist. Other subsequent versions of church have given way to where one is today.

From within church circles, the more discerning visions, those of the likes of David Gushee, Brian McLaren, Richard Rohr, John Pavlovitz, and Sam Wells, among others, are converging, and we will hear much more of this as we move forward. Though from differing church backgrounds, one hears their profound unity in faith when they all say churches must reclaim their basic elements of worship, prayer, learning, fellowship, and service.[13] These were the true weapons of the spirit in the past and the only tools for moving forward. And the perspective has to be outward, not introverted, the aim to thrive, not survive. As Loren Mead and Sam Wells put it, the church has something to live for besides itself, a reason for being—it is for and about life in its fullness. This is putting death and resurrection into practice, bringing the new life that the gospel offers into reality, not only in brick-and-mortar

---

12. Merritt, "America's Epidemic of Empty Churches."

13. Raines, "Hope for Dying Churches."

structures better used, but in the transformed Christ-bearers, the women and men who form the body of Christ in a specific location.

Shane Claiborne has been living out precisely this in Philadelphia for over two decades of his forty-three years, as Nick Tabor brilliantly shows.[14] Now the author of numerous books and often on tour in a refitted bus, Claiborne has shown the deep countercultural inclinations of the New Testament and has been challenging both mainline as well as evangelical and Pentecostal churches to come to terms with their connections to politics and society. He rejects the comfortable alliance between many evangelicals with both the Republican Party and president and their hawkish defensive outlook, opposition to health care and better services for the elderly, children, low-income, and immigrant folk, and their support for corporations, the financial establishment, and the wealthy. There is no evidence of spiritual health and congregational success having anything to do with more members and higher income in giving. Real faith is about concern for the neighbor, for justice and peace, especially for the powerless and those in need.

Resurrections in Transition and in Respecting the Local Community

In Rockville, Maryland, for over sixty years, Twinbrook Baptist Church has been an open, progressive Christian community. It made clear its welcome to LGBTQ people and became well known for this openness. Members even counter-protested disruptive actions by the notorious anti-gay Westboro Baptist Church. Twinbrook members were also very active in support of the legal rights of LGBTQ people, becoming part of an amicus brief before the Supreme Court asking protection from discrimination against gay and transgender workers.

Twinbrook supported outreach to students needing assistance with school meals, also children with autism. But when shrinkage over a long period finally led the congregation to closing, what the members decided to do was startling. Marisa Iati, covering this story for *The Washington Post*, mentions several other church buildings were either sold or demolished so that further works of mercy could continue in the community around them. Rolling Hills Baptist in Fayetteville, Georgia did this, as well as St. John's Catholic Church in Virginia, Minnesota. Rolling Hills followed the example of several other parishes they learned about, one in New York City

---

14. Tabor, "Evangelist."

and another, Navo UMC, in Decatur, Georgia, among others, which simply rented space for Sunday worship and gatherings for fellowship and study. The vote to sell off their property was almost unanimous and the proceeds from the sale and from lowered maintenance and operating costs went to local outreach projects and rental fees. St. John's Church in Virginia was only one of several now-redundant, formerly active-ethnic congregations with dwindling memberships and antiquated buildings requiring much maintenance and high operating costs. A newer parish, Holy Spirit, remains with its parochial school, while St. John's is closed and gone, along with Our Lady of Lourdes and Sacred Heart churches, also with former ethnic memberships now disappeared. Here, as with the other cases, there was the elimination of expensive heating and maintenance.[15]

Twinbrook Baptist sold its building to the Latinx congregation who had been renting space with them, Centro Cristiano Peniel, for a million below market cost. So worship and outreach continues with Centro, but also goes on with over thirty nonprofit organizations in the surrounding area. These groups support medical clinics as well as several youth programs. Community Reach of Montgomery County itself is an umbrella organiza- tion with medical services, as well as housing assistance, for low-income and uninsured people with chronic health needs.[16]

Alan Roxburgh makes an important point about how churches are responding to change. It is one that runs counter to much of the corporate culture in which we live. In thinking about how to address the profound, disruptive changes in our society affecting congregations, also the internal changes in those communities, many denominations or national church bod- ies think from their administrative centers outward to the local churches of the parishes. Often, specialists are engaged as consultants, and the vision often becomes one of structural and institutional change. After all, this is the way that response to problems looks, both in the private and public sectors. Think big. Think long term. Think in terms of modifying existing patterns, trans- forming structures, not only nationally and regionally, but locally.

And so, the recent history of mainline church bodies is littered with program after program for evangelism, church planting, parish replanting, tweaking of liturgy, hymns, preaching styles, architecture, and concepts of ministry that have been tried and eventually discarded. "Entertainment evan- gelism," churches without any visible religious symbols or creeds, the use of massive screens and projected hymn, worship, and preaching texts, relabeling

15. Iati, "Liberal Baptist Church Will Close Its Doors and Give $1 million to Non-profits."

16. Quinn, "Church's Radical Act"; Riebe, "Old Church Demolition Saddens and Improves Catholic Community."

and renaming of congregations to eliminate connections with historic church bodies—so away with "Lutheran" or "Presbyterian," no more St. Thomas or Resurrection or Transfiguration, but Joy Church, Life Community, Son Rising, Living Water, or the like, for names of congregations.

But Roxburgh's point is not to criticize faddish efforts of the past. If they have shown themselves to be short-sighted, unrelated to local conditions, not connected to a living community in the local church, this will show itself in time. That is the real point he makes. Local communities of faith show themselves much more capable of assessing their situation, even if dire, such as demographic shrinkage, buildings outgrowing the size of the congregation, diminished ties to the neighborhoods and people around the parish. As we have seen and will continue to see in several chapters here, there are substantial provocative stories of revival, reinvention, of resurrection and new life in the communities of faith across the country. When the description of the demographic and other changes I pull together become too much information and too discouraging for some, the good news of how congregations have found new ways of living out the gospel, being the body of Christ for the life of the world—these should be a balance that lies at the heart of faith—the cross, but also the empty tomb.[17] Maybe put simply: trust the local church! Allow yourself to accept that health has little to do with size and volume.

Other Resurrections—in Philadelphia, Oakland, and Winnipeg

It is possible to redesign the space that communities of faith occupy for better use. The Philadelphia Center for Architecture has been involved in a competition, "Infill Philadelphia," targeted more specifically: "Sacred Places/Civic Spaces." The Pew Charitable Trust investigated in 2017 and found nearly 840 sacred places in the city where there is dire need of repurposing and investment. With shrinking congregations and deteriorating buildings, these communities of faith faced very bleak futures unless they replanted themselves in their neighborhoods, attracted investment and input from neighbors on what was needed in their sections of the city. The Philadelphia Masjid in Mill Creek, the Wharton-Wesley United Methodist Church in Cobb Creek, and Zion Baptist Church in North Philadelphia were targets for efforts to connect these congregations to programs in which their space could be used during the week. An earlier study of

---

17. Roxburgh, "Attend to What's Happening on the Ground."

religious buildings determined that the economic impact of their spaces could be over $1.7 million a year.

The Philadelphia Masjid teamed with Peoples' Emergency Center and, while long-term engagement will take millions more and much time, they have already been able to take their space—a former school—and begin to use it for food prep and meals, as well as for offices and meeting rooms to help neighbors deal with housing issues. Wharton-Wesley UMC partnered with ACHIEVEability, a program focused on single parents trying to survive economic, educational, and other challenges. Zion Baptist connected with Called to Serve, an umbrella group for numerous family and youth-related needs and activities.

In each case, the partnership was extending the love for the neighbor that lies at the heart of both Islamic and Christian faith. One small interesting note was the importance of an entrance to the building that was both accessible and welcoming. The Masjid was able to modify an entrance facing the local park, thus not only opening the space up to residents but also advertising and attracting people to the programs ongoing inside. Too often the locked main door to the sanctuary is what neighbors see all week, even if there are side entrances to educational wings and meeting spaces. Hospitality becomes not only a scriptural mandate but a real invitation to others to come and use the facilities.[18]

The First Christian Church of Oakland began as a congregation in 1876. In 1928, the present mission-style complex of buildings was dedicated, with a 1,500-capacity sanctuary. Over time, like many urban parishes, the neighborhood changed. Residents, including members, relocated, and the decline continued till there were twenty regular worshippers on Sunday. Nevertheless the complex of buildings was maintained by the membership and now forty or more nonprofit organizations use the space all week long, the small congregation continuing to hold services. Now known as the Oakland Peace Center, the property was put into a trust with Disciples Home Missions, a division of the larger denomination, the Church of Christ/Disciples of Christ.

Sandhaya Rani Jha served as pastor from 2006 to 2013. She then became director of the center and another member, Monica Joy Cross, is part-time pastor alongside several other ministries. Jha has both an MDiv and a master's in public policy from the University of Chicago. Along with members, Jha realized that the congregation could offer low-cost or even free space at a premium in a high-rent area to groups working for social justice, health care,

18. Cunningham, "Redesigning Sacred Spaces to Serve Their Communities and Save Their Congregations."

education, and more. In 2007, the membership held a retreat which led to the decision to make their buildings a place where peace and service and healing for the entire local community could be based. They were blessed with facilities that were in reasonably good shape and eminently adaptable to use for meetings, programs, office of nonprofit organizations. By 2009, the center was partnering with the national Disciples of Christ, and the center was welcoming organizations and events.

Given the imposing size of First Christian Church/Oakland Peace Center, it might have seemed more likely that the property transformation would have been in the direction of residential housing, or a restaurant, or perhaps the space simply sold, demolished, and turned into commercial or residential space. Often, church buildings, with their distinctive sacred art and architecture, are unlikely candidates for repurposing. But this complex of parish buildings defied those presumptions. This is not always the happy end to a tale of decline, however, and the issue of what will happen to a beloved sanctuary can become an impediment to reinvention or repurposing of space.[19]

At St. Matthew's Anglican Church in downtown Winnipeg, we encounter another case of death and rising. This is a reconfiguration of space and of community mission and identity that, like the Oakland Peace Center/First Christian Church, allows both the congregation's life and ministry to continue along with very different activities. Originally begun as a house church in 1896, the present building from 1947 replaced one gutted by fire a few years earlier. Seating 1,200, it was a massive structure with sanctuary and educational buildings and rectory, the hub of a neighborhood that also came to be known as St. Matthew. But the drift of population to the suburbs, and the decline of the surrounding commercial and residential areas, led the parish to consider closing and selling the property. Roof replacement was not financially feasible to the now-small but dedicated congregation. However, Cathy Campbell, a former rector, and her vision of what outreach service the church could do, inspired by other parishes, became a rallying cause. Since St. Matthew's housed a significant ministry for the resettlement of New Canadians, many immigrants and refugees from violence, the parish was able to be funded for a new roof, saving the main building from further leak deterioration.

The transformation, really the resurrection of St. Matthew's, did not come easy. The remaining congregation, aging, experienced the range of feelings when a beloved community and its home begin to crumble—which

19. Corrigan, "Tiny Congregation with a Big Building Is Resurrected as a Center of Peace."

the sanctuary literally was doing. With many Anglo-origin people having moved and many new, diverse faces filling the neighborhood, it was an experience of almost all of the stable past disappearing. And it was. But the remaining community at St. Matthew's, much like that at Oakland's First Christian Church, engaged in sustained reflection and, despite some resistance and doubt, they saw that the future was to use what property they had to serve the neighborhood while remaining a eucharistic community there. Eventually their space was converted into twenty-six apartments, some single-bedroom units and other three- or four-bedroom ones. These would all be eligible for government rent subsidy. This was a significant contribution to the dire need for affordable housing in the area. Now the community, while smaller than its glory days, has Sudanese and Burundi members and has rerooted itself in the neighborhood. Gone is the immense nave that seated over 1,000, and a small chapel is a better fit for a smaller but cohesive, if diverse, parish community.[20]

So, another instance of a declining, dying congregation culminated in a real resurrection. However, I think it is crucial to note that the resurrection is not a return to St. Matthew's "glory days" after WWII, with lots of people who were pretty much the same, centering not only their spiritual but their social lives in the parish. Resurrection will never be a restoration of the "good old days," of the past church community that involved successive generations of families. The demographic changes that we have mentioned repeatedly here make such a restoration or return impossible. Yet such dreams persist in this country, and are even offered as promises by some running for political office.

Such "left behind" Americans, studied by Arlie Hochschild and others, were assured they would get their jobs, thus, their salaries, benefits, and pensions, back, that they would return to the middle-class, upwardly mobile prospects their parents had known, thirty or more years earlier. This has not happened, and it will not happen. As John Judis pointed out, and as Hochschild's study, done before the 2016 election, the sense of rage at being let go, outsourced, abandoned, and ignored predates the Trump era. So too the populism, with its distrust of government, universities, and experts, and the nationalism that targeted immigrants as well as various populations here as "other" and threats to economic well-being. Support for anti-immigrant, anti-government, pro-gun, pro-law-and-order stances will continue to resonate with many "left behind," and perhaps reductions in immigration, the rejection of DACA or the Dreamers, and protection of gun rights will continue to be taken as measures to protect their jobs and security. But the restoration

20. Townsend, "Lessons in Humility for a Downtown Parish."

of former better days, also dear to many of Hochschild's informants in Louisiana, is at best a political fantasy. The same holds true for communities of faith. While we will encounter quite a few stories of near-closing and rebirth of congregations here, we will not find a case where there is a rewind or restoration to the parish of the past.

But resistance to change, mentioned by the present rector of St. Matthew's, Gwen McAllister, is real. At St. Matthew's, it did not dominate the decision to become both a welcome center and place of residence for new immigrants as well as a new community of faith. Resistance and the desire to either return to the past or retreat from the present are, however, real and sometimes destructive forces. This hardness of heart, expressed in resistance to change, is often rooted in fear. The new or different is perceived principally as threatening, as the loss of what is familiar, comforting, and comfortable. Any attempt to describe community without honest recognition of this "other side" of belonging results in a romanticized vision of community. And it not only must be recognized for what it is and from whence it comes, but it must also be met, even confronted, if a community is to move forward.

This is an element of parish life that often denominational leaders recognize but would rather downplay or ignore. The desire to return to the past cannot save a parish in decline. Neither does it prevent leadership in the larger church body from taking action that changes the congregation's status and future. The UMC Church Legacy Initiative, along with like programs in other church bodies, invites members of parishes tat are in decline or dying to reflect upon and choose a path forward. That can be rerooting in their larger community, merging with another parish, or even merging into a completely new one. Or, as we have seen, radically restructuring their space and their own identity and activity, or experiencing a "good death" and passing on their legacy and property to another parish or to constructive use in the area.

Replanting in the Community and Repurposing Property: Wesley Community Development Corporation

The name of Methodist church founder John Wesley in the title of a community development corporation suggests something other than energizing deteriorated neighborhoods is going on.[21] Following Wesley's conviction that congregations must be rooted in relationship with God and living a holy

---

21. Shimron, "North Carolina Nonprofit Helps Churches Convert Property from Liabilities to Assets."

life in the world, this nonprofit has been working with Methodist parishes in North Carolina on how to better use their buildings and land to pursue the mission of connecting with their neighborhoods in loving service and witness. Wesley Community Development Corporation (CDC) was set up with help from Duke Divinity School.

Park Street UMC in Belmont, North Carolina, a growing community, had almost five acres of land for their campus, as well as a sanctuary that needed a new roof and internal repair. Wesley CDC was just the group able to assist this congregation and others in the Western Carolina Methodist Conference, which is seeing forty to fifty congregations close a year. A two-day program called "Seeds of Change" gives pastors and congregation leaders a chance to think through what they have—their buildings and land—and how better to put these to work. Wesley CDC manages 2,400 congregational parcels of property totaling more than 75,000 acres. Some are the campuses of congregations that have closed, others are congregations in transition. All are challenged by decline, some diverse and thriving, others down to few members.

Wesley CDC is neither a religious miracle machine nor simply a property developer looking for maximum profit in the sale and reuse of church holdings. Almost seventy parishes have thus far used Wesley CDC's services, and more will be doing so each month. A stunning finding, across rural and urban, white and black, small and larger congregations, is that typically a parish only uses its building 10 to 15 percent of the time. This is primarily on Sunday. Wesley CDC tries to envision with each congregation how nonprofits and their service providers might use the buildings most of the week. Underused or unused space—undeveloped land, parking areas no longer needed, buildings no longer used—all these become targets for evaluation and repurposing. Methodist parishes, like those of a number of other church bodies, turn property back to the larger church body, here the conference, the equivalent of a diocese or synod, when the congregation closes. Wesley CDC tries to go local and respect each congregation's history by working with it to repurpose right there in their area. This is preferable to the Conference, which functions at a more distant level of the church trying to do this.

With assistance from Wesley CDC, several other North Carolina Methodist parishes have been able to set up after-school programs for young people; studio space for yoga, taekwondo, and tutoring; space for clinics and screening; office space for private as well as public service—all of this in space often not used during the week. Thus, these parishes receive in return funding from rental space and help in meeting energy costs, in addition to refurbishing existing worship space, including basic tasks like new roofs.

In one case, Christ UMC in High Point, North Carolina, the best decision was for the parish to sell its entire aging campus to High Point University, temporarily share space with another Methodist congregation, and evaluate sites for a much smaller, more flexible location. No miracles, but Wesley CDC really becomes a Godsend to parishes seemingly faced with financial disaster and an end to their lives of witness and service.

Merging Congregations—Not Death, but Life—in Austin, Billings, Houston, and Elsewhere

Merging of congregations may be the most frequent strategy for confronting decline in members and disappearing financial support. In Catholic diocesan restructuring of parishes, but also in those of other church bodies, merging may mean the closing of some parishes, whose members then are urged or even told to become members of another neighboring congregation. In some cases, the result is a new congregation, which while continuing to use the space of a former parish, either takes on or is given a new name and, in principle, identity. Particularly in more rural areas, where there are multiples parishes of the same denomination no longer sustainable, such a move can be painful for those whose parish disappears in the merge, their building no longer functioning as a worship and gathering place. Earlier, merging of parishes by Catholic dioceses in Pittsburgh, Hartford, New York, and Boston were mentioned, along with others of the United Methodist Church in North Carolina.

In Austin, Texas, a dying congregation, Asbury UMC, agreed to their local UMC conference proposal to invite a new, much younger, and informal group to use their fellowship hall for Sunday services. They ended up not only providing space but also became members themselves in a completely new congregation, Servant UMC. The old chancel of Asbury was not dismantled but became an area where small children could sit and read with their parents. The long church nave was turned horizontal with the communion table of the new congregation placed in the middle of the side wall. A band played contemporary music projected on screens, and the sermon was a dialogue between pastor and congregation. The new pastors came out of the Baptist and Presbyterian churches and brought their experience to this new plant of a congregation. Their style was informal and very much aimed at a younger community.

Founded in 1948, Asbury was one of the numerous parishes that sprang up in the population and building boom after WWII. Returning veterans with new families and people moving in from the country for

work and out of downtown created entire new sections of cities. This
was the case with Asbury UMC in central Austin. But by the mid-2000s,
Asbury's families were no longer multigenerational. The children and
grandchildren of early members relocated for education and work. The
core remaining community shrank with age, sickness, and deaths from
several hundred to less than fifty. The transition was not completely gracious. A few members resented "their" church building being taken away
from them and given to outsiders. The influx of younger people and their
small children was an assault on the staid, quiet ambiance that a handful
of seniors sustained.[22] Yet, a number of the older members of the former
Asbury parish remained in Servant UMC.

When one looks more carefully at what the new community, Servant
UMC, brought in, there is reason for hesitation. Most of what was imported
was new and alien to the members of Asbury—songs projected on a large
screen, a praise band with electric guitars, drums, bass, and the very informal style of the service and the younger pastors. Outreach included
immigration and healthcare clinics, also reaching out to local businesses,
including performers at an adult club. The desire to establish a new congregation of a decidedly younger age appears to have been the aim of the area
Methodist conference, based on the view that the aging members of Asbury
could not revive and survive. But former Asbury members were welcomed
and remained in the new Servant UMC congregation.

A case that attracted media attention also involved a Methodist congregation in Cottage Grove, Minnesota. Cottage Grove UMC Church was
scheduled to close in June 2020. It had been unable to financially support
a pastor for seven years, and since then the thirty or so older members
led the congregation themselves, caring for the property and conducting
services. The area UMC conference's plan was to reopen the congregation
sometime after the closing, perhaps before Christmas of 2020, but without
the former members.[23] While they will not be physically barred from entering and attending the reopened parish, they have been counseled to go
to church elsewhere so that a new, much younger congregation may start
up, without their presence as a reminder of the past and their likely adherence to their own traditions. The area conference has invested $250,000
in the reinvention of Cottage Grove UMC, and the pastor of the larger
Woodbury UMC, with which Cottage Grove was linked, has pleaded with
older members of Cottage Grove to come over to his parish and allow a

---

22. Flynn, "Dying Texas Church Gives Life to a New Congregation."
23. Shaw, "Best Path to a Younger Flock?"

new congregation with new ways and new people to emerge in their old location. He even suggested Jesus recommended this.

This case is not an anomaly. The previous case of Asbury giving way to Servant UMC, as well as others described in various chapters here, are not so rare. There are sometimes hurt feelings on the part of the older members. They feel they are not only being left behind but are seen as an obstacle and embarrassment. This sounds like Good Friday and the silent tomb of Holy Saturday period.

Within days of the first reporting, Methodist leaders claimed that the Cottage Grove members were not thrown out and told to go elsewhere.[24] Further reporting continued to raise questions about whether the Cottage Grove members were excluded or simply asked to wait till the new congregation had actually started functioning. No less than well-known Methodist bishop and professor Will Willimon felt compelled to comment, given the national media coverage. He noted that given what is happening to congregations—what we have seen here repeatedly—there is real conflict between older members who stay and the younger members replanting parishes.

Willimon, who closed numerous parishes when a conference bishop, further observed that both the older members as well as the new younger ones were "victims." I don't think he was trying to wriggle out of a difficult situation. He was underscoring that new starts in a former congregation as well as totally new plantings of mission parishes target younger people. And younger people often cannot relate to the traditional church, the hymns, liturgy, congregational culture, and activities, all of these, paradoxically, familiar and still welcome to older members.[25] Methodist pastor Allen Stanton, a specialist on small parishes, sees a real dilemma here. There is widespread denominational misunderstanding and devaluation of smaller parishes. Church bodies and local expressions such as conferences and dioceses don't know what to do with older members of declining ones. This also holds true for new-start pastors and members.[26] This dilemma, really a clash between two different sorts of members, those left over from the past and the members of the future, is a challenge to the reality of community as church. Clearly there is also a clash of visions of what a parish is or can be. Is the past coexistence of multiple generations no longer possible in a parish? Is the model of church, minus all the traditional elements—altar, cross, candles, historic hymns—the only one going forward? This was the Willow Creek

24. Bailey, "Church Allegedly Asked Older Members to Leave."

25. Graham, "What's Really Going on Inside the Minnesota Church Accused of Trying to Expel Its Aging Members?"

26. Stanton, "Misunderstanding the Small Church."

model, also that of the Alpha Program. Where is the holy community that gathers those of different ages, political, social, economic and ethnic backgrounds? Within the death-and-resurrection mystery lies a way forward in confronting these clashes, this dilemma. Some of the parishes we have visited here show us it can be done. Out of several, I would point to Servant UMC in Austin, Bethesda at Haw Creek Commons, St. Peter/Cathedral of Hope in Houston, Redeemer Lutheran in North Minneapolis, the Episcopal Church of the Advocate in Chapel Hill, and Christ the King Lutheran in Cary, North Carolina.

Not all replanting efforts have been so contentious as Cottage Grove. The effort in Hutchinson, Minnesota, Vineyard UMC, led by pastors Jim and Sara Hein, is one with far less contention.[27] Their approach was a "soft close" of the former congregation, with a gradual transition to a different worship style and hard pastoral work aimed at not driving older members away. Methodist pastor Dottie Escobedo-Frank is more categorical on this issue. She argues that after many different efforts at revitalization, the closing-restart model, with a decided shift toward a younger target population, and thus the removal of much traditional décor, liturgy, and hymns, is the only way. She further claims it is rooted in death and resurrection.[28] Is this so absolute an assessment as she suggests? Is the past merely a cluttered attic or basement needing carting away? Are older, even ancient traditions incapable of connecting with younger people?

Gail Cafferata, an Episcopal priest and sociologist, has chronicled her journey of joy and pain in serving a parish that closed.[29] She also surveyed 130 pastors who had gone through the same process of a congregation's death. Cafferata found that the experience of a parish's closing indelibly imprinted itself on all members, especially on the pastor. When a new congregation, a replant, is able to follow, there is an Easter experience. But even when this is not the case, when the doors close for the last time and the building remains empty and locked, she says resurrection can still be experienced. Sometimes years may pass with a seemingly abandoned building and dispersed community, only for there to be, almost miraculously, another start, a new life. We will see that later in the Eagle Rock, California death of St. Barnabas Church and rebirth as St. Be's, the same we saw with St. James and later St. Jax in Montreal. All of this again underscores the complicated humanity of God's choosing to "move into the neighborhood,"

27. Miller, "Minnesota Methodists Say Rebooting Churches Can Be Helpful but Comes with Peril."

28. Escobedo-Frank, *ReStart Your Church.*

29. Cafferata, *Last Pastor.*

as Eugene Peterson's translation of the Scriptures puts it—God's choosing to "pitch a tent," to dwell among God's people (John 1:14 MSG).

Death and resurrection notwithstanding, congregations are not eternal. Buildings remain, as the numerous village churches here and in the UK and numerous other places attest. But a congregation is a living social reality. And as will all living beings, some die and some are resurrected. As the parish stories we have heard here suggest, there are ways in which to both welcome and integrate members of a closing parish into a new one that is opening in the former location. While some members of the former parish will likely stay away or go elsewhere, others do try to become part of something new, especially if there is an acknowledgment on the part of the new community of the legacy and lives of service of the former congregation. The UMC Legacy Initiative is sensitive to this, and in many locations, with the help of the pastor of a closing congregation, have modeled the transition on the death and rising of Christ rather than on a marketing model of failure and reinventing for success.

Models from the corporate and marketing world can be useful. They can also be short-sighted and not always productive. While a pioneer in the use of marketing research in the use of corporate culture and urban sophistication, the well-known Willow Creek Church, in South Barrington, Illinois, eventually had to modify some of its strategies. The church's size, though not what it once was, and their resources provided both capital and insulation against the challenge of the aging of their first cohorts of members and overall national decline in joining the institutional church. In the end, without being cynical, there is only so much innovation that one can do to the essentials of church. And what were once strikingly different and new styles of Sunday worship as "entertainment" and "performance," along with concentration on membership rooting in intense smaller groups or cells—even this becomes habituated, routine, the usual, even "traditional," in time. Most recently, Willow Creek has had to face the scandal of revelations of sexual abuse by its founding pastor, Bill Hybels.

As encouraging as the Asbury UMC-to-Servant UMC transition from dying to rising appears, like all else in Christian faith and life, it is provisional and tentative. It can be damaging to those involved. Church buildings, rituals, and congregational cultures of the recent and especially the distant past get confused for the essentials of church—the gathering and community of the people of God for worship, study, fellowship, and service. These are the components that are the real "tradition," not a particular style of liturgy, preaching, sacred music, or architecture. Death and resurrection presume incarnation, God's becoming one of us, subject to time and space, hunger and pain, capable of suffering and death. Death and resurrection are the action of God in, with, through, and for humankind. This means death and resurrection cannot avoid human nature's possibilities for wrongdoing and destruction as well as the good that can be done with God.

But to return to Servant UMC, no matter what questions of the future of such an age-specific congregation might be, in Austin something most significant happened. As we will continue to see here and elsewhere, the most basic process of dying-rising took place. A community had been there and flourished for almost seventy years. Its decline was not a problem capable of a neat or effective "solution." The demographic changes that accompanied a group of aging Boomers and their parents before them, along with shifts in the neighborhood's population, simply made the older congregation's life unsustainable. For those who remained and joined a new community, it could have been impossible or insulting, or an experience in resurrection. It appears that the newly merged congregation greatly benefited from the presence of the remaining Asbury church members who joined, just as the Vineyard UMC in Hutchinson, Minnesota, seems also to have experienced, something which perhaps in time will also happen at Cottage Grove UMC. Dottie Escobedo-Frank is right for sure in this; death and resurrection and, we could say, Pentecost were relived in these congregations. The life of the church in that part of Austin goes on, just as has happened into the third millennium of the Christian experience. The shape, the culture, and the style of the community's worship and fellowship change—they always have—but the life of the people of God goes on.

Merger and Resurrection in Rochester

Another transition, this time a merger, took place for Presbyterian Church in the USA (PCUSA) congregations in Rochester, New York. A decade ago, John Wilkinson and Judy Lee Hay, pastors of two relatively healthy congregations, regularly met for conversation and mutual support. They knew that there were in their city five Presbyterian parishes without pastors, two had closed, and two other were teetering close to doing so as well. The established model of PCUSA congregations was that each one was envisioned as an autonomous unit, linked by regional/presbytery membership and denominational belonging, but responsible for its own maintenance and survival. This model was simply not working any longer.

There were too many PCUSA parishes in the greater Rochester area, and decreasing membership and resources dictated more closures. This is, as we have seen in numerous cases here, a common pattern across virtually all church bodies or denominations in the US. Previous demographic patterns for establishing parishes, such as employment locations—factories, mines, mills, farms, commercial neighborhoods—and immigration or internal migration many years earlier resulted in these congregations gathering and planting their buildings. Sometimes the multiplication of parishes of a single denomination stemmed from growth that needed new parishes to absorb overflow. In other cases, as we have seen, ethnic/language group identities determined the creation of new congregations. This was particularly the case with Lutheran, Roman and Byzantine Catholic, and Eastern Orthodox parishes. Occasionally, doctrinal or other internal disagreements resulted in new congregations that would splinter off. This was more often the case among evangelical and Pentecostal communities.

In the time since the two pastors began talking about the future of their Rochester Presbyterian congregations, seven out of eleven parishes have either closed or left the church body. The four remaining have formed an association, Urban Presbyterians Together/Riverside Neighbors, which remains part of the PCUSA Presbytery of Genesee Valley. Like many other formerly booming industrial centers, Rochester has seen decline, deterioration, poverty, and embedded racism. The disappearance of great employers such as Kodak, Xerox, and Bausch & Lomb have turned what were healthy neighborhoods into struggling social and economic sectors. The pastors and other clergy and laity knew they could not undo the demographic and economic changes that damaged the city. But they determined to continue to be the presence of God and forces in outreach by better alliance with each other—shared worship, teaching, fellowship, and projects for the neighborhoods around their church buildings. Each parish does a "Great Lunch" annually for all their neighbors. They have also sponsored "Great Schools," a coalition of businesses, nonprofits, and community groups working with the Rochester public school system. Magnet schools have been created.[30]

The two congregations merged, sold their properties, and together became a "church without walls," meeting in rented space but continuing to work within their neighborhoods. The historic buildings had become unsustainable and, for them, the building was not the church. Church is God and the people of God gathered and at work in the world. Two other parishes in the association decided to share a pastor when it was evident that neither could support one individually. Eventually, the two merged as one of the congregations realized its time was over and that the building could be put to good use by a nonprofit group and they would continue as members of a somewhat larger and stronger community. The process was one of death and resurrection, of grieving and relief, as well as hopefulness and joy at being

---

30. Flanigan, "City's PCUSA Churches Band Together to Face Ongoing Decline."

able to continue as part of what in effect became a new entity. In the coalition, there were different resurrection experiences too.

Judy Lee Hay's parish decided in the wake of her retirement, and after forty years serving as pastor and continued decline, that it was time to move on. While several buyers visited the property and made offers, the coalition lobbied successfully to keep the buildings. They became home to the ROC SALT (Rochester Serving and Learning Together) Mission Center, where the already-existing food bank joined several new social justice partnerships in using the space. Thus, while no longer a functioning parish, the symbol of the old Calvary/St. Andrew's parish—the buildings— continued a presence and needed outreach work in that neighborhood. Despite the pain both Pastor Hay and members felt, they also celebrated the legacy of their parish living on.

Another example of a death-to-life merger can be found in the Catholic diocese of Great Falls-Billings, Montana, the closing and then merging of three parishes—St. Francis Xavier, Eden, St. Paul in Sand Coulee, and Saints Cyril and Methodius in Stockett—to form a new one—Holy Trinity, in Centerville. Again, the sense of a Good Friday, then Holy Saturday—that is, a death and burial but also an Easter resurrection—occurred for the people. The presence in the dying and rising process of retired Father Martin Werner, who had served one of the closing parishes as an accompanying counselor and teacher, helped greatly. While temporary space in a gym was used for Sunday liturgies, there was a small chapel where weekday masses were celebrated and the sacrament reserved. There, an icon of the Father, Son, and Spirit, the Holy Trinity, in some ways expressed three previous communities that had become one—what the doctrine of the Trinity teaches.[31]

Yet another story, and one different from most we have followed here, is that of an historic German congregation founded in 1848, St. Peter's in Houston, and the Cathedral of Hope, an LGBTQ congregation there. St. Peter's now-quaint white clapboard building, a chapel compared to the much larger brick church built seventy years ago, has had a long journey of ups and downs. The most recent shrinkage left it with a small group of aging members. A way to survive was renting out its now-way-too-large space. The large sanctuary was rented to the Cathedral of Hope, an offshoot of the larger Dallas church of the same name. It started small, with fewer than twenty-five members, mostly white lesbians. But once relocated to St. Peter's, the Cathedral community began to grow and become more diverse, with African-American, Hispanic, gay, and straight members, ranging across age groups. Their pastor, Leslie Jackson, a part-timer with

31. Olsen, "Resurrection Story."

a theological education from Columbia Seminary, is a fiery preacher. He is gay and African-American and his husband is a leader of the choir. Alongside Jackson is St. Peter's last pastor, Vicki Sheil-Hopper, and the two lead services for both the smaller former St. Peter's community as well as the larger Cathedral of Hope community, with sharing particularly in important church seasons and for feasts.

In this case, the two communities have merged, the larger Cathedral of Hope congregation now taking the principal role in terms of financial support. But what is striking is the diversification of the joint community's membership and deepening of their commitment not to just co-exist but flourish as the body of Christ. Leslie Jackson describes the community as a gathering of people—Greek Orthodox, United Church of Christ, evangelicals, Baptists, Catholics, new agers, Nones, and even atheists—a community rooted in God's love, and extending that love to all as well as seeking justice for all. Worship includes traditional hymns, gospel, jazz, and much more. The parish website described it as a box of chocolates—you never know what you will find.

The two congregations merged in January of 2019, and Easter was celebrated as a relaunching of their mission, going all the way back to 1848. Once in a rural area, the small clapboard chapel and the later brick sanctuary now sit amid car dealerships and fast-food restaurants along a busy commercial strip. In Houston, the very notion of not just a racially integrated but also diverse congregation, as St. Peter United is, stands as an anomaly. Dr. King once said Sunday morning is the single most segregated time in America, but this parish now contradicts that otherwise true assessment of American churches.[32]

Not long ago, this particular merger of congregations would have seemed most improbable. St. Peter's was a staid group of mostly senior citizens. Their services were traditional, restrained. Their ability to do more than worship and gather for fellowship was severely limited. The Cathedral of Hope was a gathering of gay and lesbian, white and African-American and Hispanic and more, a mix of young and old. Their worship was loud, upbeat, emotional: Leslie Jackson very much in the classic style of black preaching. Yet join together they did, honoring each other's backgrounds and experiences, but confident in expressing their own identities. The result was a merged community that now could do more by way of outreach, possibly expanding their community meal and garage sale/thrift shop enterprises. Most importantly, members and their pastors see the merger as more than survival but as an expression of the Resurrection, a proof that life triumphs over death and hate.

32. Gray, "St. Peter Reborn."

CHAPTER 4

More Resurrection

New Identity, New Life, Simplicity,
and Back to the Table

Renaming, Rebranding

EARLIER I SAID THAT much of what we would be seeing as we heard from congregations and their actions was rooted in the central theme of death and resurrection. Surely the closing of a parish and the rebirth of it or another correspond to this mystery at the heart of the gospel. But what about changes in name and identity? Are these changes in churches' names momentous in the sweep of things happening in the churches today? Are reinventing venerable parishes to be centers of gathering for prayer and outreach but also the arts? Of real significance is the reinventing of parishes as community centers for prayer, for social outreach, for other vital things like art and health care. There is true resurrection of parishes in their going public, becoming better stewards of property that serve not just the congregation but the neighborhood around. Resurrection can also mean getting simple, back to basics, learning again what table fellowship can be, seeking to listen to the community around you.

Sometimes, existing congregations can experience rebranding, that is, a renaming that expresses new identity. Trinity Baptist in Maplewood, Minnesota became LifePoint church. Maple Grove Evangelical became The Grove church, its publicity reminding readers, "same church, new name." First Lutheran in White Bear Lake became Community of Grace. While removing denominational labels such as "Baptist" or "Lutheran" achieves an opening up of the community beyond a particular historical identity, the new names also aim at being more accessible to post-denominational folk, those with little or no loyalty to a particular tradition. Marketing research has suggested that while these labels are useful to older believers, they are often misunderstood or perceived as narrow and restrictive to younger people.

In Iowa and Minnesota, more than half of the Baptist congregations no longer have "Baptist" as part of their names. Likewise, 60 percent of Assemblies of God congregations no longer identify themselves as such. Even regional associations have changed titles. The former Baptist General Conference became Converge North Central, and Transform Minnesota is the former Greater Minnesota Association of Evangelicals. Lutherans are somewhat less likely to rebrand or rename, although there are numerous cases of parishes that have, such as Tapestry in Richfield and Shobi's Table in St. Paul. Well-known pastor Nadia Bolz-Weber founded a parish in Denver and called it "House for all saints and sinners." Though officially part of the ELCA, the lead pastor who succeeded her, as well as the associate, are both Episcopal priests. House is emphatic about its adherence to traditional liturgy as the framework for worship, though with many innovative elements. Catholic and Episcopal and African-American churches have for the most part retained more traditional names and identifications countrywide.

Thirty years ago, new parish plants in the suburbs began to employ less churchy names and architecture and design, Willow Creek being a most notable example, with Woodland Hills Church a Minnesota version. It was noted by an evangelical leader that branding remained extremely important in marketing, but while it is no longer IHOP, that franchise continues to serve breakfasts including pancakes. For the most part, rebranded or renamed congregations have remained in their denominations, albeit often streamlining their building styles and worship.[1] But the deliberately corporate and secular look of Willow Creek has also been challenged as dated and confusing. Is it a conference center, corporate headquarters, or God's house?

The Park Church Co-op in Greenpoint, New York has not tried to undo or hide its traditional ecclesiastical design. The sweeping lines of the Neo-Gothic nave speak of the sense of church that is centuries old, as do the stained-glass windows, high altar, and cross. On Sunday, worshippers gather around a free-standing altar for communion, the pastor presiding in clerical collar. The former Lutheran Church of the Messiah dates to 1899 and was also identified as the "Park Church," located across the street from Msgr. McGolrick Park. In addition to Sunday eucharist, a number of groups also use the church as a space for performances and events; for example, the Brooklyn Children's Theatre and a monthly dance party: No Lights, No Lycra. There is a monthly nondenominational meditation event/session called Sound Church and weekly sessions of Dancorcism

1. Hopfensperger, "What's in a Name?"

(that is, dance + exorcism), a therapeutic, restorative approach to dance. Local musicians perform at Park Church and there is even a monthly candlelight celebration of the ancient close of day service, Compline, with local musicians performing.

Park Church pastor, Amy Kienzle, is someone who came from a no-churchgoing family and who came to faith and the ministry later in life. She has moved on to a new parish in Sacramento. Her account of Park's transformation, begun under her predecessor Griffin Thomas, is a journey of change and discovery much like that of Greenpoint, which has passed from early-twentieth-century German and Irish immigrants to Polish old-timers and new immigrants, and now to hipsters, artists, entrepreneurs, and developers, given Brooklyn's rapid and astonishing renaissance. Park Church still very much looks like church. But it also looks like a bazaar of music, dance, art, and other activities. All it lacks is a coffee house. It is very Brooklyn, a hotbed of culture. Now even an upstate reviving location, Beacon, New York, is called "Brooklyn on the Hudson."[2]

Lutherans may not always change the names of churches, but they have been engaged in changing image. Nationwide, the ELCA has gone from 5.2 million members in 1988 to 3.7 million in 2017. The Lutheran Church-Missouri Synod (LC-MS) has likewise declined from 2.7 million to 2 million, a smaller, very conservative, and exclusive denomination. Minnesota has more Lutherans than any other state and some congregations there are trying to respond to what they see (and what we have identified here) as the signs of crisis and decline—aging communities with few young families and children, declining attendance both at services and other parish activities, and declining financial support. There are niche congregations aimed at Millennials featuring nontraditional café-like locations. In these venues, very informal gatherings take place, usually not on Sunday mornings, more likely in the evening. The events appear like poetry slams or music sets, or even potluck suppers, but they are really services, worship in a distinctly nontraditional style. But in other instances, the efforts to reimagine or reinvent are less innovative.

Rerooting and Reinvesting in the Neighborhood, Going Public: Redeemer and Franklin United Churches

Changes in name and culture may seem highly effective strategies for challenged congregations, at least from marketing perspectives. However, the

2. Chu, "Rebranded ELCA Church Is a Place of Welcome for Believers and Nonbelievers Alike."

extent to which rebranding and renaming changes the identity as well as the mission of a congregation depends on the vision of that community. Things can look a lot like traditional church or hardly at all. But as the scriptural saying puts it, "by their fruits you shall know them" (Matt 7:16).

However, there are far more radical yet market-based or linked ways to go, even when many parishes around all seem to be suffering from the same factors producing shrinkage and decline. Redeemer Lutheran Church, in the Harrison neighborhood of north Minneapolis, was swiftly declining by the early 2000s. It did not change its name, but it dramatically transformed its identity and mission, especially its connection to the neighborhood. Redeemer decided to start acquiring the properties around it. It now owns twenty-six apartments, nearly all of the block on which it's located. It has a community development agency as part of its work—Redeemer Center for Life. The parish has a number of venues for service and enterprise on the block that could well be call Redeemer Street instead of Glenwood Avenue. There is the "Health Commons," a neighborhood center for health services and wellness programs. Another of its buildings houses a bike shop that repairs bikes and teaches neighborhood folk to do the same. The residents of the apartments located above the commercial units on the block are diverse just as the congregation now is, with younger Millennials and older Scandinavian-Americans, as well as lots of other ethnic and racial groups represented.[3]

Kelly Chatman, who came as pastor to a declining Redeemer congregation, is now an assistant to the local bishop. Chatman had spent most of his ordained service in higher administration in the ELCA, heading youth ministries, among other assignments. He only spent a few years in parish work after ordination, as an associate. Redeemer was indeed a challenge to him, towards the end of his pastoral career. He thought he'd remain at Redeemer for a short tenure, until retirement. He remained for almost twenty years.

In a neighborhood that had lost its solid middle-class population and become vulnerable to drug trafficking, unemployment, and tattered low-income housing, it surely was a challenge. Redeemer had a large stone Neo-Gothic sanctuary, along with an educational wing, but when Chatman arrived, there were only thirty members left, a tiny group on a large nave. Now years later, what happened? What did they do to turn into a vibrant, diverse parish that is clearly the hub of an entire neighborhood coming back to economic and social health?

3. Strickler, "Church Finds New Life."

Chatman frames the answer as taking on the world, that is, the whole neighborhood around the church as the real parish, the true community of faith. This happened quite literally. As noted, Redeemer acquired virtually the whole block of buildings next door. The parish then created Redeemer Center, an umbrella group for an array of enterprises and outreach ventures in the larger community. There's a bike repair and coffee shop, a café, a sixteen-unit apartment building, as well as seven more apartments over the café, which is also the office of Luther Volunteers Corps. There is another storefront that became the Living Room, a locale for health care consultation and clinics, classes as well as community gathering. Two single-family homes have also been built by Redeemer, which now has almost a hundred for Sunday services. The crowded monthly calendar, accessible on their website, gives an indication of just how much of a center of the neighborhood this parish has become.[4]

There are also community gardens on the property and in warmer weather, bi-weekly food fests around their outdoor pizza oven. The annual parish block party in August draws hundreds of area residents and visitors, a real feast for foodies. It is reminiscent of the Church of England's ancient village parish church of St. Peter, also to be described here, which decided to have the church again be the center of town life and business, remodeling so that a yoga studio, nursery school, child-care centers, and a collection of local craftspeople could maintain a market there on weekdays, with liturgy and church school there on Sundays as well as other specifically parish gatherings.

Just looking at the venerable stone building and its stained-glass and wooden-clad interior, Redeemer does little that stands out as unusual or cutting edge. The faces of the people of Redeemer are a mosaic of American diversity, African-Americans, Latinos, Asians, and people of European descent. There is a 10 AM service of prayer and praise that uses the music, prayer, and preaching of the black church. The 10:30 AM main service is the traditional liturgy of the Western church now used by many church bodies.

Redeemer partners with five other urban and suburban congregations, several of which have helped finance startup enterprises and which often participate in specific outreach projects during the year. For adult education, in the fall of 2018 there was a twelve-part podcast from *Scene on Radio* titled *Seeing White*. This podcast explored the conflicts still stemming from racism, something necessary in the North Minneapolis area where Redeemer is located. The death of George Floyd and the protests following confirm the need for facing racism in Minneapolis. Perhaps

4. Schneider, "Lutherans Work to Shed Stuffy Images and Kick-start Change."

being the owners and landlords of so many urban residential and commercial units is distinctive, but not so much for the income possibilities as those of witness and service in the community. Where other congregations have continued to shrink and eventually disappear, Redeemer's solid stone tower and nave have moved past Scandinavian beginnings to a community of grace that reflects very accurately the diversity of the Twin Cities and of America in the twenty-first century.

While it might seem that church, particularly in urban locations, appears to be a losing proposition, there are more than enough countercases to challenge this. We just saw the case in Rochester. Park Church is one, along with St. Lydia's dinner church, and another Lutheran innovative congregation in Brooklyn. So too are Methodist congregations written about by Donna Claycomb Sokol and L. Roger Owens.

Drawing on their respective experiences in Mt. Vernon UMC Church in Washington DC and Duke Memorial UMC in Durham, North Carolina, Sokol and Owen describe a series of issues that challenged congregations must confront. These include the process of pruning/letting go, rethinking their vision and strategy, overcoming the divide between mission and evangelism (often taken to be the same drives), excellence in parish life, worship, and in the cooperation of clergy, laity, and staff. Not unlike Diana Butler Bass's study of healthy parishes some years ago, these crucial elements are not surprising at all, rather what most would see as the critical ingredients in the life of a congregation. And perhaps also not surprising for the tradition of John Wesley and his brother Charles, their experience affirms that the pastor is neither a charismatic celebrity, as in some megachurches such as Rick Warren's Saddleback Church, nor an entrepreneur, in still others like that of Joel Osteen. The pastor best serves as the preacher and spiritual teacher who inspires imagination, helps interpret the vision of the congregation, and guides in the discernment of work the parish does together. The classic components of sacraments/worship, prayer, learning, communion/fellowship, and ministry/service are what a reviving, resurrecting congregation uses.[5]

Jason McConnell, pastor of a Congregational-Methodist parish in northern Vermont, Franklin United Church, describes how going public breaks a congregation out of its isolation, again making church part of public life and action. McConnell has been part of a school ski instruction course, worked on the rescue squad, and been elected to the local school board. He also has worked with local groups assisting those leaving correctional facilities to reenter their communities. In fifteen years, he and his family have

5. Sokol and Owens, *New Day in the City.*

become familiar faces in the town, known for their many different ways of being involved in the wider community's life.

This is mirrored in members of the Franklin United Church congregation. While such congregational extroversion may be unsettling to some who believe the parish is essentially for them and their friends, almost a "family chapel," the outreach is really a return to older patterns. Churches of the nineteenth and early twentieth centuries, as congregations long before, were vital components of the towns and villages where they were located.[6]

Honoring the Sabbath

The resurrection of a congregation need not take unusual measures or extreme changes. One such example is the Lake Nokomis Presbyterian Church in Lake Nokomis, Minnesota. This parish offers a variation on prioritizing the basics of church—worship, prayer, fellowship, service, and learning. In coming there as pastor a decade ago, Kara Root arrived at a church that had "aged out," with no young people or children, no new members in seven years, with thirty gathering on Sundays in a nave that could hold 300. There were a couple more years of the endowment to sustain them.

Root proposed what no one had ever considered—recovering authentic Sabbath as the core of renewal, a day not only free of work and messages, texts and emails, but even of coming to church for services. Few were coming every Sunday anyway. On the first and third Sundays, it was a traditional eucharist, but on the second and fourth weekends, there was a contemplative service Saturday evening and Sunday at home was a Sabbath of rest and recreation. First Sundays become a group participation in outreach, while big festivals bump Sabbath observance, like Christmas, Easter, and Pentecost, for example. Saturday evening services have some elements of the regular liturgy such as Scripture lessons and a brief homily. However, quiet music and time for reflection (using the labyrinth) for exchanging understanding of a text and connections to everyday life during the week are parts of the service that usually have from a dozen to two dozen participants.

Sunday worship is up to forty to seventy and the membership almost a hundred. Sabbath Sundays do not mean that people are restricted to staying at home. Picnics and dinners, discussions, visiting—all of these and many other things are the rest and play of a Sabbath. Probably it was the seeking to be intentional, to do things slightly differently, to use trial and error for the Saturday evening services, make mistakes, attempt new activities such as lighting candles with prayer, sitting in silence, listening

6. McConnell, "Pulpits in the Public Square?"

and exchanging in conversation as personal spiritual deepening and community/church building. Kara Root does not see any of the practices, including the Sabbath-keeping, as recipes or tricks to change directions, and they may not work for other congregations. Simply becoming more deliberate and mindful of what it is to be church, to be a holy community—these are the seeds for the growth that took place at Lake Nokomis, for its revival using ancient practice in the church.[7]

Listening to the Community around the Congregation

In the East Liberty section of Pittsburgh for over two decades, a ministry of listening to the community has been pursued by Presbyterian pastor Patrice Fowler-Searcy. This had become a deteriorated neighborhood when she arrived twenty years ago, a community abandoned in "white flight." This once-stylish area had turned into an eyesore, with frightening crime rates and massive poverty. But now, East Liberty, like much of Brooklyn and Beacon and Hudson, New York, has come back, revived with a vengeance. Whole Foods, Trader Joe's, Home Depot, and other national businesses have emerged, as well as, and more importantly, the appearance of real entrepreneurs in farm-to-table eateries, artisan bakeries, coffee and wine shops and cheese stores, and elegant cafés and taverns. All of these cater to artists, craftspeople, and well-educated young professionals as new residents.

Her parish, East Liberty Presbyterian, long ago became a partner with the like-named East Liberty Development, Inc. (ELDI). She's both a local pastor and community developer and, as such, offers a model for church being sensitive to location, location, location, to use the realtors' mantra. Fowler-Searcy took the prophet Nehemiah as a model for her ministry. Like Nehemiah, she came to understand that her role was to help rebuild the city, both for God and for her neighbors. But her task was not to dictate how this should happen, but rather to engage in careful listening to what the residents, the businesses, and the churches wanted to become. Community development, for her, was the vehicle for pastoral gathering and nurturing, not at odds with Christian ministry.[8]

She stands for many of the pastors whose efforts have been, and will continue to be, described here. As another who listens to her, seminary professor L. Roger Owens notes that Patrice often finds herself in the middle of tensions between the ELDI vision and that of the congregation. Yet, since

7. Strickler, "Minneapolis Congregation Finds New Life through Ancient Practice of Keeping Sabbath."

8. See "Patrice L. Fowler-Searcy."

the two groups share so much in terms of goals and destiny in the East Liberty neighborhood, more often compromises are reached. The repayment of a loan from the church to the development group was just such a moment of tension. The congregation had fronted funds but then needed them desperately for renovation. For the good of both, a new repayment plan was found and agreed on. The conundrum with the East Liberty neighborhood is that along with renaissance comes the displacement that gentrification always produces. The renewal of commercial and residential properties makes for jobs and a rebirth of the area. Balancing that with the fate of those left out or left behind will continue for years. Fowler-Searcy confided that trust and listening are not miracle meds, but they are essential to the church remaining a vital part of the life of a neighborhood.[9]

Getting Simple

Simplicity. Simplifying. Getting simple. These have become marketing buzzwords. There is even a magazine, *Simple*. These have been ways of describing downsizing, escaping from possessions, clutter, perhaps job stress, family and relationship strain, and disruption. Then there is Marie Kondo wanting to clean out your house and radically simplify what you own and have. But what have these trends to do with the pattern of death and resurrection? In them we find patterns for church in rebirth and reimagination of their identities and missions. Simplifying has great significance in Grafton and Worcester, Massachusetts, where the UMC has planted two communities pursuing a much cleaner, less formal or traditional model of congregation and life. "Simple supper, simple church" is the approach.

When the Grafton UMC congregation closed in 2013, the UMC sent a "planter," a mission pastor to see if another kind of community could be gathered. Now there is another community in addition to Grafton, in Worcester, and several others in other states and Canada: B3 in Denver, Kindred in Houston. These are churches "without walls," congregations that do not own a building but, in the case of Simple Church, rent space from the Grafton Congregational Church, not only for the weekly shared meal and Lord's Supper, but also for baking bread they sell at local famers' markets and shops.

At Grafton, the pastor is Zach Kerzee, himself a PK ("pastor's kid") and a volunteer at the local farm that supplies produce to the same venues where the parish's bread is sold. He brings vegetables to the community supper and

9. Owens, "Seminary Students and Their Professor Benefit from the Wisdom of a Local Pastor."

others who come to the supper all bring food they share. In the baking, they partner with Grafton Job Corps, a local employment training program for young people. The meal setting for reading, talking about the Scriptures, and sharing the eucharist is at once the ancient model of liturgy. This was the celebration in the earliest communities that met in houses of believers, who then were recognized as leaders of those churches by Paul in his letters.

The Methodist tradition of John Wesley and others as itinerant preachers, with no meeting houses except the homes of participants and the sharing of prayer as well as meals, makes the Simple Church approach both very old and new at the same time. Rather than a pastor talking at/to people, here, after the readings, a conversation is begun and continues till they feel it's run its course. The Simple Church website has prayers and hymns and those who come are free to bring and share their own.[10]

While supported by a three-year grant from the UMC, Simple Church at Grafton had to get creative with financing in order to survive. Like other communities of this model, Grafton is free from buildings and their maintenance as well as clergy-compensation packages, insurance premiums, and all the other expenses of the traditional parish. Yet each community does need to rent space as well as contribute to the support of a pastor as well as to pursue outreach work and lastly, to give from what it has. So there is a place for giving on the part of individuals and households as well as raising funds in a variety of ways, baking only one. They call their plying of trades to fund themselves a monastic funding model, as well it is, in addition to being the most ancient model, one employed by St. Paul himself, sometimes called "tent-making," since he worked in the leather-processing trade. There is website design, done by Kerzee, and also carpentry and catering. Other locations have developed their own trades. Further, there is no requirement that a member subscribe to a particular confessional statement, though in time it will be clear that the Scriptures, prayers, hymns, and sacraments are indeed "primary theology," ways of viewing God and the world. "Tradition," but a "living tradition," has a way of being spun out of the life and connections in a community of faith.

While the Grafton and Worcester communities were planted by the UMC, there are others that are sponsored by the ELCA or the Seventh-Day Adventists. There is also the Simple Church at Home Network, a lay-led aggregation of about 250 house churches in 23 countries, most in the US. The congregations average twelve members. It was founded nine years

---

10. McDonald, "Simple Church Bends Dinner, Worship and Enterprise to Create a New Model."

ago by Milton Adams, a Linden, Tennessee teacher who holds a doctorate of ministry.[11]

Back to the Table: Church as Fellowship and Food

Food and drink, bread and wine, the elements of the Lord's Supper, or eucharist, have been at the heart of Christian community and life since Jesus's fellowship meals and Last Supper with the disciples. But food and drink beyond the eucharist, almost as an extension of the sacrament of communion, of community, have also figured importantly in the ancient church. Historians point to the shared meals of associations gathered around a teacher—*havurot*, from *haver*, "friend"—as the kind of table fellowship Jesus had with his followers. There was also the "feeding of the multitude," with the multiplication of bread and fish to care for crowds in the thousands. Scripture scholars note that in the Gospels, the Last Supper appears to be a Passover meal, although there is no description of the supper itself in John's Gospel, rather Jesus's washing of the disciples' feet and the long "farewell discourse."

After the resurrection, in the last chapter of Luke, Jesus is recognized by his disciples at table in the inn of Emmaus as he breaks bread and gives thanks at the start of a meal. Just after Emmaus, Jesus also appears, apparently not blocked by walls, to the disciples gathered at table. He assures them he is not a ghost, says he is hungry, and asks what they have to eat—broiled fish, which he then eats with them. And if this does not make the point, at the end of the Gospel of John (21:1–14), he is seen on the shore, having prepared broiled fish and bread over a fire, breakfast for the disciples who have been fishing all night. The Acts of the Apostles (2:42, 46–47) and apostolic letters recognize the breaking of bread as connected to a communal meal. The best-known instance is Paul's extended statements about the one bread and cup over against divisions in the church at Corinth that fracture the community both at the meal and the eucharist (1 Cor 11:17–34).

Even when the eucharistic liturgy became separated from a communal meal, there was often feasting linked to church gatherings. I wrote about some of the adventures in food prep and sharing of my parish, with pirogi making, Easter bread baking, and an annual food fair highlighted. But to these I also featured the comforting "repasts" or "mercy meals" Eastern church congregations arrange after funerals. And of course, the Sunday

---

11. Holmes, "From Backyard Baptism to Potluck Bible Study, Church Starts at Home."

"liturgy after the liturgy" is the coffee hour, what some Lutherans consider the "third sacrament," the sacrament of refreshment and fellowship.[12]

Dinner Church

St. Lydia's Supper Church in Brooklyn, founded by a charismatic pastor, Emily Scott, and a Yale Divinity School classmate, Rachel Pollak, is the best known of micro-churches of the "dinner" or "supper" genre. Scott and Pollack, as seminary students and Millennials, were aware of the widening gaps between most congregations and people their age. Even as theology students, they felt the distance themselves. A musician, Scott came from the rich liturgical tradition of the Episcopal Church. Pollak, a Unitarian, was a sculptor and printmaker, and while not identifying as a Christian, nevertheless had a deep regard for spiritual life and practice. The dinner setting for gathering people for telling their own stories, helping to make and then share, was rooted in their experience of having little money in graduate school and wanting to gather friends together. I remember this from years ago when my wife and I were in graduate school and living in a tiny Upper West Side New York City apartment. Having people all bring something to share for a dinner was the most inexpensive, festive, and thus frequent entertainment we had. We can still not fathom how much cheap wine and how many hours of impassioned debate and conversation we were gifted to enjoy in those years. Exactly this was the seed for the vision Scott and Pollak had in a dinner church, St. Lydia's. It was named for the businesswomen in the garment industry of Thyatira, Asia Minor, now Turkey. Having been moved by St. Paul's preaching, she and her household were baptized and became the head of the local church there in her community (Acts 16:14–15).

While they got St. Lydia's off the ground, and the location moved several times, Scott and Pollak eventually stepped down from leadership as pastor and community coordinator. Now the team of pastoral leadership has entered a new phase with their departure. Christian Scharen is now interim pastor, and there is a team that includes a community coordinator, leaders for the second Sunday Waffle Church service for families, also a leader for music, and the leadership table that is the parish council for the whole community.

The eucharist is part of every meal at St. Lydia's. At the dinner church on Sunday and Monday evenings, all who come help prepare a vegetarian meal. During the meal, the presider chants the eucharistic prayer. The home-baked eucharistic bread is shared along with the cup within the meal, during

12. Plekon, *Uncommon Prayer*, 168–200.

which there are also Scripture readings, a homily, intercessory prayers, and conversation of course. At the Waffle Church, eucharist is part of essentially a homemade brunch, this a service aimed at families with children but not exclusively. It is playfully described as "sticky church" made up of songs, stories, maple syrup (and waffles, to be sure), and the love of Jesus.

Like even the most traditional of congregations, St. Lydia's has experienced change, inherent in and necessary in the life of any group from a family to a parish to a club or company. The sheer passage of time means that the founders and first members of St. Lydia's are probably now in their forties, maybe older. Time stops for none of us. What was "in" and "it" yesterday now seems nostalgic, vintage, maybe even dated.

Here is one of the not-as-yet-hidden but core realities of community and church. Some aspects need to be changed, for they no longer speak to those gathered, no longer sound or look or function as they once did. Vestments wear out. Some songs we sing are so much of a time that we need to relegate them to the "greatest hits" or some other "classics" categories. New bread and wine are needed, the candles burn down, the liturgical cycle of seasons turns round and round. A good friend and colleague of mine in the ministry remained at the same parish so long that he was marrying young people he'd baptized and then, in turn, baptizing their children. My own prayer list now has several columns of those I used to visit, to whom I brought communion or chatted with, who I have buried, who have passed into the heavenly kingdom.[13]

One might be tempted to dismiss St. Lydia's and the concept of a church/community gathered around dinner as a phenomenon of "hipsters" based, not coincidentally, in a veritable hipster, trendy paradise of an area, namely Brooklyn. St. Lydia's was conceived of in New Haven but it could have been Los Angeles or Boston or Philadelphia or Chicago or a thousand other urban settings. And while there is no Neo-Gothic bell tower and nave with stained glass windows and pews and organ, what goes on at St. Lydia's is just as ancient as it seems right now, soon to be yesterday. The earliest gatherings of disciples who would first be called the Christians at Antioch took place in peoples' homes, around tables, in the context of a meal (Acts 11:26). Jewish Christians celebrated Shabbat not just in synagogue with readings, psalms, and preaching, but at the Shabbat meal of a family, relatives, and friends gathered at table.[14]

13. Kling, "Origin Story about St. Lydia's #Brooklyn"; Sierra, "Dinner Church Finds a Home in Brooklyn"; Plekon, *Uncommon Prayer*, 95–119.

14. Green, "Secret Christians of Brooklyn."

Emily Scott thought to take what is the earliest version of a prayer of making thanks, from the *Didache*, a very early church text, for use as the eucharistic prayer at St. Lydia's. The community resembles those gathered for the "apostles' teaching and fellowship, the breaking of bread and the prayers" (Acts 2:42). The most elaborate of hierarchical liturgies with dozens of vested celebrants and assistants, massed choirs, huge assemblies in towering basilicas, trace their origins to the upper room's Last Supper and the other table fellowships with followers during the years of ministry by Jesus, and to the gatherings in the churches in the houses of Lydia, Junia and Andronicus, Prisca and Acquila, Lydia, Nympha, Philemon and Apphia (Rom 16:7; Acts 18:2–3; 1 Cor 16:19; Rom 16:3, 5; Acts 16:40; Col 4:15; Phlm 1–2). So, the concept of a "dinner church" is not just a hipster innovation, but a return to a most ancient model of church.[15]

Church without Walls

Another church without walls is St. Isidore's Episcopal in Houston, started by priest Sean Steele. A cellphone app is the network tool, and a building, with all its costs, was deemed unnecessary. Services are held in a number of locales. One is by a food truck that distributes surplus produce. But despite not having a permanent altar and pulpit, rather laundromats, brewery restaurants, and coffee shops, as well as food truck spots, Steele uses the *Book of Common Prayer*. He argues that people today really searching for God find there is much more in the church's historic liturgy, in the Scriptures, eucharist, and in the hymns and prayers, than they might expect. The rector of an established parish, Trinity, took Steele upon seminary graduation and he was ordained as a priest for this church without walls, much of which was the fruit of his own vision and planning. This parish without walls is named for the patron saint of the internet, St. Isidore of Seville, compiler of an early medieval equivalent of a search engine, *Etymologies*, also called *Origins*.

The congregation was shaped by Steele's experience in finance, including the last days of Enron. He was intent on working with the unchurched, and Trinity's rector, Gerry Sevick, himself a former social worker, and their bishop, C. Andrew Doyle (from whom we will hear later), were also committed to innovative outreach by the church. The path which led to St. Isidore's is a fascinating one. It wound its way through a gym member's talks over breakfast at a Taco Bell, ideas from a specialist in church planting, and several experiments with houses churches, most of which did not work out. There was also liturgy at a pub, ashes and prayers on Ash Wednesday

15. Vanderslice, *We Will Feast*.

at a Panera, and then a Palm Sunday service at a laundromat, in addition to time for those in need to do all their loads as well as grab some snacks. Laundry Love, as this was called, was but one of several efforts—experiments, really—in gathering a community of varying types of people and at differing locations, all of which had an effect on the kind of cohesiveness the group achieved—or did not. Originally a ministry of Trinity Woodlands, St. Isidore's now has house churches of its own, meeting on Zoom during the pandemic as well as the Abundant Harvest Kitchen, which is feeding those in need. Such a transition, as with the Grafton Simple Church, is a major reimagination and redefinition of the community, which, in turn, requires continual acquisition of funds to keep the project, even without walls, going. This is a challenge shared by most of the efforts at community reinvention, reimagination, or redefinition being described here.[16] However, that a new parish like St. Isidore's can spin off house churches on its own and develop a response to food insecurity in a time of crisis says much about the durability of local churches that strive to be the body of Christ for the community around.

Offering Space to Another Congregation

Munger Place Methodist Church in Dallas, Texas had been an important part of the city for over a century. But by 2009, the loss of jobs in the Great Recession and the decline of the section called Old East Dallas, due to school desegregation and loss of industry, meant a swift, dramatic decrease in membership and finances and imminent closing. A growing nearby congregation, Highland Park Methodist, was looking for a location on which to set up another campus. This congregation started conversations with Munger Place and with the Annual Conference's approval and took over the expenses of repair and maintenance. This was not just the takeover of a closed parish, but a kind of death-and-resurrection process. The traditional church building and worship space invited the new community there to find ways in which to take the venerable tradition of Methodist preaching, hymns, and sacraments into a twenty-first-century-accessible form. The building is traditional, as are the feasts of the church year and the Scriptures and sacraments, but the style is contemporary music, informal dress, and listening carefully to the neighborhood around the church in Old East Dallas nowadays—not the past.

Lead minister Andrew Forest, in a way similar to Sean Steele at St. Isidore's, insisted that making disciples—that is, hearing and living out

16. See "Church Has No Walls but Many Doors."

the gospel—was what Munger Place was about. Community gardens and shared space with nonprofits are frequent elements of congregations that are dying and trying to revive. These are fine ministries but the bottom line is about connection with God, and all that flows from this, especially community. Almost half of the people at Munger Place, reinvented, were not church members before. Something about the worship, community life, and pastoral care drew them there. Forrest, unlike Steele, is more opinionated about the drift of mainline churches away from what he terms "orthodox Christianity," which is clearly a very traditional vision. Here again is the clash seen repeatedly in the last half-century between traditional, "high demand" Christianity, although with contemporary music and casual clothes, and other communities more willing to adapt and change as the culture and society do. This was once Bill Hybels's claim about Willow Creek, also Rick Warren's about his megachurch. Yet despite the confrontational stance Andrew Forest takes, the now-successful effort over the last seven years at Munger Place is yet another case of the refusal of even a dying congregation to pass way quietly.[17]

Two Churches in Winnipeg

We already visited a repurposed parish in Winnipeg, St. Matthew's Anglican church. Now another two. Methodist pastor and seminary professor Jason Byassee has drawn attention to two Anglican Church of Canada parishes in Winnipeg that seem to be more than just sustaining themselves, even growing while many other congregations around them are floundering.[18] St. Margaret's, led by David Widdicombe, is in most respects a traditional Anglican parish, not only in fidelity to the historical liturgy but also to ethical teachings often debated across the churches now. It keeps within traditional Anglican canons by offering communion to baptized Christians, whereas St. Benedict's, from its start with ten people, excludes no one, seeing the bread (hearty, chewable) and wine, shared generously in ceramic cups, as the common meal of the family of God.

Widdicombe has an Oxford DPhil in theology, having studied with Rowan Williams, among others. The website of St. Margaret's is welcoming but rare for parishes today in its seriousness. All the sermons are recorded and archived, as are a number of lectures from regular series and other presentations from local theological programs at universities. Widdicombe's preaching, on the day Byassee visited, made no reference to the listeners, to

17. Forrest, "Every Dying Church in America Has a Community Garden."
18. Byassee, "Richness of the Faith."

himself, just lectionary texts and Christ. The sermon is challenging, asking listeners to think through what a text says—and this is often much more than is apparent. What the parish as a community does—worship, study, fellowship, service to the neighborhood around, the city, and beyond—this is the parish's reason for being and a good example of the basics being done and well. It is also a key to the parish's identity.

With Jamie Howison as pastor, St. Benedict's table is quite different from St. Margaret's, though belonging to the same church body and diocese. It is a striking mix of radical innovation and tradition. Its website describes it as "ancient-future," a concept Howison takes from theologian Robert Webber. Also influential is the late American Episcopal priest, theologian, and chef Robert Farrar Capon. Howison is as learned as Widdicombe but in a much more hip fashion. He has a book out on Coltrane as a spiritual force in his music. The liturgy has music composed by the local director, Gord Johnson, as well as other folk singer-composers like Steve Bell and Alan Levandoski. They are part of the Diocese of Rupert Land of the Anglican Church in Canada (as is St. Margaret's), but the choice of St. Benedict of Nursia, the great writer of the monastic rule bearing his name, shows their catholic and ecumenical sensibilities. They cite the Iona community, from which some of their liturgical texts come, in a very open and economic approach to creeds and doctrine. They use and confess the historical creeds but also acknowledge that many who come to see and listen in their community have doubts and questions and may be in conflict with traditional perspectives. Howison also credits this theological openness and flexibility to Robert Farrar Capon, who insisted on God's unbounded grace while allowing for endless diversity in our responses to God.

st. benedict's table (they use lowercase) invites all to communion and welcomes LGBTQ people, something not explicitly done at St. Margaret's. saint ben's table uses All Saints Anglican Church, sharing some weekday and feast day services with that congregation, but scheduling their own Sunday liturgy for 7 PM Sunday evenings, with twice-monthly afternoon services for families and those for whom night services may be difficult. The liturgical year is adhered to but there is flexibility, a desire to be open to change, to want to adapt to people in the twenty-first century rather than seek to preserve the past models of worship and fellowship. Both parishes are extremely keen on outreach to the neighborhoods around them and to the homeless, who sometimes pitch tents near the church buildings. Baskets for contributions of nonperishable foods surround the sanctuary at the table. Originally st. ben's was in the "emergent church" model of community and was aimed at Xers and then Millennials and did not do all that well at attracting and keeping younger adults. But in relaxing efforts to target them, it became a place for older folk and members of other parishes, for whom the Sunday 7 PM liturgy is possible and a welcome addition to their experience of church. Members at St. Margaret's are encouraged to find their own ways of living out their faith in daily life. Again, there is no anxiety about conforming to traditional patterns, rather recognition that diversity of gifts and time will make for a diversity of forms of service. Those who can help are directed toward ministry groups for visiting the homebound and ill as well as, a network of members in order to maintain contact.

What is striking but perhaps not immediately apparent is that both of these congregations do not seek to do unusual things to be church. They embody one of the various modes of parish community and life we have seen here. Neither needs to drastically repurpose buildings, yet both are anything but turned inward and isolated. In their respectively and subtly different ways, they revere tradition while not idolizing it. Just as the initial response to shrinking congregations may lead to the conclusion that small communities have little chance of a future, further contemplation of what actual parishes are doing to be the body of Christ can lead to different conclusions. This has been the case for me, and hopefully, the rich mosaic of communities presented here may do the same for those who make their way through this book.

Doing Away with Parishes?

All of the examples we have looked at in this chapter are local congregations, parishes established in a specific location for those living in proximity. This has been the parish model for over a thousand years, though we have already encountered numerous congregations that extend far beyond the area around their buildings. And we will continue to inspect others in the chapters that follow. But in the UK, at least one regional collection of congregations, the Church of England diocese of Birmingham, is exploring the possibility of doing away with the ancient, traditional geographic system of parishes.[19] All the way back to the earliest communities of faith, groups of believers were, by definition, inhabitants of a limited geographic space. With transportation consisting of horse-and-wagon and walking, this tended to be a delimited area. The earliest congregations met in private homes, which were small, almost always less than thirty or so. Over time, as has been noted, a special building was set aside for gathering and worship, and the pastor or presider of such a community, originally self-employed, was paid to care for those in that congregation. Hence the title

19. Ashworth, "Birmingham Diocese Seeks to Undo Parish System."

"curate," also "rector" or pastor or the "vicar" of the archpastor/overseer of the entire region, the bishop.

No matter whether the Eastern or Western church, and no matter, later, the denomination or church body, the parish system has endured, although with widely differing patterns of oversight and organization. In numerous spots now, the historical multiplicity of parishes is no longer necessary, due to more rapid means of transport as well as by relocation of the population (most often rural to urban locations). And of course, there is the dramatic decrease in church attendance in the last century, although a famous census that measured religion in England in 1851 already showed lower-than-expected levels of religious observance. Taken on Sunday, March 30, 1851, the attendance count was 10,896,066 out of a population of 17.9 million. There were 5,292,551 attending Church of England services, 4,536,264 attending the other Protestant churches, and 383,630 attending Catholic services.[20] Such numbers are staggering today. They were the same then but for completely opposite reasons. That so many would have not been in church was a shock to church leaders of the time, and it lead to many efforts to revive religious observance across the country, not the least of which was the construction of hundreds of new churches.

We sometimes think only of Europe having numerous village churches, many of which are now redundant—this being an official category in the UK, meaning that clergy are no longer assigned nor regular services conducted. This has led to teams of clergy covering numerous very small historic parishes, and in time these collapsed even further with services in every single church no longer possible. Just in 2019 there was a legal recognition of this reality, allowing some very small parishes to forgo Sunday services in lieu of rotating ones. The advertisements for clergy positions in *The Church Times* more often than not describe a "benefice" to include several churches spread out over an area. Larger ones may have a "team" of maybe ten parish churches in three villages, with multiple clergy covering these.

In the Birmingham diocese, a special Strategic Development Funding of £5 million alongside the funding possibilities of the wealthier parishes will enable a redistribution of clergy in several categories. There will be seventy-three "oversight" ministers, each with two to three churches to cover. Another thirty-six are "local" ministers of congregations able to compensate them. Another twenty-eight "context" ministers are involved in various chaplaincy and outreach situations. The diocese emphasizes these are but working titles or categories which may change in the future. But the redeployment is a real detachment from the historical tie to one

20. See "Two Religious Censuses."

geographic location and building. The title of "minister" also reflects this reordering. A minister may be ordained or not, full time or not, a deacon, a reader, or a reader-in-charge, that is, a lay local minster with limited liturgical duties. The reordering of the old parish system does not require the closure of parishes and buildings, although that is not ruled out going forward, when a thorough assessment of buildings, their condition and use, is completed. As radical as this Birmingham effort may sound, it is not as radical as that recently done in the Church in Wales, where 122 parishes became twenty-seven Ministry Areas. On reflection, we have encountered very much the same kinds of redeployment of clergy and parishes in the American context. Most such efforts were restricted to one or more congregations in proximity, rather than an entire ecclesiastical region such as a diocese in the Catholic, Episcopal, or Orthodox churches, or an equivalent regional entity such as a Methodist conference, Lutheran synod, or Presbyterian presbytery.

But there is more to the story. With the necessary closing of churches during the pandemic of COVID-19 early in 2020, the grim reality that the Church of England knew but had not faced made itself unavoidable. The new Archbishop of York, Stephen Cottrell, is reported to be chairing a review of the status of the forty-two dioceses and almost 16,000 parishes of the Church of England.[21] While he says the review is focused on the essential tasks of parishes, eventually the question of the number of parishes and buildings has to be faced.[22] Since over 12,000 of these churches are historically protected, the Church of England is bound to maintain them. At the same time, many have been declared "redundant"—that is, no longer needed given the number of other nearby parish buildings. To further complicate matters, as we have already seen elsewhere here, often a single priest cares for several of these parishes, usually with rotation of services on Sundays and often as a member of a ministry team. The use again of the historic "ministers"—namely, larger parishes as "resource" churches to link up for shared activities and events with smaller congregations—was another attempt to work with so many parishes with decreasing memberships.

Now, though, it is clear that the individual parishes, the dioceses to which these belong, cannot be financially managed by the national church. The Liverpool diocese furloughed its staff during the pandemic due to lack of funds from parishes. Another strategy is the merging of dioceses. Thus, those of Ripon, Leeds, Wakefield, and Bradford merged in 2014 to form

---

21. Michael, "Review Could Lead to 'Massive Shrinkage' of England's Dioceses."

22. "Reported Cull of Bishops, Cathedrals, and Dioceses Is Misleading, Says Cottrell."

the diocese of Leeds, now the geographically largest in the entire Church of England. There are now more than double the number of bishops, 108 at present, as there were in the nineteenth century. Many of these bishops came along with the explosion of church construction in that century's latter half. Church attendance has been shrinking for the last century or more. Cottrell questions whether continuing to be "church" in an area means only buildings and pastors. There are no easy fixes and likely the review will provoke much debate and conflict. Suffice it to say every church body is facing the same realities—something made clear throughout this book. Denial and delusion are responses to the reality of shrinkage and decline. Yet the core movements of death and resurrection, as incarnated in so many examples of parishes re-inventing, redefining, repurposing, and replanting, show that it is not just an arc of decline but of rebirth and new life.

Death and Resurrection Again: Trinity UMC Closes —and Becomes Open Table Methodist

The last thing even faltering congregations want to have happen is that they disband, close down, perhaps even sell off or give away their buildings, and accept the end of a history of being the body of Christ. Every year this happens, for hundreds of parishes of every church body across the country and across the world. Canada has seen a significant number of church clo-sures. The reality cannot be ignored or explained away. As we saw earlier in chapter 2, with so many—not just thirty-five and younger, but throughout the age spectrum—drifting from active participation in congregations, the closing of some, even many, is inevitable.

Methodist pastor Jason Butler was sent to Trinity UMC in Raleigh, North Carolina as the aging members were dwindling and despairing of a future—a familiar pattern. They told him that over the years they had tried pretty much everything they knew and learned of to turn things around. So in cooperation with the North Carolina UMC Conference, Butler arrived. As he noted, old habits die hard, something we know well from personal efforts to change our eating, exercising, and relationship patterns, to men-tion only a few. I can say from experience in the parish that Butler was quite correct. It is not just a question of age either, for even younger members often have patterns of engagement and expectations so engrained that even temporary experiments with change end in failure and a return to old ways, often with the mantra that these are "tried and true." Almost at the begin-ning of my parish experience, I heard of the phrase called the "seven last words of a church," that is, "We've never done it that way before."

Butler says that the people of Trinity had not used one method of confronting their situation, and he was going to introduce it—disruption. It meant that, for a time, they would stop doing everything, even the good things like study and prayer groups, Christian education, and even worship. It was a kind of keeping Sabbath, a period of inaction but reflection.

Butler observes that the six months of quiet and pondering enabled the members who stayed to realize they had distanced themselves from the neighborhood and people around them, so focused had they become on survival. This "survival theology," which I have mentioned before, easily shapes financial strategy, internal relationships, and conversation in a parish. Butler does not say this, but my colleague, who coined this term, believes such survival drive turns a congregation ever more in upon itself and blocks ideas about change, repurposing space, and replanting in the larger community.

Butler claims that the period of disruption led to reimagination, re-identification, and rehabituation. Some left but those who made a commitment to remain committed to new relationships with their neighbors, a new dedication to identity as the body of Christ. The new name of "Open Table" was accompanied by a move to weekly communion and a deliberate effort to listen to the community around and connect to it in various ways. The congregation became more diverse in every way after its disruptive Sabbath. The website of Open Table lists several ongoing forms of community engagement. These include twice-monthly meetings with civic leaders to learn what they are doing and what further needs to be done. There is also review of the work of Love Wins Community Engagement Center, which offers a place for people with nowhere to go. Open Table partners with the Wilmington Street Men's Shelter and the Wake County IAF and Open Table links to several other national outreach programs.

The weekly communion is reinforced by "common table groups," gatherings of parish members, friends, and neighbors around a potluck meal to pray, reflect on Sunday readings and preaching, and share concerns and information, and meet those who live around members. What is particularly notable is the rooting of what Open Table aims to be in the very core of the gospel. I am struck by how this congregation's solid theological vision of the parish as a community gathered around word and eucharist takes flesh in accessible opportunities to gather, to learn, and to help.[23]

---

23. Butler, "Disruption Is Often the Key to Renewal."

Death and Resurrection in Indianapolis

Broadway UMC in Indianapolis has experienced a similar death and resurrection. The typical outreach ministries of food and clothing pantries
and after-school programs are gone, along with summer youth programs.
Mike Mather has been pastor of Broadway for more than fifteen years.
Following the lead of Northwestern University emeritus professor John
McKnight, Mather and De'Amon Harges began listening to the neighborhood around the church, getting to know the people and their gifts, their
strengths, and their achievements more than the deficiencies of the area
and its residents. In time, more than a dozen other "listeners" would join
them. This was McKnight's vision of "asset-based community building,"
one that Mather described as rooted in Jesus's telling the disciples at the
Last Supper that they are friends, not servants. It is also, without being explicit or self-conscious, a deeply incarnational view, since it sees God alive
and at work in every woman and man, regardless of poverty or wealth,
education or lack thereof, success or failure in work and life. Mather had
been at Broadway for a stint from 1986 to 1991, but then he was reas-
signed there in 2002. Not long after, a kind of farewell and funeral service
were held for ministries that no longer met the needs of the area and its
people—those just mentioned above.

Slowly, Mather and Harges began to encounter individuals with talents—backyard gardeners who, when they joined together, put forward
a farmers' market of produce. There was another member with strong
entrepreneurial skills. She manages a collection of small businesses who
rent Broadway's unused weekday space—dance studio, pottery shop, a
small architectural firm, and several who do catering now that the church
kitchen is commercially licensed. The parish website shows numerous opportunities for gathering with fellow members as well as others outside in
the neighborhood. Especially important is the list of, not one, but three
Sunday services, each one of them featuring the eucharist, ranging from
an early, smaller one to another with a live band and an informal setting to
the traditional liturgy later in the morning.[24]

These last two congregations emphatically show what cumulatively we
have seen in visiting quite a few parishes in this chapter. That is that there is
no "magic," no collection of miraculous church-growing strategies, at work.
That will be the case with all the congregations we will look at in subsequent
chapters. But then, you may ask, what is the point? Can we not get a pattern

---

24. King, "Death and Resurrection in an Urban Church."

capable of replication elsewhere, a blueprint for reinvention, repurposing, and replanting for renewal and resurrection?

At the outset, I said this could not and would not happen, not out of any cynicism or being secretive but due to what was the focus here. Despite being rooted in different traditional and church bodies—Anglican, Eastern Orthodox, Methodist, Presbyterian, Catholic—there is an astonishing convergence in what defines a parish, what are the spiritual roots of the life of that community, how they relate to each other and then to the neighborhood, the people around them, whether rural, small town, suburban, or urban. At the end, these strands, already suggested at the outset, will show what, after all, the church, the clergy, and the local community are for. What is encouraging is that the basics here have always been at the core, from the first century CE, in the "primitive" ancient church, down through to our own supposedly religion-less twenty-first century.

CHAPTER 5

Resurrection in Parishes Relocating and Restructuring

Grace Church in the Berkshires

WE VISITED QUITE A few congregations in the last chapters. Some went as far as they could and then, in the pattern of death and resurrection, died or nearly did so before being raised to new life. In some cases, this meant being subsumed into new congregations: Carr UMC giving birth to Shepherd's House UMC congregation, St. James Anglican in Montreal becoming St. Jax, and Asbury UMC giving its space to Servant UMC and merging into the new parish. Some others went the route of repurposing in a variety of ways, their properties turning into residential housing buildings. Still others found new ways of existing, such as St. Matthew's and st. ben's table in Winnipeg, Redeemer Lutheran in North Minneapolis, and First Christian in Oakland. And there were completely new community starts such as St. Lydia's dinner church in Brooklyn and "churches without walls" like the Rochester Presbyterian parish and St. Isidore's. We will visit more parishes in this chapter, some with similar patterns of reinvention we have yet to encounter.

There are many ways in which churches can choose to confront the changes reshaping our society and congregations too. Great Barrington, Massachusetts is close to Tanglewood, where concerts are held each summer by the Boston Symphony Orchestra, the Boston Pops, and many other performers. It is a town of some former grandeur in western Massachusetts, close to the New York border. As one drives down Main Street through town, there is a classic lineup of important buildings, from a grand Carnegie library to a several-block stretch of restored and repurposed commercial buildings, residential space atop and numerous high-end businesses below—coffee houses, boutiques, galleries, and pubs. The town's past as a hub of entertainment and commerce has returned. Given the historical character of the main street, there are several grand churches lining it—Roman Catholic, Congregational, Methodist, and Episcopal. One especially stately collection of buildings, dominated by an imposing stone nave and tower, was once St. James Episcopal Church. It is now St. James Place, an imposing events space where all kinds of gatherings and performances are held beneath the saints and biblical scenes of the stained glass windows. For years, it has been the site, among other venues, of the nation's oldest early music festival, the well-known Aston Magna concert series. It still hosts their Saturday evening performances.

But what happened to St. James Parish, and why is their cathedral-like edifice an events space? Established September 21, 1762, by Church of England priest Thomas Davies, the parish occupied different buildings in its more than 250 years of existence, stretching from before the revolution until just a few years ago. In 2008, the present stone church's back wall nearly crushed the rector's car and the entire structure was deemed unsafe and the congregation evicted. Repair would have been a multimillion-dollar project, far from the resources of a once large and prosperous but now-shrinking parish. When a neighboring parish, St. George's in Lee, also came to a point of discernment on their future, the two communities took time to pray and discuss the future. The result, embarked on in 2010, was a decision to house the parish in a creative if nontraditional fashion.

The location of a parish is an often overlooked but crucial factor in the history, life, and sustainability of that community. I immediately think of some of the parishes looked at in greater detail in chapter 5 to follow. One that is situated right on the main street of a town that still functions as a municipality was able to revive itself. Another, in the Methodist cluster, no longer has what could be called even a functional hamlet around it, and is dependent on a few families so that it has become essentially a family chapel. Yet another, an urban, formerly ethnic Lutheran parish, has flourished after severe decline due to its location near medical and academic institutions and remarkably mixed housing and commercial venues.

It made more sense to remain in or close to Great Barrington's healthy town center. If one continues down Route 7 from the old property, now St. James Place, a performance and event space, past the Congregational and Catholic Churches still open, and past a Methodist one now closed, you can almost miss a small office and chapel in a strip mall. More likely, a bit further down Route 7, you will notice Barrington Brewery. It is exactly that, a local brewery with a restaurant and an events hall called Crissey Farm. Every Sunday at 10 AM, members of the parish community of Grace Church gather and set up the altar and worship space. During the week, the now-joined parish has office hours and educational gatherings, as well as weekday services in the small location in the mall. Just as the first pastors brought their ministry and the sacraments and preaching to hamlets in Massachusetts as well as nearby Vermont and New York state, so too today does Grace gather a community as the Episcopal presence in the Berkshires. In the past, St. James Parish had led in setting up two housing projects for lower-income and senior residents. Today, these continue as Grace members work at the Lee Food Pantry and at Gideon's Garden, a vegetable plot they run in the summer months for hungry neighbors.

Grace Church is an example of a formerly affluent, well-established parish confronting its drastic decline, being open to joining with a nearby congregation in similar straits, and then essentially using the same basic tools to replant in the town. There were no huge leaps in style or theology. No measures adopted to attract young people or mimic megachurch practices. What works for Grace in a small western New England town is a continuity with the past. The grand sweeping nave and stained glass windows of the old sanctuary remain there, a magnificent setting for concerts and other events. Such ecclesiastical grandeur is not possible at the banquet hall of the brewery nor the small strip mall chapel. And yet there is a strong sense of the sacred through icons, the cross, altar, candles, and liturgy. But there is also a persistent commitment to serving the needs of the larger community. I suspect that this fairly modest and traditional yet not stuffy approach may be the most common one found among congregations that are reviving themselves. It appears in quite of few of the congregations being looked at here.

Rearranging and Repurposing Parish Space and Life

Even in "Bible Belt" locations like South Carolina, the same changes for parishes we have been describing here have been occurring.[1] As factories and mills have left towns, so has the population, and the demographic cluster has begun to affect the churches. Younger, educated people have already relocated in order to access education and jobs. The multigenerational families which were pillars of many small congregations have been thinned out or disappeared. Every mainline church body has recorded declining membership there—Presbyterians, Baptists, Episcopalians, and Methodists, with only Catholic parishes remaining stable or showing modest growth—this due largely to immigration. In response, you see many of the same efforts at reinvention or reimagination reviewed in the chapters here. The Church at West Vista, a network of house churches, meets in people's

---

1. Ellis, "Losing Faith."

homes except for the last Sunday of the month, when they all gather in New Brookland Tavern. Church in a tavern is not a problem at all.[2] In Columbia, Downtown Church meets in an event space not far from cathedral-size historic churches, offering an informal, very open, and accessible gathering for preaching, hymns, discussion, and fellowship.

Churches don't always repurpose space that is vacant during the week or underused at other times for religious projects or even not-for-profit, service-oriented endeavors. We will note several efforts on the part of parishes to offer space for residential as well as commercial development. In these, the parish becomes an enlightened property owner. In the case of Our Savior's Atonement Lutheran Church in upper Manhattan, co-working space was made available for writers and others looking for exactly such opportunities away from their apartments.[3]

Our Savior's picked up the idea of using their space weekdays from another congregation profiled here, St. Lydia's "dinner church" in Brooklyn. The founding pastor there, Emily Scott, launched co-working at rates of $80 a month for part-time and $240 for full-time co-working use. Our Savior's rates were lower, but in both cases, as well as other parishes repurposing space this way, the aim was to connect the congregation to the surrounding neighborhood, to build bridges with people living there. Users of co-working need not fear being religiously harassed by efforts to proselytize, to get them to attend services. As with the more frequent location of nursery and other pre-school programs in church space, the aim is not attracting new members but offering a service, often at a very reasonable cost, to neighbors. Likewise, the space no longer needed or underutilized during the week is both leased and rented to not-for-profit groups, as well as small businesses such as yoga and dance studios, artists like potters and weavers, after-school programs, English as a Second Language classes, and space too for baby and maternity health services, among others. Redeemer Lutheran Church in North Minneapolis, along with Reconciliation Services at St. Mary of Egypt Orthodox Church in Kansas City, are other notable examples of such intentional repurposing and reinvention of use. We will look at the latter soon.

Pentecost near Pasadena

Ordinarily, when a church closes, there is a great deal of grief, maybe guilt. Why couldn't the members have done more? The pastor? The bishop? It is sad

2. Ellis et al., "Church in a Bar?"
3. Ryder, "Faith and Freelancers."

to look at a now-empty sanctuary, thinking services will no longer be held, no more preaching, hymn-singing, church dinners or coffee hours, church school, or the programs of outreach to the neighborhood.

Such could have been the case when St. Barnabas Episcopal Church in Eagle Rock, California closed after more than a century of life in this small community near Pasadena. The parish had a deep sense of pastoral commitment stretching across a couple generations of rectors related by marriage. One of the creators of the Navaho language code system used by the well-known "Navaho talkers" during WWII settled in Eagle Rock and was a member after the war. And the parish had a history of service to the community. But like so many other congregations in the US, St. Barnabas simply kept shrinking until it could no longer manage financially, and this after a series of priests tried to keep it going. The rectory continued as a sober house for people in recovery and the preschool program that operated in the education space also continued its presence and work.[4]

But now there is a very different kind of revival or resurrection taking place. There are Jubilee interns (an Episcopal outreach corps in Los Angeles) and neighborhood volunteers replacing dead grass and preparing new herb, flower, and vegetable gardens. Inside the parish buildings, complete cleaning and repair is ongoing. Rabbi Susan Goldberg, of independent Nefesh Los Angeles, a spiritual community not based at any synagogue, has become not just a tenant but a part of the new community slowly taking shape and called, in honor of the past parish, St. Be's.[5]

Though Sunday services stopped in June of 2018, a weekly Thursday evening gathering for song, discussion, and Bible study began. Rather than coming from the diocese with a preestablished vision, the plan has been and continues to be to allow the larger community of Eagle Rock to show how this new gathering, this resurrected parish, can serve in the twenty-first century. The revival leader is a neighboring priest, Canon Jaime Edwards-Acton, rector of St. Stephen's Church in Hollywood and head of the Jubilee Consortium, a nonprofit group with interns for community work. Edwards-Acton leads an innovative, activist parish, and seems to be exactly the right kind of one to coordinate the revival efforts in Eagle Rock without making them conform to any pattern.

Late in September of 2019, regular bilingual services began on Sunday evenings at 4 PM at St. Be's. What St. Be's will become is a story that is unfolding, an outcome yet to be revealed. Edwards-Acton is himself a resident of

4. Kawamoto, "St. Barnabas Church Concludes Parish Ministry after 104 Years in Eagle Rock."

5. McCaughan, "Diocese of Los Angeles Heralds Birth of Closed Church as New 'Exploratory Community'"; McCaughan, "Revival or Resurrection."

Eagle Rock, so his involvement was as much that of a local wanting to see good use and life return to a venerable church in the town's history. With over a decade heading the Hollywood parish, he and the people and clergy of St. Stephen's have been involved in social-justice work and protest alongside the outreach programs that most congregations we meet here support, from food banks to tutoring and inviting the neighborhood—not just parish members—to use church space, to be welcome.

With a team of willing and spirited painters, cleaners, and gardeners, a local rabbi in residence, and with some people who have been gathering on Thursday evenings and Canon Edwards-Acton, the resurrection of St. Be's, though improbable, has strong Pentecost precedent and promise—that a small band of disappointed followers of Jesus had a windstorm and fire shake them into witnesses. Then they spoke with power to a city full of international pilgrims—this is not just strategic staffing and planning. They were understood, these disciples, and the rest is history. The century-plus life of St. Be's in Eagle Rock, the hopes of the volunteers and the Canon—this is community becoming.

Resurrections in Reinvention: Christ the King, Trinity Presbyterian, and First Congregational

Christ the King Lutheran Parish has been a fixture since 1964 in Cary, North Carolina, a suburb of Raleigh. It was planted at a time of enormous church and population growth. That period now is seen as the waning years of the post-WWII church boom. Christ the King had as many as 2,000 members at its height, but it is now down to 400 at services on Sundays, a figure that immediately puts it into the upper 5 percent of all American congregations. This ELCA parish maintains its first sanctuary, traditionally appointed with altar, cross, candles, pulpit, and font, and there are two traditional services each Sunday employing the liturgy of the church's service book.

But there is also another side to the parish, best captured in a sleek, glass-walled addition where contemporary services and Bible studies are conducted. One of the pastors, often a younger associate, leads them without vestments and with PowerPoint presentations, all of which then is posted on YouTube for great circulation. The parish made a concerted effort to reach out to the parents of Sunday school students who were being dropped off by their parents. The parents, and other adults, now have an upbeat, casual, but tech-friendly class, while the young people also attend church school. Every

Sunday one can choose either a contemporary or traditional service both at the early 8:30 AM and later 11:30 AM times.[6]

Wolfgang Herz-Lane, the senior pastor, came from Germany on an international church exchange, remained, and has served the inner city as well as affluent urban and suburban parishes. When they started to decline, the community at Christ the King used strategies they always had employed—outreach, welcome invitations to the neighborhood, but especially church school parents. A team of pastors offers a range of ages, interests, and energies. LGBTQ people were explicitly welcomed by the community, which became a "reconciled congregation" in the ELCA. A local chapter of the national community development organization, Industrial Areas Foundation, was set up at the parish as a base for a food pantry, a place for clinics, and other outreach work by nonprofits.

This parish is an example of using elements from within church tradition to revitalize and replant itself. Christ the King chose no unusual programs but offers members an impressive array of ministries for their involvement, ones that have been around in American congregations for decades. There are men's and women's groups, trained teams who visit shut-ins and those in healthcare settings, as well as social outreach and advocacy teams. In addition to providing backpacks to students at the start of the school year, parishioners continue connections to an Appalachian ministry and Habitat for Humanity, which builds new homes and renovates dilapidated ones. There are opportunities for working in produce gardens and food-bank outreach, refugee settlement efforts with other churches, a pantry with health and hygiene products, and numerous other ways of putting faith into action in service of the neighbor.

As we move through congregations in these chapters, we will find some that make amazing leaps of ingenuity and creativity in reviving themselves. Some of their experiments are surprising given the inherent conservatism of church folk. But in many cases, the basics of parish life—worship, study, fellowship, and service—become themselves sources of new vision and life both within the congregation and in outreach to the surrounding neighborhood.

In the tough neighborhood of Hilltop in Tacoma, Washington, Trinity Presbyterian Church has been getting a new lease on life. While many of the newcomers are younger people and families with children, the resurrection of Trinity was not due to using alternative contemporary services and music and deliberate informality. There is some of this. Its history

6. Shimron, "Amid Decline, One Lutheran Church Strives to Live Up to Its Namesake's Spirit."

resembles the stories of many of the congregations we have described here. Started in 1891 in a downtown YMCA, the present brick array of buildings dates from 1922. Lynn Loughlin was pastor from 1987 to 1997 and witnessed the decline of the neighborhood's economy, housing, and schools and the rise of violence, drugs, and crime. Down to less than thirty for Sunday services, and most of these older people, the demise of the congregation appeared imminent when Loughlin arrived.

But a spark continued to burn within that tiny community. It manifested itself in members starting an after-school tutoring program that reached out to the surrounding neighborhood. This was nothing radical, nothing extraordinary or creative. After-school programs were staples of urban churches and other organizations by then. Trinity members were white, and the children they brought into the education complex were African-American, Latino, Asian, and more. A clothing bank, then Tony's Kitchen, a weekly soup and conversation community lunchtime, as well as a neighborhood health clinic, co-sponsored with another Presbyterian parish—these were the other beginning steps to establishing real connections with the larger neighborhood around the church. Almost two decades later, the after-school program continues alongside the Bobcat Learning Center. Harlan Shoop brought people from University Place Presbyterian when he came in 2000. A few years later, a known community leader was hired as the director of the several outreach programs and still more sponsored with other parishes.[7]

The present pastor, Matthew Robbins-Ghormley, came in 2017 as Trinity had recovered and was a very different community from what it had been most of its history, now reflecting the diversity of the area. The real drive for renewal here was clearly the desire to be part of the neighborhood once more and to serve it, even though this meant that most being served were not members. This is a kind of sociological leap, a crossing of a boundary or widening of the very experience of community that seems to be part of every congregation that has enjoyed rebirth. But from within Christian understanding, this was also a tremendous leap of faith, a story of both deepening and widening what the community of faith means and looks like. Trinity is in partnership with Allen African Methodist Episcopal, Peace Lutheran, and the Church of the Indian Fellowship to explore their communities of belonging, especially around race and identity, in a time when immigration as well as diverse peoples in America are being marginalized and oppressed.

7. Mork, "How Serving Its Community Transformed a Dwindling Church."

So at Trinity Presbyterian, it seems that neither conventional church growth nor imitating the megachurches was pursued. There did not appear to be dynamics capable of moving the parish from decline to being diverse and vibrant again. Upon closer examination though, concern for the needs of others in the neighborhood, first evidenced by just a few older members, a couple of retired educators among them, became an ember that, with some divine as well as human breath, caught fire and started burning once more.

In the end, when we reflect on what it is that church offers to us and to the people around us, we must recall this very basic but authentic passion to serve. It isn't just, as in years past, a matter of saving others and being saved oneself. It is not just "hell-avoidance" or heaven entry, but as Sam Wells puts it, sharing abundant life. This ultimately is what being saved means. Saving comes by being, as Wells so often argues, "with" sisters and brothers who need education, healthcare, food, shelter—in sum, the love we in the church say we have, and want to share, from God. Resurrection appeared in the impulse to do something for young people with few life chances.

Sometimes, resurrection is not so obvious. First Congregational Church of Bellingham, Washington was healthy enough to build a new church home in 2004. But putting up a new structure was not enough. The congregation gave serious thought to what they wanted to be and do as a community of faith going forward. They planned a new sanctuary, of course, and they wanted additional areas for other purposes. After considerable discussion and prayer, the congregation planned for the area below the worship space to have its own points of access, independent entrances and exits, this looking forward to it becoming a place for community nonprofit groups to utilize.

Now named The Ground Floor, it has opened for precisely such sharing of facilities with the wider community. It is now a drop-in center for homeless young people, run together with Northwest Youth Services. Originally, the parish was not able financially to finish the downstairs but used it to store furniture for a nonprofit helping house homeless families, as well as a clothing depot for any who were in need. The Ground Floor drop-in and service center now shares the space with the furniture and clothing depots. The congregation now has an anchor in these outreach efforts and is able to channel both members and resources toward their work. The Bellingham church is but one of many examples we have seen and will see here, not just congregations in financial need first looking for added rental income, but more importantly, finding connections to the communities around them and using their space to reach them.[8]

8. Brekke, "Houses of Worship Are Not Just for Worship Anymore."

The examples of other congregations doing similar sharing of facilities and reaching out to the larger community are impressive. We will mention and link to several others. Peace Baptist in Decatur, Georgia has hosted Celebrate Recovery since 2001. Mosaic Church, which opened around the same time, is home to Vine and Village. This is an umbrella for nonprofit agencies such as Orchard, the area's largest food distribution network. There is also space for post-foster-child counseling, other services for young adults, and the Evangelical Alliance for Immigration Services. Mosaic Church pastor Mark DeYmaz has published a book about these efforts and how others can use them as models.[9]

What is interesting to note is that, as with Redeemer Lutheran in North Minneapolis, Mosaic also rents space to business enterprises such as a fitness center and coffee shop. The deal is the church gives them lower-than-market rents in return for the businesses charging lower and more reasonable costs to the community for their services, what DeYmaz calls "benevolent ownership," a kind of capitalism with a heart and conscience. While congregations that fold often put their buildings on the market for redevelopment as residential sites or commercial space—there are examples noted here—the choice of reaching out and partnering with small businesses in particular is a sign of new life, an indication of renewed awareness of the opportunities to be of service.

Radical Relocation and Resurrection: Out of the Ashes for St. Thomas

Is it a new corporate headquarters, the space for a major advertising or media startup? No, while it may look like all the above, it is a church along with space for temporary housing in a city with high mobility. St. Thomas Episcopal Church's Neo-Gothic church burned in 1970, and the space it had inhabited was used for a temporary building the parish long ago outgrew. The real estate value of the property was enormous. It was, after all, DuPont Circle in Washington DC.

Enter Zeus Living, a San Francisco-based corporate living startup. Targeted at the highly transient population of professionals who may enter an urban area on contract for anywhere from a month to a year, the location was perfect for Zeus to create an entire building of apartments. The parish was able to have its own space for a sanctuary as well as meeting and educational rooms. Once a parish composed of Washington elites, business, government,

9. DeYmaz, *Disruption*.

and old established families, St. Thomas's DuPont neighborhood began to change dramatically in the mid-twentieth century. Galleries, restaurants, shops, and bars took over the neighborhood. The rioting after Dr. King's assassination and the destruction of buildings only a short distance away made the area less desirable for both business and residence.

Under the rector at the time of the fire, Henry Breul, the parish deliberately reached out to artists, young people, and the LGBTQ community who were the new residents and visitors. Processions into the neighborhood, outreach programs, and a new focus on social justice became hallmarks of the once toney congregation. Then the sanctuary was ravaged by fire in 1970 and the parish hung on in temporary quarters until the plan to share the property with a structure intended for housing as well as parish space passed through planning, the diocese, and the parish processes of review.

The parish's decision to sell part of the property to Zeus Living was met with substantial local criticism and opposition.[10] The case of St. Thomas is important for us to note, since it is one in which aspects of the decision to sell were debated and criticized. To be sure, the sale enabled the parish to finally have a new church home after years of using its educational space for worship and all the rest of its activities. While several affordable units were included in the new apartments as part of the contract, neighborhood leaders noted that the rest of the units were high-end. These were aimed at transient residents and contributed little to the life of the surrounding neighborhood. St. Thomas parish decided to remain in place on DuPont circle with the new apartment structure, unlike other real estate agreements noted here with urban congregations in which the parishes selling property relocated. The mixed character of this DuPont Circle arrangement underscores the conflicting factors at play—the desire to stay and offer the presence of the body of Christ in a neighborhood, over against the gains to be made for ministry from high-end real estate locations and properties.

Resurrection in Time and Space: Weekday Church and Church without Walls

St. Stephen's is an imposing stone edifice right next to the Thomas Jefferson University Hospital, a sprawling, internationally known complex in Center City Philadelphia.[11] It has a priest, Peter Kountz, who does what every parish

10. Banister, "Dupont Circle Church Redevelopment Opens with Corporate Housing Units."

11. See Cunningham, "Philadelphia Episcopalians Explore What Happens When Church Is Separated from Sunday"; also Kountz, "New Life in Old Space," 26–29.

priest does. He preaches, celebrates the eucharist, and distributes ashes on Ash Wednesday to a large daytime congregation. He does counseling as well while the church is open. There are historically significant artworks and burial places in the spacious sanctuary. St. Stephen's also provides coffee and snacks for those who come by to sit for a while, nap, read, or possibly talk to the pastor. So this sounds like any other venerable urban church. The congregation has been there for a long time, the present building designed in 1823. In the 1980s, the congregation began to shrink, a beloved, long-term pastor retired, and the decline continued until the diocese closed the parish, only to open it again, under newly elected bishop Daniel G. P. Gutierrez, who insisted on this after visiting.

The mission of St. Stephen's is to be open and usable for heat, a cooling space, phone charging, quiet, conversation, prayer, services, yes, even a nap. There is a new space where the burial vaults and gravestones of past members are visible, a kind of *memento mori*, remembrance of time, history, and death. There are daily services too for any who want to participate. The daily eucharist also has anointing and the laying on of hands for healing. Monday through Thursday these liturgies focus on the holy women and men in the church calendar celebrated on ordinary weekdays. Also, since some major feasts like Epiphany and Ascension are weekday feasts, they will be celebrated, along with a service for Thanksgiving Day, Christmas, and Good Friday. Often seventy or more visit the church on a weekday.[12]

Strange as it might seem, there is not an effort as yet to rustle up new members and return to "normal" Sunday functioning. Yet, it is clear there is really a church, really outreach and ministry going on in Center City Philadelphia at St. Stephen's. And the weekday mix of liturgy, hospitality, and care is joined to an active arts life there, with regular concerts and performances of classical and jazz, dance and drama, in the space. And the famous (or infamous) "mystery worshipper" recently visited and reported on liturgy there, when the martyr and apostle to Germany St. Boniface was commemorated. The stained-glass windows, some by Tiffany and other noted nineteenth-century studios, along with the memorial and the Furness Burial Cloister of exposed vaults and tombs, form a beautiful and historically significant, as well as holy, space in downtown Philadelphia. The parish Facebook page and website give not only the history and present mission but also many images of this glorious space.

At the conclusion of her book about encountering other traditions of faith, Barbara Brown Taylor describes at length a church without

---

12. Cunningham, "Philadelphia Episcopalians Explore What Happens When Church Is Separated from Sunday."

walls—a Sunday eucharist at Woodruff Park in downtown Atlanta.[13] It was a remarkable gathering of homeless people, passersby, and neighbors. The bishop was present as it was the installation of the priest who would be the pastor of this "church of common ground," as it was called. Taylor used her visit in several ways. One was to give a sense of her reconnection with her own Christian tradition, this after vividly narrating the spiritual pilgrimage on which she took her class in comparative world traditions of faith. Over the many years she had offered this course, it became her own spiritual journey as well. What she experienced in this church without a roof or walls was something she'd also written about in a beautiful celebration of the sacred in everyday life.

In this "church of the common ground," people are free to come and go as they wish.[14] The church, that is the people who come together to pray, gather in a public space, open to any who wish to stop or linger.[15] During the liturgy Taylor attended, a woman carried on within earshot, occasionally disrupting the service, but never reprimanded or asked to leave. The eucharist, as well as the readings and prayers offered by the celebrants and gathered faithful, are also open—available and accessible to others of whatever faith tradition or none at all. Linked to the church are other outreach efforts to those who have no lodging or care, such as Common Soles, a foot care clinic. Fifty to sixty often gather, several thousand if you count all Sundays of the year. This nontraditional church was founded by Lutheran pastor Bob Book and his wife, Holly. The Episcopal diocese of Atlanta eventually took the church and its ministry under its wing.

Until recently, Monica Mainwaring was the priest, but now there is an interim while a new pastor is sought. Others on the ministry team include an assistant pastor or curate, a deacon, a coordinator, a fellow from Episcopal Service Corps, and interns during summer months. Besides the Sunday liturgy, there is morning prayer on Monday and Wednesday, a Bible study, and the foot clinic which is held at nearby St. Luke Episcopal Church park. Several parishioners, funded by an Innovation Grant from Leadership Education at Duke Divinity School, are being trained as leaders in the community that gathers at the Church of the Common Ground. Mainwaring relates that the church is built on relationships and these are built, nurtured over time, as the homeless are, by necessity, suspicious and hesitant with others. Here we see how church can find a place without a building, without even permanent

13. Taylor, *Holy Envy.*

14. See www.churchofthecommonground.org.

15. Simon, "Church without Walls Offers Unconditional Acceptance to People Who Are Homeless."

members, as there is understandably much that is tentative about the home-less and passersby. This church is also a lesson in what Afanasiev called "the power of love."[16] With no building to maintain, the Church of the Common Ground is light, flexible, and radically inclusive. Whether hot and humid, as Atlanta is, rainy or cold and snowy, the church gathers.

Resurrection in Diversity and the Convening of the Neighborhood

Roman Catholics have discovered just how important a new recognition of ethnic and cultural diversity is, as the number of traditionally Catholic whites of Northern and Eastern and even Southern European backgrounds seems to be moving away from church. Brett Hoover and Hosffman Ospino have explored multicultural parishes and ministry.[17] No longer are ethnic parishes mostly urban and coastal realities. All over the country one finds Latinos and Asians of different language backgrounds alongside the newer Eastern European immigrants and the third- and fourth-generation de-scendants of much earlier immigrants. While bilingual masses can be good experiences on some feasts like Pentecost, Ospino suggests they are not an optimal path to follow on an every Sunday basis. There are other ways to bridge across languages and cultures such as meals with ethnic contribu-tions, like the honoring of special feast days like that of the Virgin of Gua-dalupe. The devotion to the Virgin Mary, while different for various Latino groups, as well as Vietnamese, Caribbean, and West African communities, nevertheless offers a point of spiritual convergence. Sensitivity to customs for gifts for the Chinese and Vietnamese Lunar New Year's days, or for coming-of-age celebrations such as *quinceañeras,* are other ways in which multicultural parishes can welcome and make room for different groups.

Soong-Chan Rah, professor of church growth and diversity at North Park Theological Seminary in Chicago, has studied the effects of the growing diversity of the American population on the churches.[18] Rah notes, as do oth-ers, how much cultural baggage is attached to all aspects of Christianity, from preaching and styles of worship to church architecture and the activity of a parish community, including pastoral ministry. In some cases, as in the origi-nally Swedish Evangelical Free Church, there can be a significant change in diversity over time, up to 20 to 25 percent nonwhite. But only about 8 percent

16. Afanasiev, *Church of the Holy Spirit,* 255–76.

17. Hoover, *Shared Parish*; Ospino, *Cultural Diversity and Paradigm Shifts in Latino Congregations.*

18. Rah, *Next Evangelicalism*; Rah, *Many Colors.*

of American churches are multiethnic in any serious form. That said, Rah draws on his own experience as a pastor, pointing out that it need not and should not be just the dominant white/European-shaped version of church that invites other cultures to blend in, adapt, or even add their distinctive customs. Hospitality cuts both ways. Minority groups in a congregation need to find ways to be part of something larger but also need to challenge the dominant culture being expressed in the church.[19]

There are also many examples of ethnic communities partnering with each other. As we have seen, it is sometimes the case that a congregation shrinks to the point that its best blessing is to pass its buildings on to another community. In a town nearby to where I live, this happened with an historic Presbyterian congregation that had shrunk to less than a dozen.[20] They continue to worship in the premises, but the buildings are now the home of a flourishing Latinx parish. In other cases, two different language groups may share a space, holding their services and other community gatherings at different times, and on big festivals combining in some way. The future of church in America has many demographic changes with which to contend. Rah reminds us that the growth in diversity, so feared by some political leaders and party members, is not only a core element of American history and society—a "nation of immigrants"—but, seen from the perspective of Pentecost, a manifestation of the Spirit's breathing everywhere, filling all peoples and places. The whole question of culture and Christianity remains complex and controversial. Jeannine Hill Fletcher has examined it.[21] With so much of the state, the economy, and the culture tied up with the church—in every church body and throughout history—Fletcher argues that the Crucified One at Christianity's core is the transforming theological paradigm. In Christ, every supremacy of race or class or gender is transcended.

Trinity Episcopal Church in Wrentham, Massachusetts is another example of a community of faith standing up, being present, and "convening" the neighboring area, as Nancy Ammerman calls it. The church hosted gatherings to remember those victimized and their families and all others concerned by the opioid epidemic. It was a campaign to publicize what was called #2069, the number of opioid-caused and -related deaths in the state in 2016. The campaign started with a Facebook page and then with gatherings of those concerned where signs were carried and planted all over the state. People at Trinity Church, a small congregation, were behind all of this,

19. See "Soong-Chan Rah."

20. Meyer, "Houses of Worship Do Some Soul Searching as Their Neighborhoods Change."

21. Fletcher, *Sin of White Supremacy*.

not specialists themselves but believers who felt they could offer space, a place where families of victims and others could meet.

Almost a hundred came to the first gathering and, in addition to exchanging information, learned about efforts to stem the epidemic and fight addiction. Many used the church sanctuary for prayer and reflection. This was a project that a small parish felt it needed to sponsor, one that ran its course. Yet in their actions of hospitality and convening, the Trinity community showed that even in a time of political division and social conflict in America, local churches still have great potential for transcending red-blue partisanship, for being places where diverse, even opposed individuals could gather in a space of trust and support. This effort also made the people of Trinity, and other congregations nearby, think that there were other issues that they could address together as faith communities.[22]

Of course there was no way that one congregation, or even a number working together, could defeat the opioid explosion and epidemic. But in observing the ways in which the gatherings brought comfort to victims' families, as well as raised awareness in the area about ways of confronting addiction, these proved to be revelations about what a small-town church could do. We have seen more examples of just such discoveries as congregations across the country, many of them challenged by declining membership and finances, nevertheless found new vision, reimagined themselves as small but potent forces for education, for care, and, eventually, for change in their larger communities.

Death and Resurrection: Tearing Down to Rebuild

There are also situations in which congregations that are still vital, with outreach and excellent projects for the neighborhood running, have to face dramatic but necessary changes. First Baptist on Fifth in downtown Winston-Salem faced just this challenge. At the height of its expansion, the church had over 3,000 members and a campus of multiple buildings, covering an entire city block and totalling 114,000 square feet, a virtual small town in the midst of an urban location. But today, membership is about 500, with another 700 inactive or at a distance. The congregation's first woman pastor, Emily Hull McGee, was from a family line of pastors and religious educators. And as the spiritual leader, she had to encounter a storm of issues. Several buildings were past repair. The budget just for maintenance of the campus was almost $350,000. There were major roof

22. MacDonald, "Small Rural Church Is Bringing Together People Affected by the Opioid Epidemic."

problems in the huge sanctuary, compromising other parts of the complex. Decades ago, the first integrated daycare center and after-school program in the county were a significant ministry of the congregation to the area. Now, though, the Children's Center building could not be renovated without needing to come up to code.

And there were further infrastructure issues. It would cost 8 to 10 million dollars to do repairs, and still some buildings were not capable of being saved, so big was the building issue. After long, difficult deliberations, the congregation decided to follow the downtown revitalization movement and demolish two buildings not worth repairing. Essential work to stabilize the sanctuary was coupled with a new extension that would be able to gather a crowd for shared meals, as well as a location for other outreach work. This is being discussed and planned, the tradition of focusing upon children foremost in consideration. First Baptist's difficult choice, in the face of the threat of the death of the congregation, also had resurrectional roots— a long history of commitment to serving the community around it. The congregation is part of the Cooperative Baptist Fellowship, a more open, progressive association that split from the Southern Baptist Convention in 1991. For almost fifty years, they led in efforts to support civil rights with an integrated childhood education center. So once more, the realization of faith and fellowship as a commitment to service shaped the radical decision to demolish and then repair the buildings that could be used, as well as start to identify new outreach ministry paths.[23]

Many more congregations, such as Judson Memorial in Greenwich Village and St. Mark's-in-the-Bowery, both in New York City, found that removing pews attached to the floor enabled their sanctuaries to be utilized in a host of ways for the local community's benefit.[24] Both congregations have historically sponsored and lent space to the arts: dance, drama, poetry, and performance, as well as education. Isadora Duncan, Patti Smith, Sam Shepherd, and Mark Morris are but a few of the great artists who worked at and were supported by St. Mark's. Judson has been a leader in social justice for decades, all the way back to the anti-war and civil rights movements, and more recently the protection of immigrants and sanctuary.

As the oldest Protestant congregation in the city, Los Angeles First United Methodist faced enormous challenges from changing patterns in its urban location. Major shifts in the neighborhood prompted the move of the church and eventually its disappearance—well, the buildings, at least. Started in the El Dorado Saloon in 1853, the congregation was an

---

23. Shimron, "Downtown Church Forges New Path."
24. See Schaper, "Remove the Pews and Let Sacred Sites Evolve."

essential part of the old downtown on Fort Street, now Broadway, then moving to 8th and Hope Street. With as many as 6,000 members at its height, it simply lost the neighborhood and thus most of the members as that part of downtown transitioned from residential to commercial use. When the last buildings were demolished, services continued to be held in the affordable-housing complex constructed on the site of the old church buildings. This was the pattern until an experienced pastor, Mandy Sloan McDow, came in 2017. Since Los Angeles First UMC still owned the parking lot outside the affordable-housing units, she decided it was time to get out into the world again—very much John Wesley's vision when he launched the missionary movement in the Church of England that would become the Methodist Church. Wesley used people's homes for gatherings and began to preach outdoors along with his colleague, George Whitefield. Given the year-round moderate climate, Los Angeles First Methodist relocated to a tent in what is a parking lot during the week. That is where the church continues to worship each Sunday.[25]

To give way to something so basic as shelter was not death but new life, an affirmation of Christian discipleship and service. It was a visible resurrection. Los Angeles First Methodist in a tent is still visible as a witness to the gospel, something it was for many years inside its walls. And it is also a demonstration that church is not just the building but the people of God who gather to pray, celebrate the eucharist, care for each other, and for those around them in need—precisely what Wesley himself urged in the early days of the Industrial Revolution in Great Britain.

The tragic consequences of congregations simply selling, especially to the highest bidder, then taking the money and running, occur too often. Duke Kwon is the pastor of Grace Meridian Hill Church in Washington DC. The congregation is housed in the former Mt. Rona Baptist Church, a century-old structure that had already been sold once by its Baptist congregation.[26] Pastor Kwon's congregation rented it from the owner but then suddenly found they were evicted and the building sold definitively for luxury condos in a tight housing area and market. While parishes do not always have such a market edge—particularly small-town, rural ones with very modest buildings—urban sanctuaries can often be real estate killings. We encountered this earlier, with developers actively hunting declining congregations in New York City.

Kwon and others raise the questions about the consequences left by such transactions. Redevelopment of church properties has almost

---

25. Frances, "They Sold First UMC and Put Up a Tent in the Parking Lot."
26. Kwon, "Tragedy to Communities."

tripled in the past several years. When a church building passes into the real-estate market, the losses are numerous. Not only is the witness of a praying and serving community gone from a neighborhood, so are hundreds of thousands of dollars of services to the community. Think of all the outreach ministries, from daycare and after-school care, tutoring, and summer programs with meals, safe places for seniors, perhaps cooling centers, health care clinics, thrift stores, clothing pantries, food banks, soup kitchens, space for dance, yoga, drama, exercise, study, and so much more. The list is staggering: twelve-step meetings, health clinics, polling places, emergency shelters for the homeless in extreme weather, locations for counseling services. When a congregation closes, it becomes clear that it may well have been a neighborhood hub that, as Sam Wells says, has been there at the center of community life. Or as Loren Mead said, we see the parish never existed just for itself but for others, for the life of the world around it. Kwon urges legislation that would support the transfer or sale of church buildings to other religious communities or nonprofits that serve the community. As we have seen in numerous cases, this is exactly what congregations have done as a way of keeping their history and their legacy of service alive.

New City Church in Minneapolis, a newly planted UMC congregation, has aimed at what it defines as "de-gentrification" programs that seek to avoid the destructive aspects of redeveloping neighborhood residential and commercial stock for the affluent.[27] Pastor Tyler Sit is inspired by the Scriptures and the first communities in the Acts of the Apostles. However, Sit also follows Peter Moskowitz's study.[28] In the Powderhorn section of the city where New City Church operates, also Central and Phillips areas, the aim is not to villainize start-up restaurants, taverns, coffeehouses, and boutiques, which are usually the marks of gentrification. Rather, it is to explore creative ways to enhance the neighborhood and add to household income. Sustainable micro-farming is one approach, with households using backyards and a community greenhouse for seedlings and certain crops. There are lessons to be learned from earlier efforts, such as Bob Lupton's in the 1980s in Atlanta. Lupton moved his family to an urban neighborhood that was largely African-American. His efforts led to a diverse community and for forty years he has been a leader in faith-based community development. This is especially relevant where gentrification is bringing in new investment and creating high-end housing while driving out the former residents, many people of color and those with low incomes.

27. Solomon, "Fighting Gentrification with the Holy Spirit."
28. Moskowitz, *How to Kill a City.*

What Sit and his parish are actually after is the recovery of community, a sense of welcome and acceptance and belonging in a location based on faith but extending past the smaller faith community of a congregation to the wider neighborhood in all its economic and social diversity. Often it is class—that is, economic force—that dominates over almost every other identity, whether religious, ethnic/racial, cultural, or political. Pastor Sit and New City Church, while explicitly resisting the exclusion and inequality that gentrification brings, nevertheless came to see that community was the singular gift that faith offers, and community is where and how faith is lived. This is the thesis of the entire book.

Relocations and New Life

First Baptist Church East Nashville is like other congregations, such as Zion Lutheran in York, Pennsylvania; Norwood Baptist in Knoxville, Tennessee; Calvary Temple Assembly of God in Springfield, Missouri; and Way of the Cross of Christ in Washington, DC. All of them have experienced profound, some might say seismic, changes in the neighborhoods where they have long been planted. In the case of Zion Lutheran, Cross of Christ, and Calvary Temple, remaining where they were was not a viable option. They relocated, mostly to more suburban locations where some members had migrated. First Baptist, a smaller but strong community, found itself surrounded by luxury housing, as well as Section 8 housing. An African-American congregation, it found reaching out to the condo dwellers difficult, perhaps socially and culturally impossible. The former church building of Way of the Cross became higher-income housing. The congregation relocated to the suburbs where it was able to continue its work. Walmart razed the Calvary Temple property and put up a big store, now that the neighborhood had been gentrified and shopping venues were in short supply. Despite what Pastors Kwon and Sit argue, there are locations in which the decline of numbers, deterioration of the structures, and other demographic factors make the continued life of a congregation extremely challenging and, in some cases, impossible. But this is not a blanket diagnosis either, as many of the stories of congregations we have reviewed and will examine show.

In some parishes of the United Church of Canada (UCC), something of an alternative to outright sale of property for financial profit is being pursued. This is a more entrepreneurial approach, and St. Andrew's UCC in Markham, Ontario, under Pastor Katherine Selby, entrepreneur coach Peter Miller, and the UCC's innovation director Ron Dalgleish are leading this approach. Local social activists, artists, and entrepreneurs, about a dozen or so in Markham, are able to have 24/7 access to the building where spaces are available for meetings, classes, and individual workstations.[29] The models are the medieval cathedrals and monasteries which gathered together everything from publishers and librarians, scholars and teachers, to master craftsmen, healers, and performers, not to mention clergy, choirs, and the faithful. One could hearken back even further to the early church where diaconal centers not only had liturgy and preaching but provided meals, shelter and care for the ill. Basil the Great created such a multipurpose center for service, the *Ptochoptopheion,* or *Basileiad,* in his hometown and diocesan center of Caesarea, today's Kayseri, in Cappadocia, Turkey. Benedictine monasteries were known for their hospitality to guests who were welcomed, as Benedict's *Rule* says, as Christ himself.

Inside Changing Churches: The Clergy

So far, we have looked at the factors behind the shrinkage and decline of congregations, as well as the appearance of increasing numbers of religious Nones and Dones. Central has been our observing of the pattern of death and resurrection that takes place when parish communities look to the Spirit to continue being the body of Christ, even if under very different conditions than in their earlier histories. But it is also necessary to venture into the life of parishes for someone else—the pastor.

The place and the role of clergy in twenty-first-century churches is well worth a book in itself. Where to start with the issue, even in a most cursory examination? Declining numbers going to seminaries to prepare for ordination seems right. Enrollment has dropped by half over the past decade. In an overview of seminaries in Minnesota, they averaged a drop of almost 40 percent in enrollment. Three out of four Catholic priests in the state are retired or disabled, thus not active full time, and across the US the figure for Catholic clergy is 60 percent disabled or retired.[30]

Seminaries are declining too. Bangor in Maine ended its on-campus existence, now offering distance learning. Numerous theological schools of various church bodies have closed or merged. The Episcopal Divinity School in Boston closed, sold its property, and now there is an Episcopal presence at Union Theological Seminary in New York City. Bexley Hall became part of Seabury-Western Theological Seminary. Two seminaries, Gettysburg and Philadelphia, have joined to become United Lutheran Seminary. Luther Seminary in St. Paul is soon launching an innovative two-year program

29. Rendell, "United Church of Canada Embraces Startups."
30. Hopfensperger, "Test of Faith."

with a great deal of in-parish mentoring included. Student debt, the scarcity of parishes that can support even a part-time pastor, as well as a swirl of questions about the identity of the ordained minister—thus theological, economic, cultural, and social questions along with the demographic changes earlier visited that affect all congregations—these are the crucible in which the ministry of the ordained finds itself today.[31]

The Church of England has been studying clergy well-being, with a priest who is also an oncologist and palliative care expert, the Rev. Dr. Margaret Whipp, chaplain at Oxford University Hospital Foundation Trust, providing theological commentary.[32] The study noted the rise of "unrealistic" expectations on ordained ministers, due to shrinking parish membership and financial resources for congregations. The clustering of several small village churches into a yoked parish was one of the most frequent strains on clergy, now responsible not just for one community and building, but anywhere from two to four or more. Duplication of services, parish councils, education, and outreach programs do not exhaust the challenges, which also include the maintenance of several buildings, not to mention the pastor's own health and family. The climate of downturn for the church breeds a kind of "collective anxiety" for the clergy.

One important recommendation was for pastoral supervision and collaboration, in recognition of pastors often feeling and in reality being isolated. Pastoral teams, pastoral mentors, larger churches reviving the role of "minsters"—these were other measures suggested, also noted in our survey of efforts to revive congregations here. Minsters historically were centers for missionary work. Later, these large churches with other buildings became educational hubs, schools not only for the training of clergy but the extended education of professionals. Universities have their roots both in these cathedral and minster schools, as well as the monastic learning centers. The Church of England and its proposed Covenant for Clergy urged the ordained to maintain a process for maintaining health and stability. Studies both here in the US and elsewhere indicate clergy are particularly prone to depression, isolation, and self-destructive patterns of self-medication to ease pain.

Notable in the study is the finding that, with all the changes in church and society, there is really a lack of clarity on what the pastoral ministry is as a vocation. If we consider the declining number both of seminarians in formation for ordination and the equally declining number of sustainable parishes for clergy assignments, there is abundant reason for uncertainty

31. Hopfensperger, "As Churches Close, a Way of Life Fades."
32. Davies, "Clergy Burdened by Unrealistic Job Specs, C of E Told."

as to what pastors are and what they should be doing. I would add that considering the growth over the last several decades of second-career clergy, the specter of clergy abuse, then the demographic trends already examined at length here, especially the drift of Nones and Dones of all ages away from church membership and participation, it is not surprising that this study questions whether there is a clear understanding of ordained ministry in the twenty-first century. At a debate in the Church of England General Synod a couple of years ago, Canon Simon Butler suggested that, "at its worst, the Church 'moulds us [the ordained] into a straitjacket that slowly ekes away our human goodness into a caricature of Christ.'"[33] Radical words. They are echoed though, in the memoirs of Barbara Brown Taylor, Barbara Melosh, William Mills, and Richard Holloway, among others.

Even when we look away from the deeper questions about how clergy are trained, how they should relate to their parishes, unquestionably the largest issue is that of their compensation. Across the churches, increasing numbers of parishes cannot offer a compensation package of contribution to pension, to health insurance, and to salary. This is true for mainline denominations as well as smaller church bodies and independent congregations. While some will stretch the diagnosis and speak of a shortage of clergy due to retirement, illness, deaths of Boomer clergy, and the decrease in seminary attendees and thus graduates and newly ordained, the deeper issue is a shortage of parishes for clergy, places where they can go and do the work of ministering to their communities both within the congregation and beyond.

There is no "one size fits all" response to the complex of issues and changes facing congregations today as far as pastors go. Often there is a brutal choice. Do we pay the compensation, even if not complete, to a pastor or do we pay for the utilities, maintenance, and repair of our buildings? In many of the cases of congregations we have and will continue to review here, such are the hard choices that often lead to a crisis and the need to decide on a new path going forward.

In addition to clergy well-being research, the Church of England is studying the lives and experience of its clergy for a ten-year period.[34] The findings are rich and very useful in grasping the situation of pastors in the changing, often shrinking congregations they serve. The study also considers personal and family financial situations, the well-being not only of the priest but of spouses and children, if any. There were eighty-five priests carefully followed over ten years, in all kinds of parish situations

33. Davies, "Clergy Burdened by Unrealistic Job Specs, C of E Told," para. 5.
34. Graveling, *Negotiating Wellbeing*.

and from various backgrounds, ages, and genders. Several findings will be noted in various chapters here. In particular, the lack of clarity about identity and accomplishment in often very demanding ministry situations that not even a super pastor could turn around are sources of stress and disruption for many pastors.

Clergy Alternatives and Alternative Clergy

Episcopal priest Catherine Caimano calls herself a "free range" priest.[35] She serves St. Paul's Church in Salisbury, North Carolina, presiding at the eucharist and preaching, providing pastoral care and teaching, that is, doing exactly what clergy are ordained to do. But on closer examination, these things are rather different than in the usual full- or part-time appointment. At St. Paul's, the small community of about thirty do a great deal of the day-to-day ministry. This includes meeting as the parish vestry, maintaining the building, paying bills, and the rest of what most parishes require to remain in operation. They also assume, during the week, pastoral care tasks such as visiting and bringing communion to the sick and shut-in, responding to other calls for information and assistance from the members and others in the neighborhood.

Caimano is contracted for priestly services by the St. Paul parish two Sundays a month. This means she does not have a full-time salary or other benefits as a result, nor housing either. She has an ongoing relationship with the parish but does not participate in vestry meetings and decisions. She supplies at other parishes when not at St. Paul, and is involved in a number of other online and in-person efforts that mentor clergy and preachers. Caimano has an online presence through her blog and does consulting work as well, advising on digital worship and ministry during the pandemic and beyond. A fifth of Episcopal Church parishes in the US (ECUSA) do not have a full-time, paid pastor. We saw data on this earlier. About half of clergy in mainline churches are paid for full-time work and about 10 percent of all clergy are nonstipendiary, that is, they serve without pay. While some still decry part-time clergy, clergy with employment alongside ministry such as "worker priests," the reality on the ground in parishes and with actual ordained people witnesses otherwise. The classical model of a pastor for every congregation, supported by that community, is simply no longer the norm.

Christ Church, an Episcopal parish in Bethel, Vermont, continues to be a force in the town, contributing significantly to the local food pantry and other outreach efforts. The parish is able to continue being a social hub

---

35. Caimano, "Free Range Priests Solve Traditional Church Problems."

because its priest, Shelie Richardson, has a full-time job as an insurance agent. Thus, what would have gone to her compensation package for salary, pension, health benefits, travel, and more can keep the church open. Shelie is essentially a volunteer. Clergy like her are called "nonstipendiary," serving as clergy alongside another occupation. Other labels include "worker priest," though this has more complicated origins, and "tent-making ministers." I know this pastoral vocation well, having followed it for all my almost forty years in ministry, having had a "day job" as a full-time faculty member at the City University of New York since 1977.

The ECUSA estimates that close to 14 percent of parish clergy are "nonstipendiary." If one were to count those who have some version of a part-time appointment and compensation, the percentage would likely jump more than double that figure. Nearly half (48 percent) of ECUSA parishes had no full-time paid clergy in 2014, and that number is almost certainly higher now. A quarter of ELCA congregations cannot afford to pay a full-time pastor. From 2010 to 2015, data from the Hartford Seminary Foundation indicated median parish budgets have declined from $150,000 to $125,000 and part-time clergy use increased to 38 percent. Going part-time does not necessarily mean that decline in members and support will continue. I know well a parish in which the move to two-thirds time has resulted in the budget moving back to balanced, with even a small coverage.

In an Episcopal parish in Henderson, Texas, a nonstipendiary priest, Patsy Barham, a retired educator, works the forty to fifty hours a week most clergy do, able to do so because of a working spouse, her pension, and the more affordable cost of living there.[36] Back at Christ Church, Shelie Richardson cannot devote those kinds of hours, so the result is that the parish membership has rediscovered the priesthood of all the baptized, and has jumped into visiting the sick, shut-ins, even taken on preaching. This was also the case with Catherine Caimano. Time will tell the effectiveness of either nonpaid working priests or part-time, partially compensated clergy. As we saw earlier, Grace Church in Great Barrington, Massachusetts kept a salaried priest for the two parishes merged but with both their buildings sold. In the final chapter, with Bishop C. Andrew Doyle, we'll reflect on the shape of ordained ministry going forward, these part-time, unpaid models and the traditional fully compensated one all considered. This challenge to the ministry of the ordained is ecumenical. It is shared across all church bodies, Catholic, Protestant, and Orthodox.

Still another model is that of St. Matthew's in Whitney, a neighborhood of East Las Vegas, where three priests and two deacons all have served without

36. McDonald, "Pay For a Priest or a Building."

a salary for some years, maintaining other occupations alongside ministry. This has enabled the parish to care for casino workers and a mostly impoverished parish community, and a larger one around it, with generosity. Gail Leavitt, who's been a priest there on the team of nonstipendiary clergy, calls the model "total ministry," which is precisely what is done at Christ Church in Vermont and in many other congregations of all church backgrounds.[37] St. Timothy's in Henderson, Nevada has a part-time priest, Carol Walton, as does St. John's in Gloucester, Massachusetts, Brey Hays.

Yet there is still resistance to nonpaid clergy with other occupations from seminary faculty and administration of church bodies, a distrust of something other than the model of paid or fully supported pastor by a congregation that has been the norm for more than 1,000 years. A closer look at the earlier periods reveals that clergy were supported but not as we understand this today. Clergy had a "benefice," which included a house, and part of the proceeds of lands rented to tenants—the "glebe," in English usage. And until a cash economy and expenses like a car, health insurance, and the like made a cash salary necessary in the twentieth century, clergy often were fed and clothed and their rectories heated by contributions in kind. Or, as in southern and eastern European contexts with married clergy, the clergy family worked a plot of land as well, maintained a cow and chickens, and likely did so with neighbors. So the model of a completely compensated clergy is a very recent turn in the almost 3,000-year history of Christian congregations, the very earliest parishes essentially meeting in the homes of members—"house churches," a practice revived by the early Methodists here in the US, hence the ubiquitous Methodist presence—a parish in every postal area or zipcode was once the boast, now a challenge.

The Bangor Theological Seminary Center (BTS) is now both a remote-learning formation school for clergy and a think-tank. This came about with the end of on-campus classes there. BTS has looked at a couple dozen parishes with part-time clergy. Almost 70 percent of UCC congregations in Maine have part-timers.[38] While clearly, some parishes in deep difficulty due to deteriorating buildings and declining membership and finances cannot perk up with the effects of part-time or unpaid pastoral care, many others signal that a major effect of this change is that the laity are stimulated, enabled, and better equipped to engage in parish ministry as well as community outreach.

---

37. MacDonald, "Move to Part-time Clergy Sparks Innovation in Congregations."
38. MacDonald, "Move to Part-time Clergy Sparks Innovation in Congregations."

This is the first of the effects the BTS Center study saw stemming from part-time clergy. This is a move away from the traditional "chaplain" model in which the pastor is the sole provider of liturgical, sacramental, educational, and pastoral services. While some of this was going on before—communion assistants, readers, occasional preachers, and home visitors serving on the council and committees, in education, music, and the like—even higher levels of participation show up when clergy are part time. And in turn, in some parishes, this has led to higher Sunday attendance and overall membership numbers, modest gains but real ones, as the members are really engaged and active. Cameron Barr terms this the model of the pastor as "convener" in the congregation; this a parallel to Nancy Ammerman's view of the congregation as "convener" in the surrounding neighborhood.[39] Clarendon Presbyterian could afford to have a full-time pastor, but David Ensign and the membership chose not to, recalling pastoral burnout and overwork. Linda Tuttle, pastor at Tuttle Road UMC, had a similar experience.

The BTS Center research also identifies two other roles that part-time clergy take, again with significant consequences for congregations. These include that of becoming a wider-ranging minister or ambassador of the church in the larger community—as will be noted below—and as team member. Engagement of the laity enables part-time clergy to become ministers-at-large, pastoral ambassadors to the larger community beyond the parish, as in Laura Brecht's case. This was another effect the BTS Center study identified. At St. Barnabas, Borrego Springs, California, rector Laura Brecht is called by some, or so I heard, "the pastor of all Borrego," and rightfully so. Her ministry, though two-thirds time, extends far beyond the St. Barnabas membership to the whole community. She is a leader in the Borrego Ministers Association, which is an ongoing source of direct assistance to families in need. Her deep involvement in the town mirrors that of the members of the parish. The people of God at St. Barnabas have their hands in almost all the outreach that goes on in the valley—hosting and supporting a monthly food bank, volunteering in the schools in science and the arts, teaching English as a Second Language, mentoring students on their way to college, and participating in the performing arts center productions. A retired priest who is a member, George Keith, is the Performing Arts Center's artistic director. Other members are deeply involved with music and theater productions, as well as the yearly film festival. Priests resident in the parish assist regularly with preaching and teaching. Still others are on town committees interacting with the county supervisors for the area and with local health care providers.

39. Barr, "Pastor as Convener."

All of this with a congregation of perhaps thirty-five that expands slightly during the winter and spring.

Finally, the BTS Center study identified part-time clergy redefining the pastoral role, making the pastor a team member. The team in question is that group of members of a parish who assume duties that they can canonically or legally fulfill. They can help distribute communion, do readings, visit the sick, teach, and, with training and the gifts to do so, also preach. Members, that is laity, assisting in these activities is not understood as a necessity due to fewer clergy. Rather, it is the culmination of a now long-term rediscovery of church as the people of God, not just the clergy or the ecclesiastical rules. As the BTS research suggests, the disappearance of full-time pastors and the new normal of parishes without them has led to a revisioning of what church membership means. As we have argued here, it is a return to a pattern of communal ecclesial belonging, to a sense of *koinonia* typical of the church of the first several centuries. This is not a romantic effort to recreate the past. Such is not possible. But it is a "return to the sources," a recovery of the charism or gift of community that, if not lost, then obscured or diluted over the centuries.

Lastly, part-time clergy recast the parish as the whole people of God, as a community of the ordained and laity praying, learning, working, and being together.[40] At First UMC in Hudson, Massachusetts, Rosanne Roberts is retired officially, but continues part-time, seeing a rise in participation of members in all the activities and ministries.

A Parish without a Pastor?

Sounds strange. How can a congregation function without a pastor? Actually, this is not so strange a proposition, as we have seen here. The persistent model of a pastor for every parish now has even more exceptions than those of cathedrals, minster or mission center churches, and monasteries. Parishes have part-time pastors, pastors "for the season" when snowbirds or other vacationers arrive. There are pastors who have a "day job," are "bi-vocational." There are "pop-up" pastors who serve where and when needed. Some congregations are served by retired or partly retired clergy. Some congregations contract with pastors for liturgical services and other sacramental acts only the ordained can perform. But others, from some church traditions, license or allow members to preach, or preside at communion, as well as offer pastoral care. And when there is a part-time pastor, regardless of the arrangements, it is always the case that parish members

40. "What Are We Paying You for?"; MacDonald, "Retooling for Ministry."

step up to administer everything in the daily life of the congregation, from visiting shut-ins and those in facilities to maintenance of the property, financial management, and more.[41]

While Roman Catholic parishes increasingly find there are not sufficient clergy to be assigned a pastor on a regular basis, most make do with some variation of either supply priests for Sundays and holy days or periodic visits of clergy, with lay-led services and distribution of communion from the reserved sacrament. This is also the custom in other liturgical churches, such as the Eastern Orthodox, Episcopal, and Lutherans.

Thus, St. William Catholic Church in Louisville, Kentucky stands out as a parish which since 1990 has had a lay administrator appointed by the diocesan bishop, Thomas Kelly. Previously, like other Catholic parishes, they had a pastor who was an ordained priest. Even after shrinkage of the parish membership due to massive railroad layoffs, as a center of Vatican II renewal in liturgy and outreach, the parish continued with a pastor until clergy shortage ended that. With no assigned pastor and a lay administrator, the parish continued its proactive outreach, creating new connections with the neighborhood. Earlier, when they still had a resident pastor, they had established a not-for-profit corporation to buy and rehabilitate abandoned houses for rent, at the same time reaching out to neighbors needing affordable housing while acquiring income for their own expenses. They set up a sister-parish relationship with a congregation in Nicaragua. Later, a store for local artisans and crafts people was started. The former rectory was transformed into a retreat center and it houses high school and college students learning about inner-city life and ministry. A more recent move by the Louisville hierarch to appoint a pastor became confrontational. The priest assigned was far more conservative than the parish community and wanted to be the sole decision-maker as priest. Fortunately, Archbishop Joseph Kurtz intervened and allowed the parish council to continue to administer and manage the ongoing work of the congregation.

It is telling from the parish website that the members of St. William neither deny the role of an ordained sacramental minister nor their connection to the larger church, both in the diocese and worldwide. But it is also possible to sense the strong identity they have as a community—gathered in the eucharist, in the living out of their baptism and of the gospel in being a place of sanctuary and service. The diagram in the drop-down ministries tab on their website depicts this powerfully. The circle of ministries is inseparable from liturgy and sacraments. The community defines itself by these and the specific activities of service are listed around the circle. This diagram could

41. Martos, "Can Laypeople Lead a Parish?"

well serve as a kind of icon of what this entire book wants to say about community as church and church as community, going forward. The altar and the eucharist are at the center, and in them are assumed baptism and the rest of the sacraments. All the ministries of the community radiate out from there. All members are ministers, all form the body of Christ, the parish is there at the center of life, existing for others, for the life of the world.

Pastoral Losses: A Literature of Loss

We have looked at many congregations faced with shrinkage and decline, but also rising up again to replant themselves in their neighborhoods. But the radical vision of St. William parish might seem like an anti-clerical urge implemented. Nothing could be further from the truth. It is rather an effort to restore the most ancient location of and pattern for pastors integrated into the community, who are genuinely part of the community, neither above or outside it by virtue of ordination and membership in a clerical caste. But pastors are often the chief casualties of the changes to parishes described through this book.

The situation of clergy in the twenty-first century is far too large a topic to be covered here except in a small way. In many of the congregations we have looked at, and just above in this chapter, the creative ways in which pastors work without pay or part time, something about their humanity must at least be noted, even if fleetingly. The challenges of ordained people who lead, care for, and work with communities today are enormous. When one looks at the literature about clergy, most often the issues that are most in view are the severe challenges to their health: psychological, physical, and spiritual. The "burn out" syndrome, chronic depression, struggles with eating, and substance addiction are some of the serious afflictions clergy deal with, as well as related consequences in marriage and family life. It is not surprising that a third or more of clergy opt out of congregational service within five years of ordination. And there are those who leave ministry altogether. Anyone who has worked in seminary training or in other spheres of formation such as parish internships over time knows of cases in which marriages have ended, or where ordained people have needed rehab or left pastoral ministry completely. So, at least we need to consider this matter, even if briefly.

One of the most powerful memoirs of a pastor in the last decades is Barbara Brown Taylor's *Leaving Church*. It is the first of a series of works that raise questions about faith, ministry, and the church in our time.[42] Her

---

42. Taylor, *Leaving Church*; Taylor, *Altar in the World*; Taylor, *Walking in the Darkness*; Taylor, *Holy Envy*.

work figured importantly in my own.[43] Like other memoirs, it says a lot and at the same time a little. It is a story of loss, leaving, a kind of dying, as well as resurrection. Taylor was recognized a few years back as one of the 100 most notable people in the US by *Time* magazine. She's been on the list of the country's leading preachers and her books have been *New York Times* best sellers. To her years of pastoral service as an Episcopal priest, she's now added another couple of decades as a professor of comparative religion at Piedmont College. That part of her life is soon to be the focus of yet another memoir volume.[44]

Taylor, no matter what aspect of her life and gifts you consider, is remarkable. But *Leaving Church* is an unflinching account of her leaving a parish that she had helped grow. It is not a simple story—this is why it defies being capsulized or precisely characterized. For in it Taylor shows her own weakness and shortcomings in ministry, her own humanity, in its gifts, strengths but also weaknesses. So it is an account of losing!

I was given Taylor's book by a former intern and student who had received it as required reading at a center for clergy healing. After this revelation of what can happen to clergy if they let work and continued parish growth consume them, Taylor shifted to how authentic religion cannot be kept contained within church walls, rites, and texts, but indeed there is "an altar in the world"; namely, the sacred is present everywhere. Taylor here wanted to pry religion out of the institutionalized confines where it historically had been placed. In later work, she would follow this path further, looking beyond religion's fixation with light into the darkness that was as much fundamental to human existence. And her teaching of comparative world religious traditions expanded even further the sense of the sacred that abides in a particular heritage but is not exhausted by it.

However, *Leaving Church* was not just about Taylor's own recognition of her own limitations and failures as well as accomplishments as a pastor. Her narrative also tells us that a congregation has a life of its own, a network of relationships, legacy, disappointments, and joys, as well as expectations that antedate any pastor who arrives there. Over time, all these changes, as we have seen—demographics and the host of other external factors—transform the community. More often in recent years this has meant shrinking, declining, and all that we have seen come along with these trends. Particularly when there was a "golden" age of booming for the congregation, a time remembered fondly when the parish was flourishing, such a memory can become toxic. For

---

43. Plekon, *Hidden Holiness*; Plekon, *Saints as They Really Are*; Plekon, *Uncommon Prayer*; Plekon, *Church Has Left the Building*; Plekon, *World as Sacrament*.

44. Taylor, *Holy Envy*.

the last few decades, such memories would be, given the age of churchgoers from the post-WWII era, of the 1950s and 1960s, and in some cases even down further into the 1970s and early 1980s. *Leaving Church* is also, then, very much about the church's losses, the church losing. *An Altar in the World* surely confirms this, but her other books attempt to show, as does the one you are reading, that new life is there to be received.

Barbara Melosh provides another honest and quite painful reflection on what trying to serve a parish often looks like today, and the experience, certainly, of the pastors of many of the congregations who have been described here.[45] Seeing so many ways in which a community's legacy can be passed on when that community passes away has been encouraging. Even more so to see as we have the myriad ways in which congregations attempt to reinvent, reimagine, and thus revive themselves. But these are the "good news" stories, and this was not the case for Barbara Melosh. A second-career pastor, after years of teaching and research as a university professor of history and literature, she brought a great deal of learning, professionalism, and dedication to a congregation wistfully dreaming of its past, better days. She discovered over time that the community was unable, and to some extent unwilling, to reimagine their situation as a community or to reroot in the neighborhood. The departure of her predecessor, a young, energetic pastor, had shocked them. They were still grieving when they chose Barbara to be their pastor.

Her memoir is riveting. It is a courageous narrative of disappointment, affection, and determined commitment to serve a resistant, shrinking congregation. The area was just beginning to see the glimpse of revival, even gentrification, when she arrived. As in many older congregations, most longtime members had interlocking extended family connections through marriage. There was an intricate map of the old families presented to Melosh on her arrival, a baffling record of who was from this family but married into another tribe. The longtime members themselves did not all live in the neighborhood but commuted from safer suburbs, and the new hipster residents seemed oblivious, one asking if the church was still open, as another one nearby had been repurposed into high-end apartments.

Barbara Melosh embarked on the journey every new pastor faces. She had to familiarize herself with a small world of people, objects, and patterns of behavior. There were the rooms of the parsonage and the education wing, the church hall, and the sanctuary itself. She had to learn all the intricate details of not just went on in the parish buildings but also exactly how. In so doing, she was told what was normally done and how, and that nothing

---

45. Sink, "Loving and Leaving a Church."

could or should be changed. She discovered that her new congregation was very much trapped in the past. As professional and caring as she was in reaching out to her new community, her education and previous profession in higher education became an obstacle, accentuating how different she was from the longtime members. Older herself, with an academic career behind her and without her predecessor's young children, she did not conjure up the youthful, energetic magician who would zip into their midst, quickly attract new people, especially young adults and families, and rapidly return them to the flourishing past they fantasized about.

Barbara Melosh's story is one of apparent contradictions.[46] This is captured in the title *Loving and Leaving a Church,* and the same is the case for Barbara Brown Taylor's *Leaving Church,* subtitled *A Memoir of Faith.* After seven years, the membership rolls were no larger, perhaps even smaller with attrition, and the finances were about the same, maybe a little worse. Melosh was not the savior, the magician who could make the church full again, multiplying members like the sorcerer's apprentice did with broomsticks and buckets. This was also the case for Taylor. Pastors dare not be confused with saviors! After leaving, she found her age had closed most doors to another pastoral position in a parish, but she also found a niche as a mentor to clergy colleagues. For all this, she acknowledged she saw Christ in the community at what she calls Saints and Sinners Church in Baltimore, and a sense of having tried to do what she hoped in her discerning a call to ministry as a second career.

Likewise, after leaving her parish, Barbara Brown Taylor did not return to congregational ministry but entered academic life to continue her work as a teacher and scholar. In the books since *Leaving Church,* she does not reject parish ministry but shows how faith is alive and at work everywhere in the world, not just within the confines of church. Numerous other discerning writers like Richard Rohr, Sam Wells, Sara Miles, Darcey Steinke, and Marilynne Robinson, among others, have argued the same. In our conclusion here, this will lead to the important question of what good is church, what is the point of the parish, now and in the foreseeable future?[47]

What we receive from both Taylor and Melosh is the "other side" of the story of congregations in our time, one that is seldom studied or narrated, namely the experiences of pastors in the midst of decline and efforts to revive. This is also movingly recounted in memoirs by William Mills and Richard Holloway. It is an incarnational narrative of death and resurrection

---

46. Melosh, *Loving and Leaving a Church.*

47. Rohr, *Falling Upwards*; Rohr, *Immortal Diamond*; Wells, *Incarnational Ministry*; Wells, *Incarnational Mission*; Miles, *Take this Bread*; Miles, *Jesus Freak*; Miles, *City of God*; Steinke, *Easter Everywhere*; Robinson, *Gilead*; Robinson, *Home*; Robinson, *Lila.*

too. While mostly here in this book we have observed the communities of parishes experiencing death and resurrection in these two pastoral memoirs, we see the personal experience of the cross and the empty tomb in the lives of these individuals.[48] Whether we consider it theologically or sociologically, the congregation is not exclusively defined or determined by the pastor alone. Nevertheless, enormous expectations are placed on the pastor. More often than not, the pastor is either praised for successful revival of a parish or blamed for its decline. The reality is that a congregation's existence and future is the result of a community, the whole people of God, laity and clergy, putting into practice what they receive at the Lord's table, becoming the body of Christ for the life of the world.

Ministry Years Ago and Moving Forward

In my first parish assignment, almost forty years ago at Trinity Lutheran Church, Brewster, New York, my mentor was H. Henry Maertens. He had been the pastor there for almost a decade. Maertens had much experience beforehand as an associate and then as head pastor. What was unusual was that as both the senior pastor and my mentor he considered me a peer, though I was newly ordained. He considered my previous experience as a Carmelite friar, my graduate work, teaching, research, and publishing as significant and useful formation. From the start, he viewed us as a ministry team. So we shared presiding, preaching, and other aspects of pastoral work. Both of us reported to the parish council and in time we arrived at a division of pastoral work that enabled us to complement each other.[49]

Fundraising and the construction of a new church building dominated our years working together. It was also what today would be seen as a larger parish, with several hundred members. After the building expansion, we had to come to terms with the many transitions that this new space brought and some complications as well. Not the least of these was maintaining parish income to meet mortgage payments. We had noticed that, increasingly, the parents of church school students were skipping the services. We had two each Sunday then. They dropped off and picked up their children when church school was over. Back then and now, there was a rule regarding active membership. The less present parish members are, especially at services, the less likely their contributions would remain regular. Of course, even back then, in the late 1980s, we were aware of the beginnings of shrinkage in

48. See also these very different but moving memoirs: Holloway, *Leaving Alexandria*; Mills, *Losing My Religion*.

49. Plekon, *World as Sacrament*, 233–52.

parish membership. Fewer people were moving into the area and there was a steady migration out, usually job-related. And then there was simply active members becoming inactive. In those days, the majority of parish members still had children at home. So, we attempted to meet and greet these parents between services, even going out to their cars to greet them and encourage their bringing the children to services with them.

Over the course of several weeks, our efforts to meet and greet "pick-up parents" began to connect with other trends for us. We were somewhat taken aback by the indifferent and at times almost hostile reaction to our outreach. In a lunch shortly afterwards, Maertens told me this had compelled him to reflect on what we had heard and seen from these parents and beyond in the parish. His thinking through it led him to more general observations on what was happening before our eyes. The dots began to connect. He shared with me that he saw most of the elements and expectations of parish life changing, something we had not perceived till the meet-and-greet experiment. Moreover, what he saw was the culture of parish life, as we'd known it for decades, disappearing. I have notes on the conversation in my files.

His vision was most discerning but also disturbing, given that we still served a very sizable parish in the late 1980s, with between 300 and 400 members. His own earlier experience in both suburban and small-town parishes enabled him to see patterns that were emerging in the parish we were serving, a congregation he'd served for a decade of rapid, significant growth. He was precise, too, in identifying the aspects of parish life that we both saw falling away—the couples' club and other adult groups focused on social and entertainment activities like bowling, camping, yearly festivals, trips to baseball and other sports stadiums. But also shrinking were the women's group, weekday Bible study groups, sewing circles, and the like. He'd asked my input as a sociologist of religion. I simply confirmed what he'd concluded, on the basis of studies of congregations after the boom time of the 1950s.

While there was decline in these parish groups, they did not all disappear. Some continued but in very different forms, activities, and purposes. I saw this pattern in the other parishes I served, up to the present. Even mainstays of congregational life like church school and confirmation classes were shrinking. It was becoming more difficult to recruit parishioners to teach in the religious education programs either on Sundays or those that met on weekdays. This again was back at Trinity Church in the late 1980s. We had seen that increasingly children were being dropped off at the church for Sunday church school, but their parents would not attend the service that overlapped with church school but head to the coffee shop or to the supermarket to do weekly grocery shopping, then reappear when

Sunday school was over to pick up their children. In earlier decades, such would not have been the pattern. Parishioners would not have avoided church services, especially since the earlier service had been scheduled to run simultaneously with church school.

The result of this pattern was twofold. The adults were no longer attending services regularly and, as we found, were no longer supporting the parish by contributions as they were not there when the baskets were passed. Children would then progress through grades of church school without coming to services, would not know them, nor feel at home with the texts and flow of the liturgy. Thus when they reached confirmation class in eighth or ninth grade and regular attendance at services was required as part of the preparation for confirmation, we found that most confirmands simply did not come to services, though most were dutifully brought to the classes which had met on weekdays since the clergy were taken up with preaching and leading the services on Sundays. Switching the confirmation classes to Sundays did little to change the patterns.

In time, what we saw toward the end of the 1980s has accelerated. There is, as we saw earlier, far greater mobility. People relocate more frequently, for work and other reasons. Multigenerational families, once the backbone of parishes, have become fewer. And as we also have seen, the young people I first taught in church and confirmation class back then have mostly chosen not to belong to congregations and attend services, support the churches, or bring their children there.

I share this personal memory about change and pastoral work because it echoes the accounts that Barbara Brown Taylor and Barbara Melosh give of their pastoral experiences. As they attest and I concur, pastors are often failures. Other clergy memoirs agree. And if they cannot admit this, clergy are liars. When things look difficult in a congregation, when membership and giving decline, the pastor is blamed. And not just by the council/vestry or membership, but, moving up, by the area dean and then the bishop. William Mills painfully chronicles his experience as his parish dwindled, moving away for other jobs in the Recession. What will be the aftermath of the pandemic?

Often with turnarounds and revivals pastors are given the credit when in reality, these are communal efforts. Pastors are human beings, children of God, sinners and redeemed, just as the rest of the people of God, the church. There are pastors guilty of abuse, mismanagement, deception, fraud, and a host of other serious actions which merit sanctions. Equally they often are credited or even claim credit for remarkable renewals in parish life—increased membership and giving are usually the favored metrics.

Pastors are integral to the lives of congregations. This will not change going forward. But how they function, how they earn a living, more basically how they are trained or "formed," these are significant issues. Many church bodies have not faced them, but with the growing closures as well as mergers of theological schools and experimental, creative projects for changing the education of clergy, what we have been looking at in all the chapters is crucial for such efforts.

Pope Francis has returned numerous times to the problem of "clericalism," the separate culture of the ordained as well as those in formation for ordained service. He only gives voice to what others have seen as a distancing of pastors from the rest of the people of God for dubious theological reasons, many of these having to do with an illegitimate notion that the ordained are more perfect, holier than the laity. The power differential of the clerical caste remains at the heart of the sex abuse malaise and the inability to remedy it.

Stacey Noem has called for theological formation settings in which those being trained for ordination are not separated from but learn, pray, and live with those preparing for lay ministry and from the rest of the church in general.[50] In some theological schools, the presence of partners and spouses on campus, perhaps even enrolled also in courses, are counters to the clerically segregated scheme which has persisted since the Council of Trent's establishment of schools for ministerial training. This has been normative for Catholic seminaries, given the celibacy requirement. All other seminaries have, at the least, the spouses and families of married students as part of the community. Noem notes that for Catholics there are few such institutions where there is integration of seminarians and others, including lay ministerial students. These include the Graduate Theological Union at Berkeley, Boston College's School of Theology and Ministry, and Notre Dame's Master of Divinity program. In the following chapter, on returning to the question of the place and training of pastors, we will hear one bishop's provocative proposal that the entire identity and formation of those to serve as pastors needs rethinking and restructuring. While centering on prayer, liturgy, and fellowship are crucial for those in formation, theological schools are neither monasteries nor parishes.

Luther Seminary in St. Paul, Minnesota, the largest Lutheran seminary in the US, has announced a creative, accelerated path toward the MDiv degree most often granted to pastors-in-formation. A number of factors prompted this plan, not the least of which was a gift in excess of 20 million

---

50. Noem, "We Need to Stop Separating Seminarians from Lay Ministers in Formation."

dollars, but also the specter of seminary debt looming over graduates who increasingly have been finding it difficult to find parishes that can provide compensation that is adequate to support them, even in a part-time relationship. Wartburg Seminary is yet another school that offers an alternative, albeit a somewhat less creative one. This program proposes a three-year undergraduate period and then a three-year theological and pastoral program, both at Wartburg, offering both a BA and an MDiv in six rather than eight years. A parish internship is built into this, now a widespread component of pastoral formation programs. In the UK, the growth of the number of ordinands who are nonresidential and located rather in parish settings has increased 142 percent.[51]

But looking at the question of where new clergy will go, the preceding chapters make clear the stark challenges they face. Some argue that with the increased retirement of Boomer clergy, a real shortage of pastors is approaching or already here, and the parallel closing of congregations and shrinkage of those that remain open have made the traditional model of a pastor to a parish, with a salary and housing, the exception rather than the rule. We will revisit the place of the pastor as well as formation in the last chapter here. Pastors do not define church but are essential parts. After seeing so many living examples of parishes seeking to redefine and reinvent themselves, to reshape their work and even buildings, we of course cannot forget the many parishes which have had to close, which no longer are communities of prayer, service, and belonging. To conclude then, it is necessary to get to the very bottom of it all, to ask: What is church for, and thus, what are the community and pastors for?

---

51. See Davies, "Number of Ordinands in Contextual Training Increases."

CHAPTER 6

Resurrection and the Small Church

Historically Smaller and Growing Smaller

IN HER NOVEL, *OPEN House,* Elizabeth Berg writes:

> Why isn't there a Community Center for People Who Need a
> Little Something? . . . If people would only tell the truth about
> the way they felt, it would be busy all the time. There could be
> folding chairs arranged in groups, people sitting there saying, "I
> don't know, I just wanted to come here for a while."[1]

We have followed so far quite a few congregations as these lived out the pattern of death and resurrection, facing their decline and the threat of closing.
We have also followed the movement away from organized religion in this
country for so many reasons. At the same time, and not in any magical way,
we have also seen the movement of grace that Pascal noted in his aphorism,
"The spirit of grace, the hardness of the heart, external circumstances."[2]

The entire sweep of the Scriptures is witness to these elements Pascal
connected being continuously at play. Even if we think "hardness of the
heart" too heartless a judgment on the drift away from communities of faith,
by now we have been reminded of many "external circumstances" reshaping our relationship to congregations. And there is always "the spirit/move-
ment of grace." In our last look at actual parishes and their situations today,
we need to return to that cohesiveness that keeps communities joined, and
smaller congregations are particularly apt locations for this.

Looking aside from congregations for just a moment, the desire and
need for community has been a hallmark of American life. A recent essay in
the *New York Times* by Mike Mariani focuses on "intentional communities,"

---

1. Berg, *Open House,* 196.
2. Pascal, *Pensées,* no. 507, 139.

in particular East Wind, in southern Missouri, in the Ozarks, a community of seventy-two people of all ages, from toddlers to folks in their mid-seventies.[3] East Wind began in 1974, and some residents have been there over thirty-five years, more than half their lives. There are both "personal shelters," or homes, as well as dorms for those who prefer communal living, and a flourishing farm, auto repair shop, and several industries, including nut butters and handmade apparel. East Wind is but one of probably close to a hundred such communities in existence today, with numerous others having sprung up in the 1960s and now being long closed. These communities stand in a line of alternative communal living arrangements stretching back to the mothers and fathers of the Palestinian and Egyptian deserts, Benedict of Nursia, and so many other monastic communities, to American experiments, well-known ones such as Brook Farm in West Roxbury, Massachusetts, to the Oneida and Amana colonies in upstate New York. There are also the historical religious communities which chose to separate from mainstream society, such as the Shakers and early Mormons, among others. There has been an urge to gather but also to leave the normative paths and patterns of life here. Small has always been beautiful for some.

Over the course of many conversations with pastors and parishioners in the last several years, along with gathering material for this book, I have thought quite a bit about shrinking congregations, about small and ever smaller communities of faith. And I have changed my mind about small churches. Not only do they have a purpose, as Elizabeth Berg says, they are in fact the norm in the US. What is well worth examining is the vitality and the possibilities of small congregations, and there are, in this book, quite a few examples of small parishes reviving, resurrecting, reimagining, and even reinventing themselves after shrinking and changing.

In the US, the median congregation, as noted earlier, is about seventy members with a budget of approximately $85,000. This means that half of all congregations are smaller and half larger. The average is 186 members, but this figure is somewhat distortive, skewed by the larger congregations that account for more members. So, the majority of American congregations are small—57 percent are 100 members or smaller. A study of about a thousand Protestant clergy, many evangelical, puts it bluntly: the big seem to get bigger, the small smaller.[4]

Just an aside here, and an important one, is that the very metric of attendance now is debatable. David Odum says that average worship attendance, once the key metric for assessing parish health, has lost this analytic

3. Mariani, "New Generation of Self-Created Communities."

4. Earls, "Church Growth Gap."

value.[5] Patterns of attendance have changed markedly in the past half century. "Regular" attendance used to mean three to four Sundays a month. Now "regular" can mean once a month, or even sporadically. I started noticing this at least twenty-five years ago. There are every-Sunday worshippers, but I see them as less than a fifth of the assembly. The rest have diverse patterns—from a couple times a month to every six weeks or so, all the way to never, while remaining on membership lists.

When I started in parish ministry, I was given the file of "inactive" members to contact and then visit. I also learned of the category of "members in good standing" who retained this status by a contribution of record and communion of record. Almost forty years ago in my experience, and likely much further back, personal communion records—who communed and when—were no longer kept. In some cases, the home communion on a visit would have taken care of that requirement for membership. Why was it important to maintain even such a minimal membership? In order to have a parish for the "rites of passage," which of course include funerals but also weddings and baptisms of children and grandchildren. It was also the minimum required for voting in the annual congregational meeting. Odum argues that other measures than average attendance and "active membership" must be developed. The culture of congregations is simply different.

More recently, Nathan Kirkpatrick has taken this up.[6] Since weekly attendance, which used to be connected to financial support of and activity in the parish, is no longer an accurate measure, other aspects of parish life may yield better assessment. A congregation's "footprint" is a useful tool. Historically, the "parish" was a limited geographic area, a vestige of this seen in Louisiana's use of "parish" as a designation for what most call a county. Today, it is better to see how many zip codes a parish encompasses with respect to those who come to pray as well as those who are served by the parish outreach. My colleague, assistant to the bishop in the Metro New York Synod of the ELCA, Christopher Mietlowski, clued me into what an urban parish like his then encompassed. This congregation was on the Baruch College campus of the City University of New York where I taught. I asked where his members came from, assuming that, in a city location, many were in the Gramercy Park neighborhood or nearby ones. Chris surprised me by saying there were quite a few zip codes in his membership.

As it turns out, this is now a feature of many parishes, and not just urban ones. The membership of a parish will reveal diverse, scattered zip codes, a "footprint" larger than its immediate area, thus breaking with the

5. Odum, "RIP, Average Attendance."
6. Kirkpatrick, "Are Churches Counting What Counts?"

more than 1,000-year-old model of "parish." There are likely more terms for such, but the one I know and use is "regional" parish. People "shop around" for a parish, factoring the liturgy, fellowship, and welcome, age profile and programs with which they feel comfortable, and where they could best contribute. When they find "the one," they come, sometimes from up to an hour away. I also found this to be true when I supplied at a fascinating urban Eastern Orthodox parish, St. Mary Magdalen on the Upper West Side of New York City.

Kirkpatrick points to a parish's "partners" as another more helpful indication of its identity, mission, and health. These would include all the other organizations, institutions, and nonprofit programs that utilize its buildings or with which parish members are involved in, say, food and clothing pantries, or educational and after-school programs. Closely connected are the parish's target populations—those reached by groups that may use the parish buildings for any of the activities just mentioned and others. All of these measures then provide a more accurate and complete view of a parish than the average attendance figures. I think just such measures of the life of a parish will also confirm that small parishes, really the most frequently found gatherings of people of faith, can be vital parts of the larger communities in which they are located.

Small congregations have been the church home of most Christians throughout history. In the first centuries, church was local and mostly housed in private homes. What we are used to is that later stage when buildings set apart for worship came to be the normal locations of communities of faith. Historic parish churches cover the European landscape, some traceable back to the 400s and 500s CE, with some urban churches having former structures now buried that are even older. America did not see the construction of elegant, costly church buildings (except again in urban settings) for some time. The histories of small parishes I know of well, if they have starting dates in the mid-1700s, have had by now three or even four different buildings. Outgrowth of the space, deterioration, fire, destruction by storms—these are just some of the causes of the demise of the earlier buildings. The earliest ones often were no more decorous than people's farmhouses or barns. The use of stone and brick did not occur till after the second or third building on site, and likely well into the nineteenth century.

But the point here is that while more churchgoers in the US attend very large congregations, the usual parish is small, under 100 people in membership. Roger Finke and Rodney Stark reconstructed the size of congregations for Methodist, Baptist, and Episcopal churches in 1776 and arrived at an average of seventy-five members.[7] Most congregations would have been smaller, if one is thinking as we do of those that have even the most minimal presence or contact. The notion of all those living within the geographic confines of a "parish," then as now, would be essentially meaningless for the life of the community and pastoral work. Further, they estimate that in that period only 17 percent of the population actually belonged to a congregation in some way. These numbers, as the authors suggest, replace the always inaccurate nostalgia about the "old days" of religious flourishing in America with historical realism. This is not to say that religion did not boom in certain periods in much the same way as the economy. This is exactly the perspective Finke and Stark take throughout their look at "winners and losers" in American religious organizations. What it does say is that America at that point, when beginning a new history as a republic, was nowhere near as actively "religious" as many might think.

Conversely, the rise of so many religious Nones in the past decade, indicating a significant drift away from membership and participation in congregations, bears a striking resemblance to America more than 200 years ago. Readers familiar with the perspective of religious "awakenings" and "revivals" as markers for major surges in religious activity also are aware that these are responses to times of social, cultural, political, and sometimes economic conflict, periods of stress in the world which finds its way into people's hearts and minds.[8]

And as mentioned earlier, the duplication of parishes in every hamlet and village, given the limited transportation and mobility until well into the twentieth century, has now resulted in what in the UK has long been called "redundant" churches. In short, there are now too many small parishes for a population able to travel by car. Some of the Methodist parishes profiled in various chapters are examples of congregations in transition. The itinerant ministry by Methodist clergy resulted in the church body's characterization, really a kind of boast, of having as many parishes as there are post offices or zip codes. I know that some Methodist parish researchers and consultants came to see that claim as something less than happy or sensible today.

A good friend, Wongee Joh, a UMC pastor, has worked for almost a decade within a co-op or association of Methodist congregations, all within a half-hour's drive of each other, some even closer. These parishes, most of them dating back to the late eighteenth and early nineteenth centuries, were located so that people could get to them on horseback, in wagons, or on foot, without hours of travel. The terrain of the area—very hilly, with

7. Finke and Stark, *Churching of America, 1776–2005.*
8. McLoughlin, *Revivals, Awakenings, and Reform.*

small farms better suited to dairy herds, sheep, cattle, feed crops, and small house gardens—shaped how hamlets and small towns were settled. In the mid-nineteenth century, the establishment of numerous intersecting train lines for transport of dairy and other agricultural products to urban centers thoroughly transformed the area, shifting population to stations and depots along the rail lines, particularly where different lines intersected. An even greater change took place with the construction of paved roads for the use of cars and trucks early in the last century. Eventually, some hamlets ceased to be the commercial and social centers they once were. This is true of the small town in which I have lived for decades, Holmes, New York, as well as several adjacent villages such as Patterson and Pawling.

What used to be a small village now consists of a post office, a deli, and a tiny church. The Methodist parish, formerly serving a very small and very local community, is now essentially a chapel for a few intermarried families. For some years, it was part of an association of other also very local, small Methodist congregations. The plan was to try to amalgamate most of them into two or three church centers, where members of the very small parishes could gather for worship, fellowship, learning, and service. After almost eight years, two of the original six parishes in the association closed and members joined with other congregations. Two others yoked with each other. One opted out of the association. With the departure of one of the two pastors assigned to the association in late spring of 2020, the association decided to disband after close to a decade of efforts to bolster cooperation among these now-small congregations. The New York Annual Conference will decide, at some future date, how the two or three remaining parishes will function. Likely two will remain as parishes, the other facing the situation of that in my town, Holmes.

The Holmes Church was established in 1766. The present building from the nineteenth century is the latest of several on the site, this one from the mid-1800s. Around this church are scattered a couple former hamlet stores, now parts of residences. A dairy building by the rail tracks is long gone. The former volunteer firehouse, now a community center, the post office, present fire station, and a deli are what is left of the former hamlet. Alongside older small homes, many new houses have been built in the past twenty years as this hamlet became part of the greater New York City exurbs. But other than the post office and deli, there are no commercial enterprises in the town any longer. Today, big-box and larger chain stores for home goods, food, and hardware lie a few miles away on major highways and malls and gallerias.

Several church bodies have responded to the near disappearance of these hamlets and the related shrinkage of congregations in them. In the

Hudson Valley, where I have lived for over forty years, the UMC approach, as just mentioned, has been to encourage a cooperative association of several congregations, the goal to work toward fusing them into perhaps two small but sustainable parishes, one more south and another a bit farther north. The Roman Catholic archdiocese of New York will be closing and combining several parishes in towns along a major state highway. The Episcopal diocese of New York has closed several parishes, and one priest serves multiple church locations. The Lutherans are doing the same in the Northern Dutchess Parish that combines three individual congregations with one pastor. Other church bodies have come close to terminating congregations, but thus far, one has revived and another hangs on, with most of its sanctuary and educational building transferred to a Hispanic community's use. The Lutheran parish I served as an associate pastor for a decade almost thirty years ago is a third the size it was when I worked there. Throughout the book we have heard of similar shrinkage, decline, and closure all across the church bodies and country. Jean Hopfensperger's reporting in the *Minneapolis Star-Tribune* described this in very human terms, listening to both laity and clergy. The collection of reflections by laity and clergy in *The Church Has Left the Building* echo these.[9]

Small Congregations Are Here to Stay

While there are various histories and outcomes for small parishes, the point here is that they have always been with us and they are here to stay, no matter how many appear to be unsustainable. This is not just my assessment, it is what yearly surveys show. The small parish has been the most typical one found in the United States. "Small," of course, as noted earlier, has fluctuated and for all kinds of reasons. A parish of seventy-five to 100 members was an average in the late eighteenth century and into the present. However, it is an average, and many parishes were and still are considerably smaller.

If one looks at actual congregations today, seventy-five to 100 members would constitute a sizable congregation. But of course, the very large megachurch or big-box congregations make such a parish seem small. Both a lawyer and a PhD in theology from Princeton Theological Seminary, Robert Fuggi sailed against the tide of closing parishes and megachurches in setting up the Toms River Community Church in New Jersey.[10] His account of what he was doing presents largely the same statistical view of churches in America as you have seen here. His strategy for communities of faith going forward is

9. Plekon et al., *Church Has Left the Building*.
10. Fuggi, *New Model of the Authentic Church*.

to return to the earliest patterns of the small churches, most of them house churches, in the first three centuries. Those set apart by ordination to preach, teach, and preside, as Nicholas Afanasiev points out, were not a special clerical caste. They had regular crafts or trades they plied. Fuggi sees no future for clergy who depend entirely on the congregation for housing and salary, the pattern essentially since the medieval period. He also sees the congregation as a communal project of worship, learning, service, and witness. Over and over, from Diana Butler Bass to Nancy Ammerman and Nicholas Denysenko and other students of parish life, these are the essential ingredients in a parish's life.[11] And the life of a parish, moreover, is not one ordained person held responsible for everything but, rather, the life and work of the body of Christ in this place is a community endeavor.[12]

Allen Stanton documents two UMC congregations, Salem UMC in rural Oxford, North Carolina, and Sanford UMC in Sanford, Florida, which are in the small category. Salem has around twenty people on a Sunday; Sanford, eighty or so.[13] Given their locations, growth in their membership is not likely. Oxford's historically sparse population has not increased, and Sanford's property is now hemmed in by a lake and other local buildings. Yet in both parishes there is optimism about what they can do in their small size rather than pessimism about the future. Sanford's pastor, Megan Killingsworth, aims to better use the space the congregation has to serve the community and be better rooted in it. A number of nonprofit groups have signed up to use Sanford UMC's space. Glenn Stallsmith, pastor of Salem, admits to having felt like a failure. But having realized what the congregation gives and means to the surrounding area, he now sees it differently. He pointed to the community meals the small Salem parish sponsors, as well as the community garden which invites all to come work and harvest. The area is opiate-plagued, low-income, and not seeing any development or rediscovery, which makes it like many other towns in the US. Salem, then, is a place of hope and belonging, and it can be this even with its small size.

Stanton has also raised the question of whether the efforts of congregations to recruit younger members and families with kids is missing the gifts and the faithfulness of older members.[14] While mobility, the relocation of members for work, education, and more, is a major shift, so too is the aging of congregations. We saw the marked shrinkage of those forty

---

11. Bass, *Christianity for the Rest of Us*; Ammermann, *Congregation and Community*; Denysenko, *People's Faith*.

12. Abro, "Power and Purpose of Small Community Churches."

13. Stanton, "Rural Congregations Can Thrive beyond Numbers."

14. Stanton, "Are Aging Churches a Bad Thing?"

and under in many parishes, many characterized as religious Nones or Dones. Stanton reminds us of another demographic trend among retiring Boomers. This is their relocation to areas with warmer climates, more economic housing, and artistic as well as educational and service opportunities. He suggests that parishes be aware of retiring folk entering their communities and desiring some connections in their new neighborhoods. Churches can reach out in various ways. It may not always result in new members, but it may just establish links between parish members and new friends they make in town. It may also help create contexts in which intergenerational connections can take place.[15]

Stanton also reports the tremendous support his family received from a small congregation when, just before Christmas in 2017, his six-month-old daughter was hospitalized with serious respiratory problems.[16] Both Stanton and his wife are Methodist pastors caring for small parishes. The immediate support of his parishioners when he told them of the health crisis and their fears was an enormous gift, one he knows is being given again and again now in the pandemic. With all the limitations of being small, sometimes the introverted culture of the small congregation, when there is a real community living there, creates remarkable results.

Gathering at Table: Congregations and Food

While community gardens and extended community use of parish buildings are staples of congregations reinventing and renewing themselves, as we have seen here, another move has been that of feeding people.[17] The connection between Jesus's fellowship meals with his disciples, his feeding of the multitudes, and the Last Supper is clear in the Gospels. The eucharist and a community meal is documented in Paul's first letter to the church at Corinth. Church suppers are a mainstay and the sharing of a meal continues. I have written about these in my look at prayer and faith in everyday life, *Uncommon Prayer*.[18] There are the well-known pre-Lenten pancake suppers, game dinners for those forgoing meat during Lent, not to mention special meals for events like Mothers' and Fathers' Days, as well as the start and end of church school. Such invitations to feast remain a way of not just attracting new members, but more importantly reaching out to the community around the parish. We have heard about St. Lydia's

15. Stanton, "OK, Boomer and the Church."
16. Stanton, "Gifts of a Small Church in a Pandemic."
17. Dallas, "Can a Good Meal Bring People Back to Church?"
18. Plekon, *Uncommon Prayer*.

Supper Church in Brooklyn, New York. Methodist pastor Meredith Mills created Gastrochurch in Houston, Texas, a food ministry which moves beyond the church hall to local pubs and restaurants where people are invited to talk over beers or a meal.

"Pastah J," or Pastor Jonathan Brooks of Englewood Canaan Community Church in Chicago, has gone even more basic in seeking affordable groceries for people in the community surrounding his parish, an area bereft of supermarkets and other outlets, hence a "food desert." More than 23 million Americans live in such "food deserts."[19] There are fast-food restaurants and small delis, but no place to buy fresh meat and produce, that is, healthy food for families. This is a common urban dilemma, where redlining still makes loans for development impossible and where crime statistics plus income levels deter large grocery chains from opening stores. Such an impasse was overcome by the opening, not of just any food chain store, but the Englewood Whole Foods franchise. Englewood had more than fifty homicides in 2018, and 40 percent of its population are below the poverty line. The intense commitment of Pastah J and the congregation shows in their outreach to the wider community around them.

First, they formed Five Loaves Cooperative. Large-scale shopping for staples was done at a Trader Joe's some distance from the church. Then this food was redistributed to those buying at the co-op. Later, the congregation's coordination with Chicago Neighborhood Initiatives, Englewood Teamwork, and a city program backed by Mayor Rahm Emmanuel, led to Whole Foods opening in Englewood. While there was some trepidation about Whole Foods' high prices, the company made several community-sensitive elements part of its plan to locate in Englewood. They kept their staples' prices lower than in other locations. They hired community members and put locally produced products in the store.

The Englewood Whole Foods was part of a larger shopping redevelopment project which brought other merchants to the neighborhood and created more shopping possibilities there. Five Loaves Co-op continues because the Whole Foods is a good two miles from Canaan Community Church, and bringing bulk staples in is still needed. Brooks uses plenty of biblical commentary for his description of the project to end the "food desert" in Englewood. And the parish's leadership in this is but one more example of how congregations can continue their call to worship, gather, and serve in reimagined ways.[20]

19. Ford, "Church and Community Partnership Helps Bring Fresh Groceries to a Food Desert."

20. Brooks, *Church Forsaken.*

Other Roots and Replantings:
Small Towns, Small Churches

St. Thomas Episcopal Church in Dubois, Wyoming is another small congregation that continues to be a vital part of the town, its less than 100 members notwithstanding.[21] Once the only church in town, established by missionary John Roberts in the 1880s, it is now one of eight parishes in a town with a population of about 1,000 in the town limits, and another 1,000 to 1,500 in surrounding areas. The timber industry ended when the last mill closed twenty years ago. Now there is a summer population of retired people, a few wealthy, and a number of income-challenged year-rounders. St. Thomas is known for outreach into the larger community in numerous ways, including a long-term food bank and thrift shop, where many townspeople can shop cheaply and locally. Even with seasonal residents, there is little work, and with many of retirement age in the community, there is everywhere a sense of decline, shrinkage of population, government, and community spirit. St. Thomas, however, in addition to the food bank and thrift shop, sponsors a summertime square dance every Tuesday night which brings many in the area together, as do the thrift store and food bank. Hikers on the Continental Divide Trail and bikers on the Trans-America Trail also stop in Dubois in the spring, summer, and fall, and the parish reaches out to them too.

St. Thomas's rector, Melinda Bobo, spent several years in childhood in Dubois while her father worked for the US Forest Service, and she was eager to serve the parish after some years of pastoral ministry in Minnesota. Both she and the mayor, Twila Blakeman, point to St. Thomas as a community of faith, but also a social pillar of the town and surrounding area. It is known and appreciated even by those who are not members and do not worship there.

So, it is an example of a small parish that may not bear signs of explosive growth to more local diocesan or national Episcopal church specialists. Yet it is the body of Christ in simple, yet powerful ways in Dubois. St. Thomas is but one of many congregations we will inspect here that has now found new or even creative ways of sustaining itself.

How could the demise of haystacks and the situation of the small parish be connected? R. Alan Rice thinks he knows the answer.[22] Not that anyone could or would return to the tedious, labor-intensive throwing of

---

21. Mander, "Small Church Upholds History of Outreach to Make Big Impact on Frontier Town."

22. Rice, "Demise of Haystacks and the Future of the Rural Church."

a stack rather than mowing/raking/tething and machine bailing. It makes no sense. But are small, particularly rural parishes merely sweet elements of the past like the piled-up haystacks? In the eyes of many denominational administrators, especially those specializing in growth or revival of declining and dying congregations, it is often easier to reject the small parish as a waste of precious resources, both finances and clergy. Efficiency and health would dictate that they be made to merge and, of course, some close so that there could be a few sustainable congregations rather than multiple, even redundant, dying ones.

Rice observes that while not all small parishes can survive, those that can warrant the understanding of administrators who would consider allowing retired or partially retired clergy or others who would want to be tilling small gardens, amid the trees, as it were, to serve these communities. Even more importantly, the administrators need to recognize the good that small parishes accomplish, like St. Thomas just mentioned, and numerous others referenced in these pages and others I know. There needs to be room for them too. The corporate model of congregation employed by most denomination administrators and consultants needs to see outcomes, efficiency, and careful expenditure both of financial and human resources in congregations. This, as we have seen, is why many failing congregations are simply closed. Yet as we have also seen, efforts like the Methodist Church Legacy Initiatives both help in a "good death" as well as assist in helping a community to revive, redefine, or reinvent itself, repurpose buildings, and reach out to the community. St. Thomas Episcopal is one instance, Grace in the Berkshires another, as well as many others documented here.

Rice's point is one with which we can resonate. There can be life in a small, even struggling congregation, the life of a community as the body of Christ. But it needs to be valued as such, not compared with other congregations as some congregational assessment tools do, and then found failing because it is not a suburban or, for that matter, urban parish in an area coming alive again. Small churches have their own ways of fulfilling the call to be bread for the life of the world. Further, there is need for more flexibility and creativity on the part of the larger church bodies in which small congregations are members. This would be in terms of what pastors could serve such congregations, their formation, canonical status, compensation, or not. And the parishes themselves need to be freed from what are often binding and inappropriate requirements for assessed support of the denomination and their operating procedures.

Piecing Together a New Congregation from the Old

Lisa Fischbeck, herself the rector for almost twenty years of the Church of the Advocate near Chapel Hill, North Carolina, echoes Rice's argument.[23] Advocate, an ECUSA parish, was a mission start in 2002 and, like most such communities, it moved from one rental or borrowed space to another until a piece of property with a farmhouse became available. Then an unused country church also became available, having been declared an historic structure. Said building, a "board-and-batten" space seating 125, also called "Carpenter Gothic," was moved to the new property when the parish decided on a worship space other than the farmhouse. The rest is history, with three existing parishes financially sponsoring this new parish start. The parish restored and renovated the former building of St. Philip's Episcopal Church, a rural congregation from the 1880s that had closed after massive movement to Winston-Salem from its area. So a once-small, rural church that was moved to a new location took on a new, second life as the sanctuary for another small parish, but a parish of diverse, well-educated people in the Chapel Hill suburbs.

The community of the parish is diverse, and as is the case in increasing numbers of congregations, comes from various church backgrounds and lives all over the surrounding area. Given the location of the property to which the country church was moved, with just a farmhouse on it, Advocate would never be a "village" church. I have found this pattern of a parish drawing from various spots in a region (hence a regional" parish) both in urban as well as suburban contexts, smaller towns as well.

Advocate has a 9 AM liturgy from *The Book of Common Prayer*, and then a longer one at 11 AM, with texts and music from many sources while adhering to Prayer Book's basic order of liturgy, the essential liturgy of the Western church used by Catholic, Lutheran, Methodist, and Presbyterian churches. Given the scattered character of the community, the 11 AM service is followed by a lunch which gives those who gathered for the eucharist time to be with each other. Obviously, this also works for various groups in the congregation who can link a short meeting so that people need not return on weekday nights. This is also a growing pattern; namely, clustering events on Sunday, given the often sizable commute to the church campus as well as the frantic pace of work, school, sports, and more during the week.

During seasons such as Advent and Lent, there are weekday gatherings for liturgy, study, and fellowship and a regular Wednesday evening "contemplative" eucharist with time for quiet prayer and reflection. Given

---

23. Fishbeck, "Strength and Beauty of Small Churches."

the benefit of a significant piece of property, the Advocate parish combined funding from several sources—the University of North Carolina Flager Business school and students, the diocese of North Carolina, the town of Chapel Hill, Strowd Roses, a local grower, the parish, and other private benefactors—to erect three "tiny houses," (one ADA accessible) the "Pee Wee Houses"—on the campus.

Fishbeck emphasizes that the odds were against this experiment from the outset. There were numerous small, rural parishes all over the state, few able to support a pastor or even keep their facility open, and with little or no chance of growing or surviving. But, as with the Methodists' Church Legacy Initiative, the vision of a priest and very small community, supported by then-NC bishop, now presiding bishop of the ECUSA, Michael Curry, carried off the near impossible.

To look at Advocate, one might wonder why it fits into the pattern of a reimagined or reinvented parish. Much of what it is and does is quite conventional, at first glance. But on closer inspection, the reimagined features start to emerge. There was no parish in this part of Chapel Hill before the mission started in 2002. It was a rural area that rapidly became part of the suburbs of Chapel Hill. At first, the parish moved about in various rental spaces till the present church campus was obtained. The closed country church was surely a wonderful repurposing of a nineteenth-century structure, small enough to move yet large enough to function for the Advocate community.

Will Advocate "take off," as was expected of "successful" church mission plants, and grow into a much larger congregation, at last building an imposing brick-and-mortar sanctuary? No. Like most, if not all of the congregations described here that are reviving, reinventing, or repurposing themselves, the older model of mission plant growing into full-blown congregation is neither possible nor an intention. The demographics, as we have said so many times, are against it. More importantly, the size of the community, its intimacy and dynamism, would be lost if growth occurred very rapidly. Advocate is larger than the average congregation referenced earlier of seventy members. But only slightly. This will never be a 500-plus member congregation with a cathedral-like building and array of committees and spacious education and administrative building attached. There is much to recommend the smaller faith community.

The Gifts of the Small Parish: Some Other Examples

Citing the research of Anthony Pappas's study for the Alban Institute, Duke University Leadership Education director David Odum argues that the small church is distinctive.[24] Small congregations offer gifts, both to members and the community around, that larger parishes simply cannot bring.[25] Both Pappas and Odum make the claim which is the central one in this book: the small church reveals that being the people of God is to become a member of an authentic community. Parish is all about relationships, not primarily programs, as many denominational and high-level church leaders persistently argue, though there will always be programs and projects. Members of a community, of a body, the body of Christ, enjoy being with each other. Not only do they sing, pray, give thanks, and break the bread and share the cup. They also want to eat, laugh, and cry together.

And they are not just a social or country club, with contact open to "members only." People of a community want to do good things together, both within their fellowship and beyond it. They love giving what they have to those in the area around them. But more than anything else, the gift they receive and the gift they are able to extend is community. This is not just emotional warmth, not just preference for these people and the desire to spend time, even grow older, together. If there is a single point to this entire book, it is this: The New Testament word *koinonia* suggested earlier is a way of remembering this rich complex of realities that comprise the community of faith we call "church," and primarily at the local level of the parish.

By being a community, members experience something that takes them beyond themselves, something that reaches into the community that stretches back to Christ and the first disciples, then all over the world, down through more than 2,000 years. It is a community of the word of God listened to, a word that challenges, consoles, moves them. But it is also a community of the table from which the bread of life and the cup of salvation come. And surely it is a community in which others challenge, just as much as the community is of the water by which all become sisters and brothers, no matter their gender, sexual identity, job, income, ethnicity, politics, or any other characteristic. Lastly, lest we think community is mostly the energy and hard work of members, *koinonia* means that the Spirit is the power who makes anything and everything happen. My colleague and good friend David Frost, whom I cite elsewhere for his helpful concept of parish "survival" theology and behavior, regularly stresses the primary force of the

---

24. Pappas, *Entering the World of the Small Church.*
25. Odum, "Reclaiming the Distinctive Gifts of the Small Church."

Spirit in our life as the body of Christ. And of course St. Augustine also insists with St. Paul on Christ as the head.

We have already heard from Allan T. Stanton. From his pastoral experience, he argues that the small church can offer hope for those in its community.[26] Members can immediately and very tangibly experience what Christian community is without the many layers and gates that larger congregations have. One element Stanton notes in particular is the ability to get an idea into process, to follow through on a project rapidly and effectively, with less waiting simply due to the face-to-face, first-hand, first-name quality of the relationships in the small church. There is nowhere to hide in such a community. When you are absent, people notice, and likely they will ask after you, if not by a call, then the next week. And this will not feel pushy in the least. Stanton points out how making space available to a wider community food bank came about with very little delay. Likewise, members who knew each other well could get behind a bill to enable grants to local stores and those volunteering for service projects.

Steve Willis finds much the same in his research, that small churches do not spell gloom and death, but their intimacy and community witness to life. And yet, there is another side to the intense intimacy of the small congregation. Ideally, the intimacy of a small parish respects and nourishes members. However, it can also be hard, even harsh, and something that drives some out and away for good.

St. Andrew's in Haw River, North Carolina appears completely unremarkable on first view.[27] Haw River mills were the leading producers of corduroy fabric years ago. But the mills have closed now, and the 2,000-plus residents are income-challenged, the median income almost $20,000 dollars below the national average of $53,000 per household. With seventy or so members and at best thirty to thirty-five who come for the Sunday eucharist, the parish seems like hundreds if not thousands of others that are the median size and surely within the category of small congregations. The white clapboard exterior houses a simple, unremarkable interior. There is no regular choir. The rector is part-time. The profiles of members, as is increasingly the case in American parishes, show aging people, with fewer families under forty with children.

Yet a couple times a week, the church hall welcomes a dozen kids from the trailer park next door after school. There are snacks and then they sit down to do homework and receive tutoring from members of the parish, almost all of them retired. When some of the children's parents asked

26. Stanton, "What Can the Rural Church Offer a Declining Community?"
27. Shimron, "Small NC Church Reaches Out in Big Ways."

for help, not only in ELS but in preparing for citizenship, Norine MacArthur and Jane Gould, two of St. Andrew's members already volunteering for school tutoring, offered their services. Then there is another member. Sharon Ranew is a retired marketer for a phone company. She doesn't even come regularly for services on Sundays. Her ministry is in the kitchen. Every day, she bakes birthday cakes for foster children in the town and the parish subsidizes her supplies. The Social Service Bureau of the county provides her the names and address and birthdays of foster children in town. She does up to 100 cakes a year. And there is a crew of almost a dozen who throughout the year tend a large vegetable garden behind the church to feed themselves and their neighbors. You need not be a member of the parish to get a plot, but you do have to get on the list.

Not much spectacular or unusual going on here, you may say. Sure, the actual parish community is quite small and unlikely to grow. What they do is also not very radical, so much so that some community organizers would likely want to steer them into more meaningful projects like voter registration or hosting health care clinics. But, notice, that as with other congregations we have peeked into, even if very briefly, there is life here and real solidarity. If there is room for the quiet member, the introverted, then this is truly a compassionate community.

Such a living community, sensitive to the neighbors around, is a real movement of the Spirit, I would say, as one who has experienced such motion in very powerful ways in parishes I have served and in others whose pastors I know. Even where you would suspect the middle-class or even blue-collar backgrounds of members might make them shy away from social outreach, they do not. I saw this over the years as people from my parish in the Hudson Valley prepared Sunday dinners and then served them at the Lunch Box, part of the Dutchess Outreach ministry in Poughkeepsie, New York. Serving such a meal is another kind of eucharist. Such a gift. And what a revelation to see that many who are food insecure look just like you.

Maybe the people at St. Andrew's or St. Gregory's, my parish, would not put it this way, but their actions incarnate what they believe, the God they love—this is at the very heart of Christianity, after all, a God who takes up space and time, becomes a human being, one of us. The ECUSA presiding bishop, Michael Curry, when the bishop of North Carolina, said the people of St. Andrew's were like Gideon's tiny, ragtag army in the book of Judges. Despite their small numbers they do more than congregation three or four times their size.

Another small church in Appalachia offers still more ways to not just survive but thrive. Wild Goose Community calls Indian Valley, in Floyd

County in rural Virginia, home.[28] It is close to the Blue Ridge Mountains, and on first view, it seems like a convention of aging bluegrass musicians and craftspeople. They worship on Tuesday evenings, after a potluck dinner. You don't see pews, but there is a large wooden cross and rocking chairs. It is part of the PCUSA and while it had a pastor, it is now looking for another. There may only be twenty or so members who come to what they call their weekly "Uprising Service." There is a significant amount of wit and humor here, from the "Wild Goose" name of the congregation to the characterization of their service. Communion is passed around, the bread in a basket, the wine in mason jars. The congregation cooperatively celebrates the liturgy. They have nothing against having a pastor—they simply did not have one at the moment and carry on as a community that makes church happen for itself.

Wild Goose is but one of the fascinating congregations profiled by Tim Schapiro and Kara Faris.[29] What distinguishes the congregations is not just that they are different from the usual parish but rather that they have at least one feature or activity that has become "church plus," as they put it, a concern that is a focus for those who are members. It can range from that of Wild Goose, which is Appalachian music and culture and a hospitality for those tired of and turned off by ordinary church life. Food, service to the larger community, artistic expression—Wild Goose's use of bluegrass music for its service—something beyond the ordinary serves to gather people. Shapiro and Faris studied a dozen of these "divergent," or better, creative alternative congregations. The foundation of a community around a shared supper, thus giving rise to a more family-type gathering, is but one of the diverse models they found. Another, Galileo Church, a Disciples of Christ community in Texas, chose to focus upon their own written liturgies, services that the members wanted to be anchored in the tradition of the church but open to the demands and issues of the moment.

Small Parishes and Repurposing in the Church of England

A study from the Church of England from 2015, *Released for Mission: Growing in Rural Churches,* and related research yield some fascinating things. A page on Facebook, *Churchcrawling,* posts members' photos and descriptions of all sorts of churches, mostly from the UK, mostly Anglican, but

28. Shimron, "PCUSA Faith Community Takes Flight Celebrating Appalachian Music and Culture."

29. Shapiro and Faris, *Divergent Church.*

with others. Some are in use still, connected with other neighboring ones, while others have closed, been declared redundant, and listed as historically protected sites. Thus, no modifications, only work to stabilize the structure, maintain the roof and masonry, and other aspects of the fabric.

Much like the case of Methodists in the US and the actual precedent for it, virtually every hamlet, village, and town in England had a local parish church, some dating back before 1000 CE, numerous ones with the bulk of the existing buildings from the Middle Ages and into the fifteenth and sixteenth centuries, as well as beyond. In another age of people remaining where they were born and raised, continuing to work in agriculture, in sheepherding, cattle, and dairy herds, the local church became the main public building, and in some rural areas still is not just the oldest but still principal local space of any consequence.

The data on churches from the Church of England are telling. While only 17 percent of the population live in rural areas, two-thirds, or over 8,300 parishes, are in rural settings, more than 10,000 buildings all told, some now closed but protected. Forty-two percent of all clergy serve rural parishes and 40 percent of all worshippers also come to church there. The figures for growing churches—18 percent—are the same both for rural and urban locales. Rural churches have six or seven times more buildings for every unit of population. Three-fourths of rural parishes have thirty-seven or fewer members attending, a fourth less than ten, yet rural attendance is twice that of urban areas—not surprising as sociologist have long identified cities are more diverse and secular.

Population shifts, mostly to cities over the last centuries, massive change to agriculture as well as to small-town, craft economies, leaving these behind for massive-scale manufacturing—these are just a few of the well-known changes that have transformed not only the rural English landscape but most of the world. All of the changes we have seen earlier have happened in the UK. So thinking not only of the Church of England but of the Presbyterians and Church of Scotland, the Methodists and the Reformed there have involved pretty much the same strategies as those tried here in the US.

However, a recent conference on rural parishes and the studies noted have turned up some interesting finds.[30] While consensus on these is not possible, there now seems growing rejection of the almost surgical procedure of closing many small rural parishes, putting the closed buildings on the protected lists, and amalgamating people in those remaining. There is also a strategy of "festival churches." In this approach, otherwise closed parish

---

30. Wyatt, "How Rural Churches are Fighting Stereotypes of Neglect and Decline."

churches would be used for Christmas time and possibly Easter services, along with the "occasional" or "rites of passage" services—baptisms, weddings, funerals. The rest of the time they would be maintained, open for visitors usually on weekends with "keyholders" located close by. However, this strategy now seems to be better than total closure but ineffective for the life of the communities based in the rural historic buildings.

Then there is the concept of "resource churches," briefly mentioned earlier. This is a contemporary version of an ancient system of "minster" churches, many founded originally by Benedictine monasteries as centers for missionizing. In time, these larger congregations continued to support and sustain much smaller outlying parishes. Today, in some locations, this model works, one in which a larger, thriving parish serves as a hub for smaller ones, with shared clergy, church schools, learning opportunities, and outreach programs. Many of the multiple-point parishes operate in this way. But clearly there are difficulties. There is not a flexible supply of clergy. Resolving local attachments and reluctance to go elsewhere even occasionally for worship, resistance of a small community to any different or creative use of space—these are just some of the many challenges that emerge when trying to work with networks of very small parish communities. There are experiments in not linking communities so tightly to existing historic buildings like "mountain pilgrims," where hiking enthusiasts gather not only for walks but for worship and conversation. Sometimes a group will use a village hall so as to avoid the conflict among smaller communities reluctant to bridge with others.

And there are some parishes in which the medieval understanding of the church nave as a public space has been resurrected. The chancel, with the altar, remains always a sacred space. But the body of the church building can be used for meetings, for town fairs, and special festivals outside of worship times. In some churches, a café or even tavern occupies a corner or back of the nave during the week and on evenings. On Sunday mornings and big feasts, the building reverts to worship space, perhaps reopening for food and drink afterwards. St. Peter's is an example in the Hereford diocese. So central to the life of the village was this parish church, stemming from the ninth century, that it gave the village its name: Peterchurch. Refitted inside, it remains the parish church for Sunday and festal services, baptisms, weddings, and funerals, but during the week it is not locked but open every day. Inside there is a café and a branch of the county library otherwise unavailable. There is also a daily preschool nursery. Regularly, there is a crafts fair. And it is still the gathering place for the community of faith. St. Peter's in Peterchurch is now one of the five churches of the Wye Dore parish or benefice, others being Madley and Turnstone, minutes' walk from each other, Tyburton and Vowchurch. Services alternate among all five.

St. James Church in West Hampstead, London, is another example. The Sheriff Center, a market plus café, operates there during the week. The nave has returned to what it was in the Middle Ages and long afterwards, a center of neighborhood activities. On Sundays and holy days, and for the rites of passage, it still is the meeting place for the people of God at St. James.

In short, the cases of rural and small-town parishes in the UK suggest that, as many here in America have found, the small church need not be seen simply as a vestige of a time now past, unsustainable, not worth supporting. Rather, as countless observers, including clergy who serve such parishes, attest, there is vitality in these communities. They are part of the great diversity that is the people of God, that is the faith. And the gift they preserve but also cherish and share is what is the central focus here—community, in all its dimensions, complexity, and possibilities.

On Troost, Downtown in Kansas City: Service and Ministry on Troost Avenue

Downtown in Kansas City, Missouri, Troost Avenue is the historic divide between black and white parts of the city. On it stands a four-story commercial building. Until 1991, this old building on Troost sat empty until it became the home for Reconciliation Ministries (RS) and St. Mary of Egypt Orthodox Christian Church. Recently the parish has relocated not far away.

RS began with a pastor, his wife, and a dream of opening the doors beyond a few loyal parishioners. The parish was dedicated to St. Mary of Egypt, a fourth-century woman who turned from prostitution and became a desert-dwelling ascetic. While her life is a model for the parish, yet another saint of our time also figures importantly for the whole Troost Avenue set of initiatives. It is Mother Maria Skobtsova, who took for her name as a nun that of Mary of Egypt.[31] Born Elisabeth Pilenko, she was a gifted poet and writer, a protégé of the great Russian poet Alexander Blok. Fleeing the Revolution, she settled with her second husband and three children in Paris, and upon the death of both daughters, she asked to be made a nun upon the end of her marriage. For over a decade, through the worst years of the Great Depression and then the Nazi occupation of Paris, she set up and headed houses of hospitality in Paris and the outskirts. These took in, as the Catholic Worker houses in New York and elsewhere would do, the homeless,

31. Skobtsova, *Mother Maria Skobtsova*; Hackel, *Pearl of Great Price*; Plekon, *Living Icons*.

starving, unemployed, distressed, and helpless. The houses provided, as RS does today, a range of services from a soup kitchen to medical care and counseling, as well as emergency housing. In the house of hospitality was a chapel, and prayer and the eucharist were the house's heart. Thus, Mother Maria's houses and RS today are not just locations for the delivery of vital services. It would be better to say that they had the heart of a church, that really, they were a very different kind of church.

During the occupation, Mother Maria and her chaplain provided baptismal certificates and memberships in the house of hospitality parish to protect and hide Jewish people, members of other communities, and political groups targeted for annihilation by the Nazis. Betrayed to the Gestapo, Mother Maria, her chaplain, and the house treasurer, as well as her remaining son who worked and lived there alongside seminary study, all were sent to concentration camps and their deaths. In 2004, they were recognized as martyr saints for giving their lives to save their sisters and brothers.

The story of RS is about how a visionary priest and his wife thought church was not complete without service to the community and a radical commitment to living in community with the poor. Today, though the parish has moved, the church remains as RS and Thelma's Kitchen serve the community. Thelma's Kitchen is a donate-as-you-can restaurant, and is one of several other programs operated by Reconciliation Services. A former financial services salesman, David Altschul and his wife, Thelma, were the founders of St. Mary's Parish and RS. David became Fr. Alexii as an Eastern Orthodox priest.

In time, RS became an independent, not-for-profit organization, though still linked historically to the parish which was part of the Serbian Orthodox Archdiocese in America. Later, Fr. Justin Mathews, who I knew as an intern in my parish in the Hudson Valley of New York State, became part of the pastoral team and eventually followed Fr. Alexii as director of RS, and then pastor of St. Mary's when Fr. Alexii entered monastic life after Thelma's death.

With a new pastor at St. Mary's, Fr. Justin's "parish" is now RS and Thelma's Kitchen and Troost Avenue and all the people surrounding it as he continues as the director of RS, also doing liaison work with local government and other not-for-profit agencies, companies, and foundations. He is a gifted pastor of the streets, with years of experience in business and not-for-profit organizations. Likewise, when the archbishop in Paris received Mother Maria Skobtsova as a nun, he told her that her monastery would be the city, its streets, and those struggling to survive there. She took this even further. Her house on Rue de Lourmel would not be a duplication of the local municipal *cantine* for residents of the neighborhood. Her house had Christ living there, a chapel and the eucharist at the core, and loving hospitality was the language spoken. This is precisely the resurrection that took place on Troost—the "parish" of RS and Thelma's Kitchen.

RS stands on what was once land of the Osage people, driven out by settlers. It was also the site of a large plantation with a significant slave work force—owned by one of Kansas City's first ministers. That it is now a place of prayer, racial reconciliation, and service is a powerful response to a sinful past of hate and division. For thirty years, RS and its predecessor, the interfaith organization Reconciliation Ministries, have made the Troost Corridor a focal point of ministry efforts to support Kansas City's most vulnerable neighbors. The RS mission is to cultivate a community seeking reconciliation, to transform Troost from a dividing line into a gathering place, revealing the strength of all.

RS has an innovative theory of change which furthers its goal of seeking racial and economic reconciliation one heart at a time. This is done through Thelma's Kitchen (now Thelma's Box Lunch, during the pandemic), the REVEAL Social and Mental Health services, the Foster Grandparents Program, RS Social Ventures, and the newly launched Social Leader Essentials e-Course. RS commits to coming alongside those in need by offering companionship, tools, and skills necessary to help them discover their strengths and succeed. Further, each person is challenged to understand her or his own success to be tied to the success of one's neighbors. RS's core values are dignity, community, and advocacy.

The majority of RS clients suffer from combinations of mental and behavioral health issues, underemployment, housing and food insecurity, and social isolation. All are below the poverty level, 55 percent of their food access comes from corner stores, and the life expectancy in the area is fifteen years less than other parts of Kansas City. RS clients mirror results of studies showing rates of depression and PTSD in poor, high-risk urban populations in the US are as high as in returning veterans. These conditions, coupled with high instances of mental health illness (Health Forward Foundation of Kansas City reports 1 in 10 adults in Jackson County suffer from serious mental illness), increased risks of homicide, suicide, accidents, chronic illness, and substance abuse.

Taking seriously the gospel challenge to love the neighbor, RS approaches each person with dignity and love, seeing each one as made in the image of God—a "living icon." Its programs strategically address community needs for affordable food access, safe environments to gather (combating social isolation), and access to social and mental health services that lead to improved health and self-sufficiency.

At the core of RS is the REVEAL Program (Restore-Engage-Value-Encourage-Act-Lead). It offers individual and group therapy and intensive case management and stabilizing resources such as ID/Document assistance, rent and utilities assistance, and medical and dental services through a partnership with the KC Medicine Cabinet. Case managers engage with guests in Thelma's Kitchen, building relationships and earning trust in the community and enabling RS to reach out to neighbors who may not otherwise seek help. RS calls their noninstitutional approach "stealth mental health."[32] As evidence of the effectiveness of their approach, in addition to receiving referrals from outside agencies, nearly 90 percent of all REVEAL therapy client-guests come from internal referrals from Thelma's Kitchen or social services.

While the approach may be noninstitutional, RS offers evidence-based, clinical support under the direction of a Licensed Clinical Social Worker (LCSW) through Individual and Group Therapy and Aftercare Support Group, and intensive case management for client-guests struggling with depression and the effects of trauma. This combined approach to mental health empowers individuals to build resilience, find healing from trauma and depression, find meaningful life work, secure stable housing, and access the resources they need to have sustainable health and well-being.

In 2020, RS will help clients secure 1,800 IDs and birth certificates, assist at least 450 clients with needed medical and dental supplies and services, and offer rent and utilities assistance to at least 800 clients. RS will serve at least 3,000 unduplicated individuals across all social and mental health services, and offer more than 2,000 hours of case management and therapy. Thelma's Kitchen will serve more than 25,000 meals. More than 2,000 volunteers will offer over 90,000 hours of volunteer service.

Thelma's Kitchen has a strategic engagement model. Thelma's offers a safe, inviting environment that fosters relationship-building among people from vastly different racial, social, geographic, and economic backgrounds around shared meals, while reducing the stigma for those seeking social or therapeutic services. This innovative approach provides pro-social and protective interventions deeply embedded in RS's program design that increase access to mental health services and brings normally segregated people together to overcome fear and normalize integrated social interactions—powerfully manifesting kingdom values, economy, and equity.

Thelma's Kitchen is more than a place to eat, no matter your circumstances. The Kitchen's tables pull people together around a meal and conversation. It is very much a eucharistic table, a place for guests to gather and

---

32. For statistic, see the RS website: https://www.rs3101.org/.

talk over food and drink, and to share to become friends of God and of each other. One could easily imagine the actual liturgy of the eucharist being celebrated there. Thelma's Kitchen is at the very center of RS, and RS is hardly just a platform for delivery of needed services. Rather it has the heart, the look, and feel of church. It is not too much to say that Thelma's Kitchen and all that stands behind it at RS is a welcoming congregation, where people can be fed and find healing, and where they can find sisters and brothers who will, as Sam Wells says, walk *with* them—not do for them.

So RS and Thelma's Kitchen are a bridge that brings people together, very much what a community of faith is supposed to be. RS is not just a church program or "outreach tool" for the community—something the church does "charitably" from its excess—but a relational entry point, a presacramental baptism into the church's love and gospel solidarity with the poor. By extension it is then also an invitation to partake of all of the services offered at RS.

To round out the picture of what RS does, the RS Foster Grandparents Program should be mentioned. It connects low-income volunteers, aged fifty-five and over, who are living in extreme poverty with opportunities to provide one-on-one mentoring, nurturing, and support to children with exceptional needs, or who are at an academic, social, or financial disadvantage. They are there to help the kids of the community in a caring and consistent way, but they are also improving their own well-being. RS partners with CNCS (Corporation for National and Community Service) and their Senior Corps program, which enables seniors across America to use their time and talents to give back to their communities. The RS Foster Grandparents Program serves Jackson, Clay, and Platte Counties. RS is present in thirty civic institutions, including schools, early childhood centers, hospitals, and Family Court. Whether RS Foster Grandparents are helping with school readiness, emotional support, tutoring, or offering other physical and educational support, they are first and foremost a caring adult role model committed to seeing young people thrive and succeed. Further, the Foster Grandparents are paid a volunteer stipend which, in most cases, enables the most vulnerable seniors in the community to combat social isolation, continue to age in place, and meet their basic needs.

Lastly, RS just launched the Social Leader Essentials e-Course to help faith-leaders, volunteers, and those with a social justice vision from every walk of life to operationalize their social priorities and learn to lead with greater social impact. Covering a rich and timely set of topics ranging from adopting a social venturing mindset to becoming bias-aware and trauma-informed, this course is aimed at helping leaders from all sectors move from charitable intentions to integrated priorities. All proceeds from this course support the work of RS in the community.

This remarkable ministry is really a church. That is, Fr. Justin's parish is not just St. Mary's, but Troost Avenue and all the rest of Kansas City. RS, along with Thelma's Kitchen and all of the RS services, offers a splendid example of a faith community extending itself, replanting in its neighborhood, and offering space to the many ministries pursued by the organizations all housed there.[33] Even though the traditional parish of St. Mary's is elsewhere now, the heart of church, its living tradition, and its inclusive community and service remain in RS and Thelma's Kitchen. It is the body of Christ for the life of the world. Its liturgy continues. Those who are hungry, not only for a meal but for God's abundant life, are fed, and their strength, and the strength of their community, is revealed. The word of encouragement and empowerment is heard. Hallelujahs are raised along with thanks. The church icons are no longer saints of old but, as Mother Maria Skobtsova called them, the "living icons" of women and men searching for God and God's kingdom. And the works of lovingkindness are done—all the outreach and further gathering of those in need and those who want to contribute and help is also as current as could be imagined.[34]

Church and Coffee

As coffee is a kind of sacrament, it is not surprising that congregations are pursuing coffee lovers as part of rethinking their mission. In Fort Worth, St. Luke's-in-the-Meadow Episcopal Church started "Coffee on the Corner" as an experiment in fall 2018, and it has continued it ever since.[35] The rector, Karen Calafat, and member Donnell Guynn explained that the simple setup of a table with coffee and some breakfast bars was envisioned as a way of connecting with the students and their parents from Middlebrook Middle School just down the block. Every day, church staff and those present for weekday events would watch the morning and then afternoon stream of parents and students pass by their buildings. Coffee and breakfast bars fostered conversation with school parents, which led to a parish effort to gather college-branded t-shirts for students on days dedicated to sessions on further education. Conversations also opened up the concerns of school

33. Garrison, "Orthodox-affiliated Nonprofit Helps Neighborhood Heal a Legacy of Trauma."

34. Bender, "Priest, a Chef, and a Hunger to Feed Kansas City."

35. Schjonberg, "Coffee on the Corner Helps Fort Worth Episcopalians Get to Know, Serve Their Neighbors."

community members that many parishioners, who commute from their regional scattering of residences, were unaware of. Often, members of congregations can only think of outreach and most other activities as ways of finding new members (and their wallets). Presence *with* others, as Sam Wells says over and over, is really the heart of service.

Los Angeles is but one of numerous cities in which churches have decided to again enter the marketplace as they have been doing since the first century CE, not just to stand on boxes and preach but, as Francis of Assisi is claimed to have said, "Preach the gospel, use words if necessary." On the grounds of Bel Air Presbyterian, the Parable Coffee Lab offers spectacular vistas of the San Fernando Valley and Santa Susanna Mountains while java and conversation flow. There are more such sacred cafes. Holy Grounds at St. Monica Catholic Church in Santa Monica, Steeple House Coffee at Grace Community Church in Sun Valley, Ignatius Café at St. Agnes Korean Catholic Church in University Park, and House Roots Coffee at Valley Korean United Methodist Church in Granada Hills are a few more.[36]

Parable hired Isaac Mason, who worked at several local artisan cafes, and he helped redesign the space to make for access to the views and create a comfortable space for coffee and interaction. This is not Bunn machine, coffee-hour-weak brew, but a two-group La Marzocco espresso machine, pour-over cones, and nitro-cold brew. House Roots Coffee at the Korean Methodist church sums up mission as "coffee, community and cause,"[37] since whatever is left after costs covering goes to social justice issues in the greater Los Angeles area, particularly ones in which the church is engaged. Similarly, Holy Grounds at St. Monica's is linked to a community center and provides a place for neighbors as well as parishioners to stop, enjoy good coffee, and talk. At the center, there is a meeting place and employment service aimed at young adults, and many of the baristas come from this program, having struggled with school dropout and brushes with the justice system. While Ignatius Café is not a business, but an outreach taking donations for costs and various service projects, Steeple House at the Sun Valley Grace Community Church is a business, with profits directed toward social and educational programs. Again, as in Fort Worth, with preschool and afterschool programs operated by congregations, the aim is not just bodies and bucks for that congregation. As with the sanctuary in Peterchurch, the productive use of sacred space all week long provides service to the larger community. As Sam Wells will argue in the next chapter, such action on the

36. Lurie, "LA Church Cafes Provide a Fresh Blend of Jesus, Community and Coffee."

37. Lurie, "LA Church Cafes Provide a Fresh Blend of Jesus, Community and Coffee."

part of parishes signals their return to the center of life in their communities, their existing not just for themselves but for others. Endeavors that are run on commercial models enable the projects to stay open, hire staff, maintain equipment, and then help fund other good work in the area, not just pay the congregation's bills. Those who really understand communities of faith in the twenty-first century say bluntly that launching efforts simply to increase parish income are limited in effectiveness. These are poor choices when ministry and outreach, that is, the ultimate purposes of a community of faith, are concerned.

The Return of Circuit-Riding Pastors

Jason and Jess Felici met while in seminary. Now they are married and both Lutheran (ELCA) pastors. There are other clergy couples, to be sure. But what distinguishes them is that they are twenty-first-century versions of a common form of pastoral ministry in American small-town and frontier congregations both in the 1700s and 1800s. They are circuit-riding Lutheran pastors, leading services, preaching, and providing care for five small parishes in West Virginia, spread out over a mountainous rural area where most of two counties are a Radio Quiet Zone for research, with even home wireless internet service difficult and no cell phone service at all.[38]

There are five different locations for services on Sundays, and the Felicis have got it down to a hectic, if exact, schedule. One of them embarks just after 7 AM on an almost sixty-mile drive to the furthest congregation for an 8:45 AM service, then all the way back for an 11:15 AM service at the church next door to their rectory or residence. The in-between services, all three of them, are covered by the other spouse in a well-choreographed route of driving from one to another.

Obviously, there are gains and disadvantages in such a way of celebrating the Lord's Day. Every congregation does have a pastor preaching and leading services. And there is regular exchange of the two pastors among the churches. However, more time to interact has to happen at other gatherings that bring together more than one location's community. For the pastor covering three services each Sunday, there is often no time whatsoever for meeting and greeting until the next Sunday's go-around, when the parishes can be reshuffled. The number in the communities varies too, from as few as eight to several dozen.

Despite the energy and dedication we see in Pastors Jess and Jason, clergy in similar situations know that such a schedule cannot go on

38. Zauzmer, "Circuit Preacher Was an Idea of the Frontier Past."

indefinitely. The wear and tear on both pastor and people is considerable. In earlier times, horse transportation would not have allowed five different services in as many churches on a single day. Congregations would have had to wait a week or longer. Likewise, even the coverage this modern circuit-riding provides does not address the underlying trends that we have seen over and over again in this book, the factors that appear to be behind congregation shrinkage and decline. Underemployment in the two West Virginia counties in which these Lutheran parishes are located has led to members relocating where better jobs exist.

Jess and Jason, as well as their scattered parishioners, know well that all five churches will not be open in the future. Already there have been church closures. The decision must be a local one, unlike in the UMC where a more regional conference ultimately says it is time to disband. That said, the local parish often is the last social association or community remaining in an area, this after the schools have shut and been relocated to more central settings, likewise the post office and small businesses. The Felicis know this part of the world well, Jason coming from Wheeling and Jess from Harrisonburg, both much larger communities. They have come to love the people in their five churches, many of whom are elderly and for whom church is their social lifeline. There are memories going back generations of people who worshipped in the small buildings, quite a few now buried in the churchyards surrounding the sanctuaries. It may be putting off the inevitable: the Felicis forestalling the death of these congregations. But the Felicis seem to sense that there will be a resurrection here, that somehow one or more of these five churches will survive. The yearly filling of the pews at Christmas is not taken as a sign of disinterest the rest of the time, since many of the Christmas and Easter worshippers are visitors, family, and parish members who long ago moved away for school and work—the pattern we have seen everywhere. But perhaps out of the five parishes, there may be enough members, enough of a community, to continue. That is these pastors' hope.

Going Forward to the Past: House Churches in the Twenty-First Century

A UMC pastor, Dave Barnhart, helped plant and now serves in a house church, St. Junia's, named for one of Paul's colleagues in ministry who, with her husband, Andronicus, led a house church in the first century CE.[39] In the

---

39. See Worthy, "Pastor David Barnhart on What Love Looks Like in Public."

online Methodist website, *Ministry Matters*, for almost a year he shared in ten essays some of the ingredients of a contemporary house church. House churches were the very first congregations in apostolic times. Paul indicated their locations in his letters to Thessalonika, Corinth, Phillip, Galatia, and Rome. He mentions a number of his co-workers in whose houses such congregations gathered, Junia and Andronicus, Lydia and Phoebe, Priscilla and Aquila and Nympha, to mention a few. Quite a number of names are noted at the end of the letter to the church in Rome.

Barnhart originally was assigned to a regular planting of a new Methodist congregation, but after a couple years shifted to the house church model. At the start, the targets were the Nones, whom we have come to know quite well, and the Dones, those who, having been active members of congregations, had left them behind for a variety of reasons.

Contrary to the conventional, building-oriented church plant, it is not the accumulation of new members, the growth, as some sarcastically put it, of "bodies and bucks," that signal health or success. With house churches, which obviously remain small, it is not unusual to have other house churches spring out of the first one. There are many advantages to the model, as well as some disadvantages. Chief among the plus factors are the intimacy and growth in knowledge of each member which the small size offers. Likewise, the lack of enormous costs for a building, advertising, salary for a pastor, as well as the institutional, hierarchical, clerical and other aspects ordinary parishes entail. House churches welcome everyone regardless of identity or background. They include whatever generation joiners happen to be.

However, the small, intimate community can be unbearable when personality conflicts erupt. There is nowhere to hide. For some, being in another's home, not a neutral place, is threatening. Such small groups can easily get isolated and sectarian, becoming alienated from other, more ordinary churchgoers and nonchurched folk. And house churches are enormously time- and energy-intensive for the pastor and other leaders.

After house churches disappeared when Christianity became legal and even state-approved, they turned up again in later centuries in various guises. The Methodists themselves preferred them for itinerant clergy and to avoid all the encumbrances of buildings and land. House churches enable members to focus on the practice of the faith in all its various expressions, from worship to learning and outreach and witness. They make clear the goal of faith informing everyday life, and life coming back to inquire of faith.

There is no one size fits all. Some contemporary house churches gather around a meal, some value singing and playing worship music, but others less so, or not at all. There are very culturally conservative versions as well as radically egalitarian versions. While Barnhart wrote as conflict was growing in the UMC, and now has come to a head, he had in mind house churches as an alternative for those who wanted church without the institutional and doctrinal fights but also without the overhead costs of a standard building, pastor, and the rest.

Barnhart offers a great deal more from his experience in house churches in the ten parts of his series. Unlike the usual planted parish, which he calls a "attractional, event-oriented, building centered"[40] congregation, house churches do not have such a goal in mind (though only the Spirit knows where a community will eventually go). Worship is central and is what sets a house church apart from a friendship circle or supper circle. Barnhart does not provide a recipe or action plan, but some aspects he notes are interesting. One is that it takes at least three households to get going, a trial run for starters, and then in a short time a commitment of those who want to continue, as some may find it too unusual or demanding to stay on. He terms the ones who commit "partners" because they have a vested interest in the work of continuing their existence.

There are plenty of specific suggestions Barnhart offers, based on experience, running the course from how not to burden hosts for gatherings to the cardinal rule of keeping things simple—from the liturgy to what is served or a meal or refreshments. Preaching, in particular, requires radical rethinking and reshaping. No longer can one person rise before even a modest gathered congregation and simply speak, even if eloquently. In a house church, there is no pulpit, no altar, no long nave down which to roam as one preaches. There will be a dozen people of all ages, maybe fewer, maybe a couple more, seated round a table or a living room. Right away the communal character of preaching stands out, and this means that whatever is said by the one preaching must soon become a conversation, an interaction among the gathered. Barnhart likens the traditional solo sermon in a house church to watching a star soccer player doing personal warm-up drills or practice kicks. The preacher needs to pass the ball to teammates. Thus the "narrative" style of preaching, stories, and lots of images "do the lifting," in his view.

Quite intriguing is what Barnhart has to say about the significance of intergenerational community in such close quarters as house churches. The traditional Sunday Church School segregation of children and adolescents with a church publishing company curriculum will simply not work, and this is, in the eyes of many, a disaster anyway. It becomes a clear path to exiting church as soon as possible. Even adolescent confirmation, where this is the practice, is now a rare event. Yet it is also not possible to simply

40. Worthy, "Pastor David Barnhart on What Love Looks Like in Public."

have kids rolling on the floor and carrying on, creating what Alexander Schmemann called "holy noise."[41] With around a dozen people all told, kids included, little of substance could go on with such distractions. Perhaps it makes better sense to think of dinner at one's home with invited guests and their kids, or a family celebration of Easter or Christmas. It works best when kids have some space of their own, even if this means their separation from the adults. Older ones, of course, can be included. Barnhart notes that involving children and teenagers in the service is a fundamental element of catechesis. They can do readings or prayers, if able, and help prepare the table and whatever else is necessary. He makes it a given that every house church liturgy culminates in holy communion. There is no need to legitimize this because it is the tradition to gather around the Scriptures, prayers, and breaking of bread.

House churches cannot abide by the strategies and rules employed for years in ordinary parishes and planting of congregations. The previously assumed goal of building a sanctuary and other buildings, what he calls "steeple churches," is not there. When it comes to bringing new members into fellowship, this too undergoes transformation. The adage that it takes disciples to makes disciples needs no debate. But the direction is essentially different. "Attractional" congregations seek to bring people in and the financial aspect is always there. In the much smaller world of a house church, the process is not attractional, not getting new folks to events or programs. Rather, the aim is to spawn off new house churches, but even more importantly to urge people toward outreach, toward service in their own neighborhoods, their homes, jobs, and schools. Still, one sees congregations showcasing "parish projects," whether staffing and supplying soup kitchens, food banks, or thrift shops, or visiting assisted-living and skilled-nursing facilities or the like. Barnhart's point is one that pastors of more typical congregations have long ago realized. To serve the Lord and the Lord's people need not be a joint effort with the parish logo on it. Rather, and especially when membership is dispersed—not a "village" church—the everyday ministry will not be visible. The everyday work of a parish community will take a myriad of forms. It will go on wherever members are living out their faith.

Barnhart has some insight for us when it comes to the obsession of many in the church in the face of shrinkage and decline. Popularity, "going viral," amazing growth—these are highly valued in our consumerist, capitalist culture. Bigger is always better, and our visions of the past

41. For Schmemann's final words, see his commemorative website: https://www.schmemann.org/byhim/thankyoulord.html.

almost always are tinged with nostalgia for packed churches, huge Sunday Church School classes, and corresponding abundance in related aspects of church life. Our church buildings, especially the historic, older, urban ones, were built for crowds of worshippers we rarely if ever have, except at huge funerals and weddings.

House churches are most definitely not the newest strategy for halting denominational and church shrinkage. Barnhart suggests that there is a "math" that best expresses what happens over time in house churches. "Addition" of members or of new house churches is a very slow process, often taking years, and the results are modest. However, when a new house church is spun off, it is psychologically moving, a real "multiplication" not of loaves and fish but of disciples and their own new fellowships. When there is "division" of members to a new house church, there is need for a kind of "maternity/paternity/parental leave."[42] In the life cycle of families, this is the case when children leave and eventually it is an "empty nest," a misnomer as well. There is a sense of loss and even grief as former partners are no longer present but at another house church plant. Also there is exhaustion as the very process leading to the departure and new start likely was draining. The "subtraction" of even just two or three members is felt much more acutely than in a more traditional congregation, even when it is a small one. The New Testament makes clear people became disenchanted or fearful or angry and stopped following Jesus. But as the parable of the sower (Matt 13:3–9) insists, scattering seed everywhere will result in seed consumed, ground up, dried out, and choked, but there will also be amazing growth.

Barnhart observes from experience that house churches are different enough from normal congregations that some who are otherwise alienated or threatened by the latter may wonder what in reality these gatherings are. And some who come may find that even in this most minimal, basic, and small version, the core of Christianity still is not for them. Others may follow an invitation and after a few visits wonder when the other shoe, as it were, is going to drop—what is really going to be asked of them? Is this a cult or a collection of extremists? St. Barnabas in Borrego Springs, California moves the Sunday eucharist from the nave into the parish room. With perhaps a dozen or so gathered around a table, the bread and cup become, in a striking manner, ever more simple yet powerful, the sense of being together heightened after being in the nave. The exchange of the peace is warm, even boisterous on Sundays during the service, but even more moving when it is so few. And rector Laura Brecht confided that it was a breakthrough in terms of preaching as well as presiding. The homily had to be a give and take, a joint

42. Barnhart, "Methodist House Churches."

effort of the gathering. Every word and gesture of the liturgy seemed more significant when so up close and personal. Now, months into the pandemic, when the Sunday service is a Zoom gathering, there is the loss of being in the same room, being able to see, hear, and touch others. But there is still a true gathering. On the Zoom screen, others' faces can be seen, when unmuted, their voices heard. There is a sharing of what is essential in the sacrament of assembly around Christ.

Linking to Barnhart's series at *Ministry Matters* is worthwhile. But for me, the most valuable of his observations came with respect to group dynamics of house churches and, in particular, the ever-present reality of problematic, toxic personalities. Every parish, sooner or later, will experience such things, and most often it is not obvious or apparent. Those looking to vent, to control, to dominate, or to manipulate will have a field day in the intimate space of a house church. "Hurt people hurt people" is wisdom among pastors, whether church planters or not. In standard congregations, even with more mechanisms to divert and block toxic personalities, these can do great damage to both the pastor and the rest of the community.

The key to group dynamics is contained in the Greek word *dynamis,* or power. Who leads, who follows, who speaks, who remains silent? Whose ideas are listened to and whose plans pursued? Who almost disappears into whatever limited woodwork there is? Of course, therapists realize how complex even one family of less than a half dozen can be. Power is not just an articulate, thoughtful individual. Power is also wielded in terms of race, gender, sexual identity, class, and age. As in the family, so in the house church, fear, threats, and vulnerability come into play, along with dominance. There is always need for boundaries and for vigilance.

Barnhart draws on John Gottman and other sources for observations about what builds up rather than destroys community in church.[43] Complaining about specific problems or conditions can but constructive, a way toward resolving issues and better connections. Criticism attacks the person rather than the behavior or situation; it is antagonistic and does not offer much constructive feedback, so much as a verdict on another. Respecting the role of someone who has taken on a task means there can be different opinions. This is the "dishwasher principle." If you have better ideas, share them. If you are attacking the other, this is out of bounds.

Barnhart suggests what many other pastors have concluded after years of experience: what is needed among members is "pastoral care" for each other. Private lives often collide with the tasks and needs, and thus the life, of a church. But the "private" lives of members are really not private.

---

43. Barnhart, "Methodist House Churches."

They are part of the substance of that community's life together. So a broken marriage, serious illness, death, major problems in kids' lives—all of these shape how we feel and act. They must be or become the business of the community, whether of the house church or the more usual "steeple" church. Have I had lunch or coffee or a phone chat or extended conversation even at church, with this other fellow member? Do I even consider her or him to be a sister or brother? Am I even in the slightest way interested in his or her life, family, feelings? Do I share more than an hour of worship or church council service or other parish work, having a real connection with this fellow member? These everyday connections in time are just as sacramental as the breaking of the bread and sharing of the cup; indeed, they are extensions of that action of communion. How much more crucial community connection has become during the pandemic, when we cannot be gathered in the same space.

Barnhart does a fascinating historical nod back to the apostolic churches in clarifying whether a network of house churches constitutes a "single" parish. In looking at similar networks known to Paul and addressed by him, there was no contradiction between the "one" and the "many." Paul greeted the "church that met at the house" of Priscilla and Aquila, Andronicus and Junia, and so on (1 Cor 16:19). But as Nicholas Afanasiev stressed, while each of these small house churches was fully the church, each could only be that, the church, in communion with the other churches. Anastacia Wooden, a specialist on Afanasiev, points out that precisely this Pauline vision of the participation of all local churches in "the church of God in Christ" comes in for attack whether from Catholic or Orthodox critics troubled by their seeming inability to detect here the arrangements they presently know in their own communions. There was in the first century CE, of necessity, both stability of a one communion of the many local churches in communion with each other.[44]

As one moves through the historical timeline, the Methodist experiment, of which Barnhart is part, returned to the apostolic model. Bishops appointed itinerant ordained elders and licensed pastors very often at first, to churches' meetings in peoples' homes. This enabled the spread of small house churches more than the purchase of land and the erection of a church building, and helps explain why the Methodists used to have as many churches in the US as post offices. In time, itinerant ministers disappeared in favor of residential pastors who were appointed by the bishop and transferred when they desired. Barnhart argues that for house churches there has to be a

---

44. Wooden, "Eucharistic Ecclesiology of Nicolas Afanasiev and Its Ecumenical Significance," 543–60; Wooden, "Limits of the Church."

broadening of how pastoral leaders are trained and then authorized to serve. It cannot continue to be that one ordained elder is sufficient for a network of house churches. Each house church wants and needs to have the weekly gathering for Scriptures and communion. The more traditional church-developing/planting model would seek out an area with the most beneficial demographics and economic possibilities. But this was in order to eventually, after renting space, raise funds sufficient to build their own sanctuary and whatever other space was needed. While this will continue, at the very least house churches will also continue as alternatives to this model.

Where Barnhart's analysis of the shrinkage and decline of churches in the US converges with what has been argued here most emphatically is in the corresponding changes to American culture, society, and economy. Marriage and childrearing as normative, ownership of a home, a car, the increased mobility distancing generations and siblings, marriage outside of religious and ethnic communities—these are some of the factors, the "de-mographics," that we have called up over and over again as instrumental in changes in belonging to religious communities. Of course, other factors are also at work and we have seen them appear and reappear, including distrust of institutions generally, estrangement from official church teachings, and the abusive behavior of church leaders, among others.

Yet what is behind the consistent inequality in America for the last several decades (the decline of salaries and wages, the disappearance of traditional pensions, massive outsourcing and downsizing—all of this and more that is familiar to us) has led to the end of the "middle class" to which the American dream aspired, as well as all that accompanied it. So declining participation in unions, in voluntary associations, is paralleled by declines in attendance at church and belonging to a church. There are notable regional, racial, and ethnic exceptions, but Americans who perceive themselves as "left behind," displaced, "strangers in their own land," are not necessarily clinging to churches any longer. Most American churches are small congregations, under seventy in membership, and they are the ones most often closing. The few and exceptional megachurches continue to grow, but when seen against the larger backdrop of American churchgoers, these larger congregations do not change the overall picture of decline.

Barnhart does not propose house churches as the miracle-working replacement for ordinary congregations and their houses of worship. He does, however, see the Methodist recognition of licensed local pastors who have employment elsewhere—"day jobs"—as what can make house churches possible. At present, the UMC guidelines for ordained clergy make such impossible even within a very large network of house churches and impossible as well for most small congregations. The minimum salary

and benefits, not to mention debt from seminary and university training, the need for health insurance, a place to live or housing equity, and
more—these have already put local congregations of every church body in
the situation of being able to have either self-employed clergy, part-time
or shared clergy, or retired clergy willing to serve. Barnhart astutely notes
that in many ways the "gig economy" has now come to the churches. I
know this to be the case. There are numerous parishes which take what
they can get, give what they are able, which often amounts to essentially
the stipend they would pay for a supply pastor, with no benefits or housing, just paid week after week to the same pastor to lead worship, preach,
do visits, and take funerals. Like so many small stores, these eventually will
go out of business. We will shortly hear from Episcopal bishop C. Andrew
Doyle a call for revisiting not only how ordained clergy are educated but
also how they could be better integrated into communities of faith. This
would be at the same time a return to the most ancient patterns, as described by Afanasiev, as well as a doing away with the clerical class or caste
in which clergy are truly "set apart" from mere lay people.

While Barnhart has a PhD in homiletics and ethics and went through
traditional seminary training himself, he makes a similar case as Doyle.
Barnhart argues that for five centuries or more, there has been insistence
on a learned clergy. Also insisted was that a parish care for the pastor's
need, provide a "living." Both of these are now parts of an unsustainable
model of parish life and pastoral ministry. He sees that an ordained elder
can function exactly as that, as a mentor, possibly even a "local bishop" like
the ancient "country bishops (*chorepiskopoi*). House churches would have
licensed local pastors leading them. Women and men should be given the
training they need, not an MDiv degree. These pastors would of necessity
have jobs on which they rely for themselves and their family. They would be
on the same level as other members. He dares to call them entrepreneurs
too, which they will have to be, like the early house church leaders and the
first Methodist itinerants.

Barnhart is trying to find a way for communities to work for house
churches. They are start-ups, new gatherings. Barnhart thinks they may
be particularly useful for the Nones and the Dones, that is, those at some
distance from ordinary congregations. The house churches are small. They
offer immediate and powerful experience of how church is community,
the people of God gathered in prayer and worship and working together
locally. All this is without the "overhead," the costly structure of a church
building, a clergy salary, and so on.

However, it is not Barnhart's intent to offer house churches as cure-alls
for the many-faceted malaise of American congregations. It is something else

to try to stretch such methods as he describes from house church experience to the "steeple" church, the conventional one with a building and the rest of the typical parish elements. Yet as we have seen and will see further on, there is already a diversity of paths to follow. And even if the house church may not work for an already-existing parish, many things Barnhart learned first from planting traditional churches and then from house churches I believe are helpful—which is why we have given the space to his account here.

He calls house churches a return to the distant and more recent Methodist past. They are neither solutions to all the issues confronting congregations today or escapes from turmoil in the churches, such as the coming split of his own UMC or any other church body. Barnhart is emboldened to say that house churches can also be disruptions in a "colonizing theology of Empire" and alternatives to a model of the parish rooted in white supremacy and capitalism.[45] The boom in church-building and congregational planting from the end of WWII on into the 1980s may have had "plausibility structures," as my mentor Peter Berger called them, suburbanization and the spread of the myth of "middle-class" stability and success. Robert Putnam and Nancy Ammerman also note the contexts of church growth from the 1950s on. In the next chapter, we will hear from a major voice in that era, Loren Mead, who inspired at least a generation of church-planting pastors.

Alongside the move to the suburbs were red-lining, white flight, segregation not just by race but by class—just as powerful a tool of division. Corporate America financed the Levitt and other track homes in the suburbs and made veterans' benefits, the FHA, and the GI Bill unavailable to blacks. The urban churches of immigrants and African Americans found themselves in crisis as early as the 1960s. Some were able to slow the migration to other parts of cities and to the suburbs while others held on.

Barnhart is radical. He is right in showing how all the major churches in America accommodated the system, whether the political marginalization of blacks or newer immigrants. Eventually, some churches were given new life by successive waves of new immigration—the Catholic Church, in particular. Others found themselves continually challenged and had to change. Episcopalians, Lutherans, Presbyterians, and Barnhart's own Methodists were among these.

The Economy and the Small Church

A Mennonite pastor, Melissa Florer-Bixler, heads one of the small congregations that make up more than 85 percent of all American parishes—one

---

45. Barnhart, "Methodist House Churches."

with fewer than 250 members.[46] The average parish, as we know, is seventy members. She repeats the oft-heard and widely held perspective that the missing demographic in most parishes are the Millennials. They are online, on-call, seeming available, wired, and working all the time. They take fewer vacation days a year than any group in history. Florer-Bixler cites the *Harvard Business Review* that tracked such patterns.[47]

Now, we are seeing fewer house and car purchases and much less involvement in community organizations, except those required, such as fund-raising efforts for their kids' school and athletic teams. They are drastically underrepresented in churches, the wisdom goes, because they simply have no time or, for that matter, income left over for membership and giving. Florer-Bixler does not challenge such a profile of Millennials and their obsessions about work and advancement. However, she does not stop with the driven, time- and often sleep-deprived Millennials, many of whom creatively string together positions and contracts in a "gig economy," as Barnhart observed. Just as crucial for the life of a parish as financial support is time: time members have to be at services, gatherings, in short, real participation in the life of a holy community. We cannot foresee what the long-term impact of the pandemic will be on the economy, on peoples' jobs, on peoples' lives, nor the long-term consequences of four years of nationalism, division, anger, and fear. No return to the "normal" past is possible.

Recalling the church's stances supporting labor unions, fair wages, and the rights of working people, as well as work conditions, Florer-Bixler argues that if churches want to move into the future, they cannot afford to remain apolitical and disengaged from economic and financial realities. Most importantly, she calls for churches to regain their prophetic stances, not on these issues only, but across the board on many other questions that have become dilemmas for ordinary people. Surely among these must be the massive unemployment the pandemic created, the widespread food insecurity, the stirred up mistrust of the "other," and so much more which the past few years have brought. In sum, the churches, if they are about the work of the kingdom of God, must show what that kingdom looks like not after death but here and now, in our lives. Of course this is the only truly biblical vision of how disciples need to engage with the world in which they earn a living, raise children, and live out the gospel.

C. Christopher Smith is pastor of Englewood Christian Church in Indianapolis, and he has written some intriguing things about the life of

---

46. Florer-Bixler, "Capitalism Is Killing the Small Church."

47. See the Association of Religious Data Archives at http://www.thearda.com/ConQS/qs_295.asp.

parish communities today.[48] He distinguishes between a parish being a religious community and being a real community. Some may grimace at such a distinction, thinking it a put-down of the integrity and the work of a congregation as a spiritual body. But Smith's case is that as it shrank to it smallest size in its history, the Englewood church came to grips with the disparate visions of the diverse groups that comprised its not-small membership. These ranged from those still nostalgic for the old days and a traditional piety to those who wanted serious engagement with their neighborhood, as well as those who wanted to be part of the booming culture of American evangelicals.

The usual structure of Sunday worship, Christian education, and fellowship had become a closed circle. There was no opportunity to get beyond continued decline and divisions among the small community left and becoming smaller. But an effort to sit people in a circle and with minimal taking off from scriptural texts eventually grew into a transforming experience. Some left because the revealing of differences became too much. Others came to know their fellow members as they never had before. Eventually, in a move we have come to recognize as one of rebirth, renewal, and outreach, the Englewood Community Development Corporation (ECDC) was created, a 501 (c) (3) not-for-profit corporation to gather several very effective programs directed at the lives of neighbors and the neighborhoods around. The enterprises include computer repair service, a commercial cleaning service, a book-keeping service, as well as a lawn-mowing service. But in the area of housing, that ECDC has made an almost unheard-of contribution, though sweat equity, limited partnerships, advocacy, consulting, acquisition, rehab, and pooling of personal resources with government and private funding. Over 25,000 households have found affordable, quality housing in the neighborhoods around the Englewood church. Seniors, immigrants, young, single, and married folk—the gamut of people in the area. No wonder that now most members come from close by rather than commuting in, which had been the pattern some decades ago when the congregation started to seriously shrink. The prophetic word to "seek the prosperity of the city where I send you" (Jer 29:7), even if it was Babylon where the people were held in captivity, took shape and became incarnate in that Indianapolis neighborhood.

In North Minneapolis, in Seattle, in Oakland, and elsewhere, we have seen this pattern of discovering for the first time (or rediscovering) what it means to be a community, the body of Christ, by congregants. And the movement then is not the inward introversion of a terminally ill parish to

48. Smith, "Cultivating Cultural Proximity."

hunker down, watch pennies, and stay open as long as possible. Rather, like the horizontal thrust of Christ's arms on the cross, the movement is out, to others, to share what the church and members have, whether space in the buildings, professional and technical expertise, financial resources, or labor power—to do the liturgy after the liturgy, not on the sanctuary altar of wood or stone but that of the hearts of the sister and brother in need.

CHAPTER 7

Visions Going Forward

"The Church is its future as much as its past."[1]

Never Just Dying, but New Life

THROUGHOUT THIS BOOK, WE have been looking at two realities of the church in our time. One is the shrinkage of congregations, the disappearance of members, the decline of church bodies. In some projections, the very existence of a church body by the year 2040 is called into question. Such was the case not long ago in media accounts of the future of the Anglican Church in Canada by 2040.[2] As alarming as this sounds, other mainstream denominations there, as well as in the US, are, by data projection, in similar situations. Churches will not disappear, but they will be much smaller. This will be the case after a period of even higher numbers of parish closures than we have at present. And there does not appear to be any change in the exodus of people from churches, no matter the age group. Earlier, we looked at the tangle of actual events and factors involved, from marrying out and relocating to those who are "done" with the church and those who have no connection, participation, or membership in a religious congregation.

Shrinkage at the national level, that of entire church bodies or denominations, is one thing. However, location is everything when it comes to any kind of social belonging. The situation at the level of congregations in our own towns and cities is no less striking. We have seen many congregations that faced crises of declining membership and resources, and we have explored what seem to be factors contributing to congregations' shrinking and declining.

1. Congar, *Église Catholique et France moderne*, 10.

2. Longhurst, "Anglican Church in Canada May Disappear by 2040, Report Says"; Virtue, "Anglican Church in Canada Faces Extinction by 2040."

However we have seen something else that such data as those pro-jecting the "end" of the Anglican Church of Canada, the Episcopal Church in the US, or the Evangelical Lutheran Church in America cannot convey. Larger bodies face the same future—Methodists, Baptists, Presbyterians—as do the many smaller ones like the various Eastern Orthodox churches. Even the Catholic Church would look somewhat threatened if it were not for immigrants.

We have seen the diversity and persistent endurance of local con-gregations, many stories of reinvention, repurposing, and replanting. The bulk of this book has been a journey through many of them. Following the central paradigm of Christianity, we know there is death, but beyond this, resurrection. What we have seen of this is not just a hope or a vision but the real lives of communities of faith. These are as striking as the data on shrinkage. Equally impressive are the creative, sometimes ingenious ways they found to redefine or reinvent themselves. Buildings were repurposed. New ties to the neighborhood around the parish were investigated and pursued. Coalitions with other congregations, with not-for-profit agen-cies, were established. In many cases, while there were real breaks with the past, even then it was possible to see the continuity in praising God, being a community in faith, and love and serving God's people in that particu-lar place. Is it possible to see in all these some visions, going forward, of church as community, community as church?

The Local Church—the Parish—Does Not
Live for Itself: Loren Mead

Loren Mead died in 2018. His stature as an interpreter and advisor on parish life in the US is unparalleled. An Episcopal priest, he was an experi-enced parish rector and church planter. He was personally involved in that great time of church expansion in the 1950s, successfully planting a parish in Chapel Hill, North Carolina. After parish service, he led "Project Test Pattern," an endeavor of the national Episcopal Church for better shaping parishes in postwar culture and society. In 1974, Mead started the Alban Institute. For years it has been the leading organization devoted to the study of the local church, the parish, and it remains under the auspices of Duke Divinity School.

From the 1950s onward, parish life seemed to have a life of its own, as Mead noted in an interview a few years before his death. So many former service people were returning from WWII, getting married, hav-ing children, going back to school, beginning careers. More people than ever were entering higher education as well as graduate and professional school. Mead was then in the Chapel Hill seat of the UNC and close to the Research Triangle. There was growth as there had not been for many years, and with a burgeoning population—all those Boomers. There were new parish starts everywhere, along with new schools, shopping centers, parks, and roads. Expansion was taken for granted and church was still a social necessity, a standard aspect of the lives of most families, a badge of identity and important location for all kinds of networking. Attendance at services and church school were at record highs, and year after year, there was need for even more new parish starts, so much so that the future appeared to be one continuous time of flourishing.

A Time of Division and Discontent

We know that by the end of the 1960s, this pattern began to shift and we have repeatedly reflected on the shrinkage and decline that are now as much the standard as growth was sixty years ago. Dave Barnhart echoed this perspective in assessing the larger picture of the shrinkage and decline of congregations in the US. After the population boom post-WWII (hence the "Boomers") and the accompanying economic surge, it was not just the destructive counter-culture rebellion of the 1960s that changed the course of American life. For sure, the youth rebellion and alienation and experimentation of the 1960s did reshape the country. Still today, we hear conservative critics blaming this for everything from clergy sexual abuse to the rise in divorce rates and numbers of those addicted.

Yet Barnhart observes, as others like Joseph Stiglitz and Paul Krugman have done, that the dream of becoming middle class gradually was extinguished. Along with this was the economic gains of the middle class after the Great Depression and WWII. Stretching as far back as the Reagan administration, there has been a series of policy decisions, pieces of legislation, modest at first, that have escalated. There was the deregulating of Wall Street and the banks after the Great Recession. The economic policy of the last decades has provided corporations with tax breaks and incentives. Some of the largest corporations, close to a hundred, such as Amazon, Netflix, Delta, JetBlue, Whirlpool, Chevron, Halliburton, IBM, Gannett, Goodyear, US Steel, GM, and Eli Lilly, to mention just a few, pay no taxes whatsoever.[3] There has been refusal to fund Medicaid expansion by a number of states, an important component of the Affordable Care Act, which itself has been the target of numerous Trump administration

---

3. Pound, "These 91 Companies Paid No Federal Tax in 2018."

demolition efforts. Unions have been attacked and public higher education starved of funding. Efforts to spread healthcare and fund education
are labeled as "socialism." The attempt to establish a universal health care
system in the US was seen as taking away Americans' freedom. Suspicion
of "big government" became revulsion for the "deep state" of government
and its employees at all levels. The promise was that retracting entitlement
programs and refusing expansion of food security and aid to education
would result in both starving off "big government" and creating enormous
tax breaks. But these tax cuts have consistently benefitted corporations and
financial institutions and wealthy individuals rather than most Americans.
Now, the earlier conservative political concern for reversing deficits has
disappeared. With growing military spending and tax "reform," tax revenue
is down. Huge deficits exist in the federal budget and entitlement programs
and other educational, health, and assistance programs are the targets of
cuts rather than sizable corporate and personal profits.

Stiglitz is but one of a number of other economists and political ana-
lysts who have identified all of the above as leading to the rise of a now widespread and intractable inequality. The economic policies of the last almost
fifty years have been most beneficial to corporations and the wealthy, but
economically, socially, and psychologically corrosive for millions of Americans. The number of Americans living paycheck to paycheck, with hardly
any savings or retirement funds, is shocking. A year ago, it was 78 percent
of workers.[4] Sixty-three percent of Americans, in a study a couple years
ago, would not be able to come up with $500 in an emergency.[5] This "other
America," as Michael Harrington called it decades ago, still exists, after the
"war on poverty" and much cutting of entitlements that sustained them.[6]
Those of the poorly and low-paid workers who have now in the millions lost
their jobs in the pandemic were there in the economy long before the Co-
vid-19 virus appeared, changing everything. Like so much of our inequality,
racism, discrimination, and hate for those who are different, "other," these
fellow Americans were suffering already and likely will suffer more than
others in our society. These "other Americans" shared none of the surging
economy the Trump administration boasted of.

Charles Murray, J. D. Vance, Arlie Russell Hochschild, Joseph Stiglitz,
and Paul Krugman, among others, point to the array of social and economic
realities and the accompanying powerful resentments building up in America

4. Friedman, "78% Live Paycheck to Paycheck."

5. McGrath, "63% of Americans Don't Have Savings Enough to Cover a $500
Emergency."

6. Harrington, *Other America*.

in the second decade of the twenty-first century.[7] These difficult conditions are all over the internet, TV, and the political campaigns leading up to 2020 elections. The landscape is one of disappearing jobs, a "gig" economy where there is no job stability, few if any benefits, and stagnant salaries. We live in a country of enormous affluence that is concentrated in less than 1 percent of the population. Even a conservative social commentator like Murray notes the scourge of addictions, the fragility of marriages and families, and the culture of scapegoating people of color and immigrants. Increases in anti-Semitic attacks, as well as attacks on Muslims and people of color, are expressions of rage. Those who feel "left behind" by a "rigged system" blame, all too often, the "other" who is not the source of their discontent, and they target those who appear "other" as the takers of their jobs and benefits, no matter whether this has any basis in reality. I have mentioned Hochschild's study of a Louisiana "parish" or county several times throughout this book, precisely because it is often painful to read accounts of the fracturing of community, the erosion of any sense of belonging to one another. Rather, it is particularly telling in describing this syndrome of failed blame. Lines are drawn long before walls and laws of restriction are promulgated. Immigrants, both legal and nondocumented, have been made the targets of rage and hostile policies, along with those fleeing hostile gangs and violence as refugees. And even one's fellow citizens, one's neighbors, become "strangers" because all that is perceived any longer is their otherness, whether African Americans, Muslims, or Jews. There has been a rise in the incidence of all kinds of hate crimes—anti-Semitic, homophobic, anti-immigrant—in the past four years. Kevin Kruse and Julian Zelitzer argue that the "fault lines" dividing Americans stretch much further back.[8]

All of these developments and policy shifts in the last almost half-century have reshaped the country and the churches as well. While politics have always been partisan, the level of suspicion and division among Americans has dramatically heightened in the Trump years, though some observers feel the racism and resentment of the "other" have been perennial features of American culture.

---

7. Murray, *Coming Apart*; Vance, *Hillbilly Elegy*; Hochschild, *Strangers in Their Own Land*; Stiglitz, *Price of Inequality*; Williamson, "White Ghetto"; Krugman, "Armpits, White Ghettos and Contempt"; Case and Deaton, "Mortality and Morbidity in the 21st Century."

8. Kruse and Zelitzer, *Fault Lines*.

Church Communities Do Not Just
Live for Themselves

But despite the developments just described, Mead observed something that gave congregations a reason for being, a sense of life and purpose. Mead recognized from his own pastoral experience, even before starting the Alban Institute, that faithful, generous, and therefore healthy parishes *did not just live for themselves*. He discerned that the healing, the sense of belonging, and the impulse to reach out and help were ways in which a congregation brought healing and fellowship and often concrete assistance like food, clothing, shelter, and counseling to the larger community.[9] Community—and all that entailed—made a congregation truly church, the body of Christ. As church, a parish could share its community of faith and service with the neighborhood and the larger world around. The congregation was, as Jesus, bread for the life of the world, there not to condemn the world but to bring it healing.

While Mead's Alban Institute published extensively on parish life, noting ways in which both laity and clergy could better interact, deal with change, and find new ways of being the body of Christ, his most basic instincts about the parish are useful for us here at the end of reviewing so many efforts to survive, revive, renew, or reinvent themselves as a community of faith.[10] Mead realized that the era in which he began parish ministry and then developed the Alban Institute to study and advise clergy and laity started to end in the 1960s.

But his sense was that, despite the decline, the parish was still the place where the encounter between God and the world, between church and society, took place. The parish is really the local church, the expression of the church that most people experience and know. The parish is what they think of when they hear "church," not some invisible "diocese" or distant bishop. There are factors, realities of how people earn a living, how and where they live, how they understand themselves and their neighborhoods, marriages, families, and the world that profoundly influence the local church of the parish. Coincidentally, in striking continuity, Mead preached at the liturgy which inaugurated the Church of the Advocate outside Chapel Hill in 2003, a parish featured earlier here.

But there are also tendencies in the opposite direction, ones that make the parish the center of all interest and activity. These centripetal forces turn a community in upon itself. As my longtime friend and fellow

---

9. See "Loren B. Mead."

10. Mead, *Once and Future Church*; Mead, *More than Numbers*.

priest Alex Vinogradov always reminds me, the suspicious, selfish, and spiteful sides of people are absolutely part of community too.[11] This other, all-too-human side manifests itself in diverse ways. Barbara Brown Taylor and Barbara Melosh, among others, effectively describe the often destructive sides of parish life.

My own experience in the first parish in which I served showed me this, and so has every other parish in which I have served, five in all. How could it be anything else? Early on I saw a great deal of jousting for influence among various groups in the parish which turned out to be power clusters. The obvious one was the parish council, but over the years this body, despite some challenging members, functioned quite effectively, working well with parish clergy and enabling the construction of a new church building. The real conflict occurred among the choir, the couples' club, and the Sunday school.

In the early 1980s, there was also a kind of parish myopia or congregational inversion. This included a limitation of vision in which the larger church, as well as the world beyond, was not particularly important. And the parish, as is often the case even today, was turned in on itself. The outlook within was shaped by the culture of the congregation—the people there, the financial picture, the accustomed activities and events, the yearly cycle of seasons, including liturgical ones. I recall that the school year and summer vacation probably shaped the consciousness of what the parish did more than the liturgical cycle of seasons and feasts. Only after Labor Day, when school had started again in September, was there a sense that most members would be returning to Sunday services and church school, to choir and to groups like the women's circle, the couples' club, and the youth groups. Once, a gifted lay leader publicly criticized this very "popular" pattern, saying we shouldn't act as though church was "closed" all summer, when it was assumed many were taking a vacation from attending services while all other activities were on hiatus. Only gradually did the rector and I realize we were seeing the start of less-frequent church attendance that in time would be a more decisive distancing from parish life.

I also remember the senior pastor's feeling that every fall was really the start of a "new year" in the parish. And in marketing mode, we needed to have a "new" theme, new activities and events for church school, as well as all the other parish groups. He had learned that offering the membership a new and interesting parish "program" was the way to retain old members and attract new ones. In the time there working with him, almost a decade, we both came to recognize that this market approach to

---

11. Plekon, *Uncommon Prayer*, 168–200.

retaining clientele, maintaining brand loyalty, moving with the membership's patterns, was in eclipse.

Patterns of life in America were changing and rapidly. As we have seen earlier, the multigenerational families which were the backbone of many congregations ceased to be that, what with people relocating. Children married out of the ethnic and church communities, and many simply moved away for education and work, never to return, except for family events. American society across the board became more mobile. It became the exception that someone was born, grew up, lived, and died in the same town or part of a city and parish.

There was little interdenominational tension with other parishes. Forty years ago, many parishes were flourishing. Lots of kids in church school and confirmation. The clergy were members of the town ecumenical ministers' association. There were joint concerts, a local chorale that drew upon choir members from all the churches. What was seldom noticed was the already ecumenical character of the membership. Probably less than half, maybe only a third were cradle Lutherans, the rest having married into the Lutheran Church or simply chosen this congregation because of its size and many programs. Gradually, we pastors began to see the lines of much deeper change that was to come.

Mead likens our period to earlier ones in American history, where economic and social shifts ended some ways of life, only to give rise to new ones which further changed the country. The changes in technology and production moved many Americans off the smaller family farms toward the end of the nineteenth century, and large agricultural industry moved in with more effective ways to plant, cultivate, and harvest crops. Smaller towns started draining population to industrial hubs and urban areas. The life we have come to know, taken for granted, lay ahead of these former small-town inhabitants and farmers, their children and grandchildren. In the cities, they met up with thousands of immigrants, became part of a society more diverse in religion and ethnicity and race than it had ever been. The next generations would experience the Great Depression, along with two world wars and an almost continual series of political and social changes. Mead's point is that apparent downturns, historical moments of decline, are never the whole story. We cannot yet see with accuracy what the passing of the thousand-year-old model of parish may lead to in the future.

Mead's main argument, that the parish does not live just for itself but offers healing and life to the wider community, is at the very heart of the vision of this book, namely community as church, church as community. The experience of death and resurrection in this smaller community of a congregation can be the good news of healing this congregation brings to the neighborhoods around it, to those it both prays for and to whom it reaches out. As we have looked at so many congregations that faced challenges of decline from various demographic changes, we have also seen two features that seem to be present wherever we see revival.

The first is almost self-evident. It is the persistence and strength of a community in the parish. Put another way, it is the will, the desire, to be the body of Christ. The second feature follows on this. It is the trait Mead observed and which Sam Wells has also described, along with others. It is the commitment of the congregation to not merely survive, not just pay the bills, keep the roof, heat, and air-conditioning on, and perhaps balance the budget while trying to compensate the pastor.

The local church of the parish does not live for itself. As the body of Christ, the parish has its own rich life, connected by liturgy, prayer, and fellowship. The parish then works to be part of the larger community, to give back, to reach out, and to serve those in need. The most effective way to show the gospel is by putting it into action. Here we are back to where we began really, to the rich New Testament vision of community—*koinonia*—which is not just people wanting to be together, enjoying each other's company, but praying, talking, and working together. This is what the church is for.

What Is the Church, the Parish, for?

We hear another take on what the parish is for from Sam Wells. He is a priest in the Church of England and at present vicar of the well-known London church, St. Martin-in-the-Fields, on Trafalgar Square. He is a most prolific author who has taught at several universities, as well as Duke Divinity School. In his publications and preaching, Wells is a tireless witness for solidarity rather than philanthropy or altruism.

Examining the prepositions we use and the vision behind them, he stresses "with" over "for" when it comes to our relationship with others— those with whom we share community and most especially those with whom we share time, resources, and assistance. One could argue there is a kind of purist attitude at work here, a dedication to an extreme ethic of identification and solidarity with others rather than a privileged superiority from which service and aid are dispersed. Not so. Wells is decisively in sync with the vision of the New Testament, of the desert mothers and fathers, of the visionaries and leaders of the monastic movement, and with the great prophetic witnesses of our time such as Bonhoeffer, Dorothy Day, Daniel Berrigan, Thomas Merton, and Mother Maria Skobtsova.

Wells has examined aspects of the life and activity of the community of faith seldom if ever thought through. In recent volumes, as well as in earlier ones, he works through many of the possible ways and others with whom we can "be with." He casts his net far and wide, looking at how we are "with" the chronically ill and the dying, the challenged, the hurt, and the troubled; with pregnant mothers and the parents of children; and with the wider creation. The focus is not just on the preposition "with," but all the connections we have and might have and how we relate to these as well as with ourselves and with God.[12]

Wells refuses to be content with the usual view of the church and the ordained existing in order to somehow change or better the conditions of those in need, whether in the household of faith or in the world. We are somehow off if we can think of ourselves as doing "for" others, contributing "to" those in need. The state operates this way, as do the helping professions and philanthropic organizations. But so doing perpetuates our privilege, puts us somehow above others. Most importantly, it rejects our relationship, our community *with* them! And to be clear, Wells will not stop at the boundaries of the parish community. Do our lives stop there? Of course not. So he also asks us to reflect with him further.

In *Incarnational Mission*, Wells's list expands to being with the lapsed, seekers, those of no professed faith, those of other faiths, the hostile, neighbors, organizations, institutions, governments, and the excluded. Methodically, he examines each of these encounters in the following dimensions of being with—presence, attention, mystery, delight, participation, partnership, enjoyment, and glory. In this, Wells tries to cover all the bases of interaction, of connection with another, as well as the place of God in them all. The wealth of his insight in what all these different interactions can be is significant. The different ways of "being with" imply that ministry and mission are actions of the *koinonia*, of the community not just "for" the larger community, but indeed "with" that larger community. By now, it should be clear that at its core, this is what a congregation is, not just the local branch of a larger organization or merely a club of like-minded or possibly family-related individuals, but the body of Christ in the world, an extension of the bread of life and the cup of salvation.

If you think back to the various congregations presented in earlier chapters, one thing sticks out. Those that somehow reinvented, renewed, repurposed, and replanted themselves experienced new life as they were reaching out to share beyond themselves. As with Christ, death led to

12. Wells, *Incarnational Ministry*; Wells, *Incarnational Mission*; Wells, *Nazareth Manifesto*; Wells, *Future That's Bigger Than the Past*; Wells, *Face to Face*.

resurrection. So too for Christ's disciples and friends. These congregations bear out what Loren Mead claimed. They rediscovered and recommitted themselves to living for others. Every one of them in some fashion established new connections with the neighborhood, with the people around who were not members. And at the same time they saw again what held them together, what made them communities. Buildings that in the past were closed all week and open just on Sunday became places of healing, feeding, play, learning, and more, from Oakland, California to Haw Creek, North Carolina, from Englewood Church in Indianapolis to Redeemer in North Minneapolis, Grace Church in the Berkshires to the Church of the Advocate, and so many others.

In most instances, it is not the case that the congregation as a whole is able to launch into initiatives with the larger community. In many congregations, as we saw, the wider community's not-for-profit groups are invited to use the congregation's educational space and fellowship halls and offices during the week for a range of services. In some cases, such as St. Mary of Egypt Orthodox Church in Kansas City, what was once a ministry of the parish in time developed into a related but independent service organization. This was the situation of Reconciliation Ministries and Thelma's Kitchen, also of Englewood Community Development Corporation. At St. Martin-in-the-Fields, Sam Wells's parish in London, there is a new program, HeartEdge, that embodies many of the features of the resurrected parishes we have described through this book.[13]

In all congregations, however, the essential task of community, of life together, is the equipping of members to be the body of Christ in their own homes, businesses, schools, and neighborhoods. This could also be described as what the New Testament, more precisely, the Acts of the Apostles and the apostolic letters, tells us about the life of the earliest church communities. This fundamental vision of community as church and church as community has not changed, though virtually everything surrounding it—from the location, building, organization, and connection to other communities and the world around—have changed, and dramatically. Were one to think, romantically or more innovatively, that the house churches Dave Barnhart talks of or St. Lydia's Dinner Church are twenty-first-century throwbacks to the first century CE, one could not be further from the truth. The size and even the location may be similar. However, just about everyone and everything else, of course, are different.

So the gathering around the breaking of bread, the prayers, the sharing of resources and one's lives and the serving of others—all these are

13. Wells, "At the Heart, on the Edge."

the core of church, what *koinonia* means. This heart of the church has not been in question or doubt throughout this book. But what is happening to church has been our focus.

Throughout, we have looked at what has been happening to congregations. We have seen how they have changed profoundly by mobility, diversity, by shifts in the economy—where people work, what they do, where they are educated, who they marry, and more. We have gathered these changes by the shorthand of "demographic changes." We have also looked at quite a few examples of parishes that countered their decline and shrinking, even likely demise, with efforts to revive, to reimagine themselves, to find new ways of reaching out to the neighborhood around them, new ways of living the life of faith themselves.

So it is necessary to ask a question so basic that it is easily overlooked. In the opening chapter, I did look at this by examining what are a congregation's defining activities, the actions that gave it identity, meaning, that gave life to the community of its members and their connection to the town or city or area around them. Both Loren Mead and Sam Wells are clear that the parish lives when it lives for others. But what is the community able to give?

The Community's Gift: Abundant Life

Wells has something powerful to say about what church is for, what the community's gift to others is. He considers this in writing about efforts to better put to use the space of the hundreds of churches that stand in every hamlet of the UK where historically every village had a church. These are not buildings preserved by the Church Conservation Trust, but parishes "still open for business," even if part of a multiple parish cluster. Wells hones in on a question that could not be more basic: What is the church here for? What is the church's mission, reason for being, in the twenty-first century?

He goes right to the New Testament for a powerful statement of the church's purpose. "Christians don't have to look far for a mission statement for the church: 'I came that they may have life, and have it abundantly' (John 10:10)." Wells continues:

> Jesus is our model of abundant life; his life, death and resurrection chart the transformation from the scarcity of sin and death to the abundance of healing and resurrection; he longs to bring all humankind into reconciled and flourishing relationship with God, one another, themselves, and all creation.
>
> Discipleship describes inhabiting that abundant life. Ministry involves building up the Church to embody that abundant

life. Mission names the ways that abundant life is practised, shared, and discovered in the world at large.[14]

A Brief Detour on Reward and Punishment

It is hard to argue with this, that church is for life and in abundance, rather than keeping people out of hell, where they'd otherwise go. What else could church be for, given the way of Jesus, death, and resurrection? But what is Wells's point? For a moment, let us reflect on profound change in religious faith, one that may not seem connected to parish decline and equally, a lot of examples of congregations coming to life again. However, it is very basic, a matter of who God is and what our relationship to God entails.

It was not that long ago that church, and for that matter, most of Christian faith and practice, was all about not going to hell and about salvation, which was the opposite of hell. I can remember, and vividly too, the emotional weight of hell and eternal punishment. Heaven as a goal or a reward was always much more vague. Anyone who had years of religious instruction, Protestant, Catholic, or Orthodox, over fifty years ago would have had a similar experience. It was truly ecumenical, though not by intent. And even recently I have heard in sermons the echo of that perspective when keeping fasting rules, attending services, and contributing to the support of the church are spoken of as if they were an insurance policy for salvation, particularly gracious because this plan was provided by God. Surely, the church as a ticket for heaven and insurance policy for avoiding hell is still around and at work.

Despite his consistent message, Pope Francis's opponents attack his consistent appeal to God's mercy, his willingness to entertain the possibility of not doctrine but church discipline being modified in the name of mercy. It is not only the alleged unchangeable character of doctrine and discipline that is being maintained and celebrated. There can be no deviating from these. To round it out, certain and painful punishment cannot be left out or put to the side. It is no sarcasm to observe that hell and eternal damnation are alive and well among many Christians today.

Wells appeals to the arguments raised by Sergius Bulgakov in our time and by Gregory of Nyssa and Origen of Alexandria, among others, centuries ago. David Bentley Hart is now the major voice about the resurrection and salvation of all, but the matter continues to receive attention.[15] Is such

---

14. Wells, "It's About Abundant Life, Not Hell-avoidance."

15. Bulgakov, *Apocatastasis and Transfiguration* (originally an appendix in Bulgakov, *Bride of the Lamb*); Balthasar, *Dare We Hope That "All Men May Be Saved?"*

certain and eternal punishment reconcilable with God's mercy, with the triumph of Christ's resurrection, with the original and timeless plan of God for all God's children?

This is neither the place nor is there space to embark on an extensive narrative of how salvation and damnation have developed in the church. I am constantly reminded by the, again, ecumenical, indeed, universal presence of images of "Doomsday" or the last judgment in medieval churches East and West. Sometimes placed over the doors entering the nave, sometimes on the back wall to be viewed as one leaves, and also above the rood screen or chancel arch, the again almost-universal image with Christ the Judge in glory, the Virgin, the Baptist, and the ranks of prophets, apostles, martyrs, confessors, and others interceding, and then the paired scenes of the blessed being invited and accompanied to heaven by angels, with the damned being hauled off kicking and screaming by devils, sometimes dragged into the voracious mouth of a monster.

It is hard to say when this salvation-damnation rationale for church started to weaken or when it was replaced by vision of God's mercy, forgiveness, love, and the ultimate and eternal victory. The debate, often a battle about the resurrection, the saving of all souls (*apokatastasis*), has never really halted.[16]

For our purposes here, it is enough to say that certainly with the Vatican II renewal, and with the "back to the sources" and other theological work before and leading to it, there was a movement away from church as keeping people from hell to a more immanent, present, and positive invitation to life with God, and to the transformation this brings. Wells again:

> God is no longer an instrument for conveying us upstairs rather than downstairs. God is not fundamentally a means to the end of securing our eternal survival and bliss. God is an end: "If I love thee for thyself alone, then give me thyself alone."
>
> The central purpose of the Church is no longer to reconcile people to God, so that their eternal salvation will no longer be in jeopardy: it is to invite people to enjoy God just as God enjoys them. God embraces them for their own sake, not for some ulterior purpose: evangelism means inviting people to embrace God likewise.[17]

While the view that we are surrounded by and in peril from "the world, the flesh, and the devil" has by no means disappeared, another and surely

---

16. McClymond, *Devil's Redemption*; also see Daley, *Hope of the Early Church*; Ross, "Severity of Universal Salvation."

17. Wells, "It's About Abundant Life, Not Hell-avoidance."

equally scriptural view has come to take its place. One might argue that after all, the last judgment dominates the latter part of the Gospel of Matthew, but as David Bentley Hart has noted, coming out of his new translation of the New Testament, even the word that expresses "eternal" in many translations (*aiónion* of Matt 25:41, 46) does not have to be limited to "eternal," but could connote an age or period or dispensation of a long but not limitless duration. Hart reminds us that Jesus did not teach in Greek but in Aramaic, and that the Hebrew word *olam* and the Aramaic *alma*,

> both of which most literally mean something at an immense dis-
> tance, on the far horizon, hidden from view, and which are usu-
> ally used to mean "age," or "period of long duration," or a time
> hidden in the depths of the far past or far future, or a "world" or
> "dispensation," or even "eternity," and so on; but it can also mean
> simply an extended period, and not necessarily a particularly
> long one, with a natural term . . . It is almost certainly the case,
> that in the New Testament, and especially in the teachings of
> Jesus, the adjective *aiōnios* is the equivalent of something like
> the phrase *le-olam*, but also the case that it cannot be neatly
> discriminated from the language of the *olam ha-ba* ["the age to
> come"] without losing something of the theological depth and
> religious significance it possessed in the time of Christ.[18]

Following the lead of church fathers and more recent theologians, Hart pries open this most consequential scene of eternal salvation and damnation in the New Testament. There he finds, as did the others, something less than absolute eternal condemnation, something Christian thinkers old and new have thought it possible to ponder, pray about, and hope for—the salvation of all. There are many alternatively merciful, generous images of God in the Scriptures—the forgiving Father in the parable of the prodigal son, of the sheep herder who goes after the missing lone sheep while the other ninety-nine are safe, the woman kneading the dough and then baking an extraordinary large number of loaves to feed not just her household but the entire village—the examples could go on, so many that the fourteenth-century Byzantine writer Nicholas Cabasilas and theologian Paul Evdokimov speak of the "absurd" or "crazy" love God has for us (*eros manikos, l'amour fou*).[19]

If God is seen more as the merciful Lord, the Loving Creator, then the world becomes less dangerous and threatening, less lost in evil, and likewise each human being is, at the very least, simultaneously sinner and redeemed (*simul justus et peccator*). As Paul Evdokimov claims, echoed

---

18. Hart, *New Testament*, 541–43. Also see Hart, *That All Shall Be Saved*, 119–27.

19. Cabasilas, *Life in Christ*; Evdokimov, *In the World, of the Church*.

more recently by Pope Francis, the church is more a place of healing or therapy, a "field hospital" than a court of judgment and condemnation. The church is there to give abundant life to all the world. And the world is the place of the Spirit just as, from the earliest times, the church is the Spirit's dwelling. Irenaeus of Lyon in the third century said where the church is, there was also the Spirit and all grace (*ubi spiritus ibi ecclesia et omnis gratia*) and the spirit of truth (*spiritus autem veritas*).[20]

Wells believes that one of the reasons for the distancing of so many well-educated, socially conscious, and ethical people from the church is a sense that the church remains something like a repository or bank of religious knowledge and practices that few nowadays were raised in or understand or want. These practices and the religious teachings remain, at least in the church's mind, necessary as spiritual capital for life now and beyond the grave. The church could be said to have the antidote to misery, some kind of spiritual "fix," otherwise unavailable. The truth is, increasing numbers of people have no need for this, no interest in supernatural, other-worldly realities or solutions.

Wells points to the earliest days of the disciples of Jesus as offering the rest of their first-century world something other mystery religions and the official state cults did not. We cannot decipher this anymore, the radical, revolutionary community and spirit the early churches possessed. The later institutionalization of the community, as Afanasiev describes, its transition to being a formal organization, based on law, with a clerical elite, these developments so hardened over the centuries in both East and West, despite the monastic alternative and even after the Reformation and the earlier reform efforts of the friars—Carmelites, Dominicans, Franciscans, Augustinians, and other small communities—Beguines, the Brethren of the Common Life, the *Devotio Moderna,* and many other movements, all the way down to the "reforming" councils, that of Moscow 1917–18 and Vatican II.

Back to the Center of Everyday Life: Where Church Should Be and Should Be Going

With years of very practical urban pastoral experience in addition to teaching and writing, Wells makes a proposal much in keeping with many of the pragmatic efforts of the parishes we have surveyed in earlier chapters. He argues that the church must return to the center of town/village/city life, that is to the heart rather than the periphery of the social life of

20. Irenaeus, *Against Heresies* III.24.1.

our time. This is also a very savvy moving away from the church's special-ization, often evident whenever the media deals with the church or inter-views church leaders. Church has a monopoly on the sacred, the mystical, both the "religious" and "spiritual" dimensions of life. Clergy are called, as Alexander Schmemann once put it to me, "to say something religious" in the face of a disaster or catastrophic loss of life, though in my view, law enforcement and terrorism experts, as well as scientists or medical profes-sionals, are way ahead of them these days.

Sam Wells thinks that social entrepreneurship, once a major role of the church, is a role to which the church should return. Once the principal patron of architects and builders and artists of all sorts—musicians, writers, painters, carvers, sculptors, and actors, the church was also most often the very location where the arts were exhibited and works of music and drama performed. This has long been recognized and put into practice with one of the Church of England's great legacies, its cathedrals.

He has in mind the hundreds of village parish churches all over the UK, more than half in rural areas, many no longer used for services due to redundancy, remote location, or deterioration—though hundreds are preserved as historical sites under the Church Conservation Trust. The Church of England legally controls the destiny of these buildings, but the many other non-Anglican ones there mirror the hundreds from every imaginable denomination all across the US that no longer function as they had for decades.

So, as previously noted, in parishes like St. Peter, Peterchurch in the Hereford diocese, at St. James, West Hampstead in London, among other locations, the church has been refitted so that it is used on a daily basis. Peterchurch controlled the dampness and need for better illumination and now houses a community nursery school, local craftspeople, and a café. West Hampstead is very much the same. St. Peter's operated a daycare cen-ter, but now calling itself the Hub at St. Peter's, there is a variety of activities hosted there. There are art exhibitions, community meals, dances, classes in yoga, pilates, and there is a café and library and children's play area. This historic sacred space has once again become a many-dimensioned community space, very much at the center of life in its town, exactly what Sam Wells suggested has been and can still be the place for a local church building and community.

In addition to "festival" churches used for feasts in warmer months, and the rites of passage, there are, as previously mentioned, "resource cen-ters," parish buildings that serve as the main locations for educational and outreach projects for clusters of smaller parishes, these all sharing a team or a single pastor. As promising as "resource churches" sounds, Madeline

Davies has looked more closely at some of the costs and side effects of concentrating funding, personnel, and efforts on them.[21] Like minster churches of the past, resource churches were envisioned as vitalizing agents, sources for renewal of mission starts, planting of new communities, recruiting ordinands and lay leaders, able to provide both personnel and materials for the surrounding area. Evidence that they are doing just this is positive. However, resource churches now take up significant funding from the national church's Strategic Development Fund (SDF).

Almost half the overall SDF grant will be used to train ten "planting curates," all trained at Holy Trinity Brompton, where the Alpha course originated. These curates will then develop new communities in fifteen urban locations, with optimistic targets of growing congregations to add 30,000 new church members by 2025, among other goals. Closer inspection and listening to neighboring parishes and their clergy suggests that the movement toward revamping most everything in church practice does attract some who had never been to church, others who had drifted, and still others who found the new, nontraditional style—usually with "praise band" music, vigorous evangelical preaching, and little if any elements of the liturgical past—was not the only way to go forward. In a few cases, when a building was provided for renovation, reordering, and use in the planting model, older parishioners found they were in effect left behind or cut out. Their Sunday eucharist was either shifted to a very early spoken service or done away with completely as a relic of the past.

Here in the US, the desire to break completely with most of what looked like religious practice of the past is commonplace. "Church growth" and "entertainment church" strategies in all the mainline denominations dispensed with altars, crosses, and vestments in favor of large screens, empty stages, and praise bands for rollicking contemporary music. There is an imperialism of a particular evangelical mode of worship, décor, piety, and behavior. As contemporary as it appears to be, this project remains in family with the procession of pietist response to modernity from the eighteenth century onward. It too, in time, will become dated and much more so than the more traditional style.

Writing about contemporary resource churches, Canon Alan Bing notes a trend toward taking the evangelical model as employed by Gumbel and the Holy Trinity Brompton program as the only effective model for church renewal. This needs to be challenged, just as Willow Creek, Calvary Chapel, Joel Osteen, Camelback, and like ventures. Twenty-five years ago, Randall Balmer, a priest and American church historian, did precisely this in what is now a

21. Davies, "Mission—But at What Cost?"

classic study on evangelicalism.[22] Other approaches should not be discarded, especially given the diversity now typical of our populations. Parishes are not only havens for aging Boomers. Yesterday's and parishes of the future will neither be those in their 20s nor 30s indefinitely.

This deeper look at resource churches and the performance of their clergy is not merely a conservative reaction on Davies's part. As noted earlier here, there has been a tendency to "canonize" one or another model of church renewal, and the evangelical one has dominated both in the US and the UK. The idea that anything looking like the church of the past hinders renewal, drives religious Nones and Dones away, is a bit of cultural myopia. It is also culturally reductionistic and often ahistorical. Remembering the praise bands and their contemporary music of thirty years ago, I know those styles have changed. Likewise, is it helpful to rule out other expressions of church life at the local level, from the more sacramental to ethnically specific?

As for churches seen as highly successful in attracting members in an otherwise declining market, how much do we know about their long-term performance? We seldom have "exit data" from new megachurch or non-denominational or pop-up church starts. We know that many have limited lifespans, sometimes due to problematic leadership, but also to the wants and needs of those joining them. Those who were attracted to evangelical styles in their 30s may not be interested in their 40s, or more basically, may not be around to continue with the same congregation, what with work and others things leading to their relocating. Tina Hodgett, a priest of the diocese of Bath and Wells and former secondary school teacher and administrator, raises the significance of long-term outcomes. The gospel should not be reducible to how many members and how much revenue can be expected in five or ten or more years.

Perceptive students of ministry and parish in our time, such as Andrew Root and Sam Wells, choose not to get hung up on the details of how services are celebrated, the church layout, and musical genres. For Wells, a lively yet traditional liturgical and pastoral approach, such as at St. Martin-in-the-Fields, works. For him, the more deliberate use of the historic and other parish buildings is part of the ministry and mission—incarnational, to be sure—of a parish.

There are other ways in which community members can be engaged in local outreach, and in previous chapters we saw many examples—visiting shut-ins, offering space for food and clothing pantries, also space for clinics, for after-school and tutoring programs for kids, and so on. One parish cannot do everything. Rather, parishes can aim at whatever a particular urban

22. Ballmer, *Mine Eyes Have Seen the Glory.*

area or town may need, and seek to help with or provide whatever programs are available. In some cases, rental of space can be an important source of income. But seen as a whole, the better use of buildings is but a very practical translation of his insistence that every community of the faith, the church itself, is there not just for moral formation, for worship, and education, even for outreach, but for abundant life, for the life of the world:

> What I'm describing is transforming church buildings—under-used, seen as moribund, and a drain on resources (in other words, a metaphor for the whole Church)—into dynamic centres of abundant life, receiving, evidencing, dwelling in, and sharing forms of social flourishing, and being a blessing to, their neighbourhood. I'm not talking about a revolution, but I suspect that I am talking about a reformation. And, at root, I'm describing what happens when we cease to use God as a device for acquiring the ultimate goods that we can't secure for ourselves, and start to adore and imitate the God who in Jesus models, offers, and advances abundant life, now and for evermore.[23]

It is of course not just about church buildings, no matter how beautiful, historic, and precious they are as part of a country's or a church body's heritage. Especially when a congregation shrinks or ceases to be, it becomes clear that the building in the end is a home for the people of God in that place and their work. We have learned here much about how in reviving themselves, even reinventing their identities and missions, parishes can use their buildings in ways previous generations could not have imagined. It is not just the decades of children attending church school but the many youngsters who could continue to benefit from those spaces for daycare, for tutoring, for after-school care, for clinics providing check-ups and immunizations, as well as care for pregnant mothers-to-be. We have seen so many examples of buildings becoming space for new businesses to start up, as affordable housing, as places where all kinds of community organizations can meet.

Sam Wells and the examples from the UK, along with those from the US we have looked at here, remind us that when parish churches return to the center of social life where they are located, they are not heading off and away from their spiritual mission. Rather, they are returning to the examples of Basil the Great's multipurpose service center in Cappadocia, to the example of countless cathedrals and monastic communities which were the first schools and hospitals and soup kitchens of their time. Perhaps this is one of the real blessings of the current picture of shrinkage, decline, and closure. To revive a parish and resurrect the community of faith seems to

23. Wells, "It's About Abundant Life, Not Hell-avoidance."

almost always include returning it to concern for the town or city around it, not to mention connections with other communities of faith.

What Is the Parish, Church, for? Community and Church, Going Forward

All throughout the book, we have looked at community and church. The claim has been that, at heart, church is community. And it has been argued that community does not mean just the delight in being together with others in a way unlike most of our other usual associations and connections in everyday life. This community is not like the one based on membership in a political party, country club, hobby group, or even a sports team or artists' studio. All these and the numerous other groups to which people belong brings individuals together over a common interest or point of view.

The experience of Israel, the people of God chronicled in the Hebrew Bible, as well as that of the followers of Jesus described in the New Testament, make it clear that the life of persons of faith is communal. Religion is not just an individual phenomenon, a private affiliation or preference. God's word is addressed to the people, a community. Worship and its ritual details are a communal undertaking. The commandments are social in nature, concerning virtually every aspect of human life, from the body and possessions of others to domestic animals, fields, houses, food, and sex. Everything has to do with God, and vice versa. All of the prayer texts we have, the most ancient of both these traditions, are in the plural. God deliberately communicates with a community. Throughout I have emphasized "community," because for some "religion" and "church" are seen as an individual reality, a private experience, a personal thing. Most everything we hear, say, and do in church or any other place of worship is communal—we are always part of a whole. But of course, the community has to be made up of individual women and men, each with her or his own life and experiences, gifts, and defects. Far be it from me to downplay the intense personal experience each member of a community has, each experience of God, of sacred texts, rites, music, also of the others in that assembly, as well as of oneself. There is no contradiction between the individual and the communal—both are aspects, dimensions of the same reality, in this case, a personal as well as shared life of faith.

So as we have seen, it is communities of faith that are changing, shrinking, even dying as corporate entities. When I submitted a short piece for a church publication that summarized both the shrinkage and rebirth of parishes, one negative comment was that the review of all the demographic and other changes contributing to decline was an exercise in pessimism and despair. Some of this was presented earlier in *The Church Has Left the Building* and in the first few chapters here. As we have seen, the data are challenging. The number of those who are Nones and Dones is growing, as is the number of congregations closing. The very first response must be to confront what is real in the churches, not just what one hopes for or imagines.

I have seen that in actual parish memberships there are often diverse reactions to change, particularly downturns in membership numbers and the congregation's finances. Some prefer to remain in denial, opting to ignore or downplay the changes occurring. Others find excuses such as difficulties with a pastor, changes in the services, positions on political and social issues that are deemed either too liberal or too conservative, and even the choice of hymns sung. The remnant of a once-healthy congregation may take the efforts of their larger church body as a rejection or discrimination against them as failures, aging ones at that. The Cottage Grove Methodist Church case has some of these elements and feelings. Of course, there is the stance that sees the world outside the church as to blame for decline. It is all the result of a lack of faith, or worse, evil at work. It is not possible to seek to better understand community without recognizing the toxic, destructive side. Sergius Bulgakov and Solzhenitsyn were only two of many who noted that the line between evil and good runs down through the center of each of us.[24]

Despite the range of such reactions and their depth of feeling, the data on the membership of church bodies, and that for individual parishes, cannot be wished or explained away. Even the few success stories, often of megachurches with charismatic preachers, does not work. The cases of once-effective megachurch pastors being dismissed and larger bodies experiencing decline are there to see. The recent history of Bill Hybels and Willow Creek was the most notable story of rise and fall for one of the highest-profile megachurch enterprises in the last twenty-five years or more. Many more failures, if one can rightly use that term with respect to the parish as the body of Christ, are invisible. Yet congregations have a life span. We see closed church buildings for sale. Some disappear, giving way to residential units. Some reopen as new congregational plantings.

But as we also have seen, confronting the realities of change and their consequences for congregations is but half the story. There are so many specific cases of parishes finding ways of sustaining their existence and work, so many examples of resurrection through reinvention, replanting, or repurposing of congregations. Even the sampling here is a partial presentation, but it

24. Solzhenitsyn, *Gulag Archipelago*, 168.

makes clear that such is never the work of one person, no matter how charismatic she or he may be. Not surprisingly, communities with new life gather for worship, prayer, study, and service. They want to be with each other and be of service to the people around. All of the fascinating efforts of renewed or reinvented parishes reviewed here are communities that live not just for themselves but for others outside their boundaries.

When the national administration of a church body has supportive programs, as well as consultants for parishes that are challenged and struggling, these agencies often are effective. We have seen this with the UMC Church Legacy Initiative and like programs. When the local congregation and its members assess their situation, and then decide to act, whether that means closing, merging with another nearby congregation, or undertaking some of the truly fascinating activities, one sees communities in action. It is the church being community and community expressing what church is about. There really is a seemingly endless number of possible directions, and we have seen quite a few here. Closing and selling a venerable building or buildings as in the Berkshires with St. James, Great Barrington, and St. George Lee parishes, did not mean the end of the community of faith in western Massachusetts. The parish that emerged from their closing, Grace Church, was a sign of Christians wanting to continue centuries of faith and presence, as well as continued service to all the communities there in the Berkshires.

By way of concluding, I want to come back to the question of what the parish will look like in the future, and I mean not the distant but proximate future. The model, or better, models, of parish we have had for the past thousand years remain for some the unchangeable pattern. But of course, this is a delusion, as even the most traditional congregation of today is different in so many ways from that of fifty or 100 years ago. While there is no question of a single model going forward, there are some features that we have already seen are essential. These do not, taken as a whole, constitute a formula or recipe. They are simply what makes a parish hang together, make it work.[25]

Going Forward: Again Pastors and
Community as Church

While we have touched on the situation of the clergy in looking at parishes, clearly this is an issue worthy of a volume in itself. Yet something more must

25. Feuerherd, "Road to the True Vatican II Parish Is Downward Mobility."

be said even at the end of this book. Who the pastor is, what the pastor does, how we understand and relate to a pastor, as well as how pastors are trained and how they relate to other levels of the institutional church—these are basic questions, essential as the ordained are to the life of congregations.

Pastors teach, baptize, break the bread, and offer the cup. They preside at marriages, bury the dead, and counsel the troubled. They provide leadership but also belong to the community with their families. They have to be able to support themselves and their families, need a place to live and other basic things. So, part of the matter here is the identity of the ordained and then the relationship of the community to them. Throughout our looking at parishes today, we have in fact been looking at how different the vocation and work of pastors is, not just in principle but in practice. So to conclude, some attention to the place of the pastor is necessary.

The church, the people of God, is a community. This may seem obvious but it is not always grasped when we think of church as a building, as a chain of command from bishop on down, as rituals and rules. Or as a budget that should ideally be balanced. Within the community are those chosen and ordained for particular service, but these ministers are first and foremost members of the community. Students of the early church like Afanasiev remind us of the communal roots of the church's ministers, one no less than Augustine echoes this: "What I am for you terrifies me; what I am with you consoles me. For you I am a bishop; but with you I am a Christian. The former is a duty; the latter a grace. The former is a danger; the latter, salvation."[26]

Clergy are not above or other than the community, as later theology has claimed. The different orders or levels of clergy and laity have resulted from this thinking and restructuring according to rank. From the start, as with the synagogue before it, the reality of church is that there are many gifts, though the body is one, as St. Paul observed. Earlier, the question arose of how the clergy best relate to the rest of the community. This is a serious question in itself, considering all that we have seen here—in the panorama of demographic changes, of people distancing themselves from communities of faith, of those very communities shrinking through aging, mobility, and so many other factors we have examined.

The situation of pastors in twenty-first century communities of faith is complicated. In some ways, clergy are assigned sole culpability for congregation shrinkage and decline. I surely have experienced such targeting on the part of alarmed members. If only the pastor were a more exciting

---

26. Augustine, *Serm. 340, 1:PL 38, 1483*.

preacher, a warmer personality, could find younger and wealthier people to join, and so on.

The identity and place of the ordained, as said, deserves a study in itself, something I plan to do. Yet, questions about the vocation and life of the ordained raised by Barbara Brown Taylor, Richard Holloway, Barbara Melosh, William Mills, Sam Wells, and others show how pressing a matter it is. The Church of England study, launched by debate at a 2017 General Synod, identified a lack of focus and clarity, and I would add, consensus on what the vocation of a pastor is, also what this calling looks like in action, in everyday life.[27]

That said, there are positive, hopeful signs. A recent study in *The Journal of Prevention & Intervention in the Community* drew on a survey of clergy and their situation—flourishing or hampered by issues of medical and emotional health. The survey found that compared to average Americans (58 percent), 68 percent of clergy reported they were healthy, flourishing. We saw this study earlier, and a co-author, Rae Jean Proeschold-Bell, a professor of global health at Duke, observed that in other studies, clergy were not found to fare so well as in this one, with higher rates of depression, cardiovascular disease, hypertension, obesity.

There are a number of centers focused on clergy health and healing, the Davidson Clergy Center for example. The strategies, or better, tools, clergy can use to flourish are neither new nor surprising. They include proactive measures like a sabbath day each week, self-care, that is time set apart for exercise, reading, prayer, family, interaction with fellow clergy, and meaningful connection in the larger community.[28] Foundational to all such very important measures, though, is a healthy sense of self, identity based not solely on ordination and pastoral success. Also clergy have the tendency to be reactive, to feel as though they are on call 24/7 and constantly responsible for parish members, no matter the circumstances. Such tendencies are, for Episcopal priest and counselor Edward Henley, self-destructive to pastors. As priest and writer William C. Mills describes, in his memoir, there are parishioners whose intent is to damage and destroy their pastor.[29]

In some ways, we have heard partial answers to this question, as well as looked at the situations of a number of congregations. The Church of England, as noted, has been engaged in a long-range study of clergy, some findings of which were noted and discussed earlier. An important one of

27. Becket, "Change Is Worse Than a Rest, Say Stressed Clergy"; Davies, "Clergy Living Comfortably, Long Term Study Suggests"; Davies, "Clergy Burdened by Unrealistic Job Specs, C of E Told."

28. McDonald, "Steps for Flourishing in Ministry."

29. Mills, *Losing My Religion.*

these is that often the external circumstances of parishes, and the church more broadly, put clergy into a situation where their purpose and identity is called into question or so poorly defined that it incurs even more conflict as well as stress and depression for them. While the data on what happens to graduates of theological seminaries in the first years after their ordinations is not as chilling as once believed, the number of theological schools is steadily decreasing as well as those entering them.

There are other more positive findings. The 2017 report of the Church of England study, *Living Ministry,* says that among four cohorts of those ordained in 2006, 2011, and 2015, and ordinands who began training in 2016, there were high levels of well-being and financial security.[30] These students preparing for ordination spoke of good health and contentment in work. Overall, there were 579 ordained clergy and 113 ordinands in formation. A more recent report asked these clergy and ordinands to respond to over thirty items covering most aspects of ministry, as well as individuals' spiritual lives and faith and their feelings about their work in and outside of the parish. The significant majority of respondents (90 percent) had positive reactions to items such as "people experience God's love," "both pastors and people want to grow numerically," and that "both clergy and parishioners feel good pastoral care is being provided."[31]

Data from denominations show a range of persistence in parish ministry, varying from only 1 percent attrition after five years of ordination up to 11 percent. On the other hand, the Association of Theological Schools notes the outright closing of schools as well as the continuing pattern of mergers. The Washington Theological Coalition closed after decades of consolidating theological faculty and students in the DC area. Gettysburg and Philadelphia Lutheran Seminaries are now United Lutheran Theological Seminary. The Jesuit School of Theology at the Berkeley Union merged with Santa Clara University. Columbia South Carolina Lutheran Theological Southern Seminary closed, released many faculty, and relocated to Lenoir-Rhyne University in Hickory, North Carolina. Seabury-Northwestern Episcopal and Bexley Hall merged, now operating as Chicago Theological Seminary. Cambridge Episcopal Divinity School closed and there is a program of study at Union Theological Seminary in New York City. Bangor Theological School in Maine is now an online/distance-learning institution.[32]

30. Davies, "Not Doing Too Badly, Clergy Tell Survey."

31. Davies, "Not Doing Too Badly, Clergy Tell Survey."

32. Wheeler and Ruger, "Sobering Figures Point to Overall Enrollment Decline"; Bonfiglio, "It's Time to Rethink Our Assumptions about Where Theological Education Happens"; Bonfiglio, "Let's Make the Church a Center of Theological Education Again"; "How Many Quit?"

Stepping back from theological schools to the public perception of clergy, a recent AP-NORC survey found that fewer and fewer people would call on clergy for help. The headline of reports on this study ask, "Are clergy irrelevant?"[33] It follows from the distancing of people from all sorts of organizations and institutions, religious ones included, that it will no longer be instinctive to call upon professionals when in need. Those who are "done" with church, or have "none" when it comes to belonging to a congregation of faith, are less likely to reach out to a priest, rabbi, or minister. The specter of sexual abuse by the clergy, the consequent denials and coverups by church administration—this too has cooled people on seeking pastoral care or spiritual guidance from clergy connected to established religious organizations. There are numerous nondenominational, nonsectarian, essentially secular consultants available—life coaches, counselors, therapists.

Rethinking the Place and Ministry of the Ordained

Texas Episcopal bishop C. Andrew Doyle has put forward a provocative vision of the parish and ordained ministers for the future.[34] Doyle's basis for reimagining church is to return church to a missional status rather than the more established, institutionalized form, derived from the temple and state imperial organization, with their codes, laws, hierarchies, and stratified layers of officials and members.

He calls for nonstipendiary clergy, that is, pastors not dependent upon a parish for their income, to become the norm. We saw this earlier that increasing numbers of clergy are doing ministry alongside professions and occupations and not being compensated by a congregation. No longer is the parish actually a "living" for many pastors. In at least two dioceses of a church body I know, the majority of parishes cannot offer a compensation package to a pastor. Nor can these parishes afford to offer benefits such as health insurance, contributions to a pension plan, housing equity, or even housing. Some or all of these used to be standard elements of compensation packages. Now a stipend or honorarium is the most that is possible, thus requiring secular employment by both the pastor and spouse. In one other diocese, an alarming number of clergy families depended on food stamps as well as state programs for children's health insurance and Medicaid coverage for low-income families. Clearly, this is unsustainable.

33. Shimron, "New Poll Shows Growing View That Clergy Are Irrelevant"; Karoub, "AP-NORC Poll."

34. Doyle, *Vocātiō*; Doyle, *Church*.

In addition to wanting clergy freed from financial ties to parishes, Doyle realizes that the most ancient models also argue for compensated pastors (1 Cor 9:9–14; Phil 4:16–19; Acts 10:7; Luke 6:2), as well as those who earned their own living. Paul argues that pastors are worthy of support, while at the same time plying his trade of tentmaking, or craftsmanship in fabric and leather (2 Thess 3:7–10; Acts 18:1–3; 20:33–35). It seems, from much of what we have seen here, that going forward, increasing numbers of congregations will not be able to compensate their pastors except in a partial, symbolic way.

Doyle further calls for a deprofessionalizing of the clergy. This is not a rejection of clergy education and formation but a change in the social category or caste which later political situations and theology created for them. Drawing on Roman and Byzantine imperial models, clergy became a stratum or caste separate from and above the nonordained. Later, the ordained were seen to be ontologically different from the nonordained, ordination giving them a different identity or character that gives them higher status and power in the church, bishops enjoying the highest level of such.

But to be clear, Doyle does not propose elimination of the ministry. Rather, he thinks there are distinct roles for all three ordained offices. Bishops could be area ambassadors or consuls, able to circulate among the parishes in their dioceses, not tied to a particular parish as its pastor. This does not stray very far from the practice of the last thousand years, in which the bishop was in principle the chief pastor in an area, with special bonds toward his colleagues, the presbyters. One can already see the ways some bishops use online communication to be a regular presence for the clergy and people of a diocese, not just a once-a-year visitor to a parish. Some bishops have tried to create a much more collegial relationship with their presbyters, not just one of constant fear of top-down decisions in the future.

In the early centuries, bishops had a particular relationship to deacons who were their direct assistants in administration of the diocese. Today, in practice, across the Anglican, Catholic, Lutheran, Methodist, and Orthodox churches, the diaconate is a stage in the progression toward presbyteral or priestly ordination. However, there has been a rediscovery of the permanent diaconate, especially in the Catholic Church. Such deacons routinely function as parish administrators, that is, as pastors with the exception that they cannot preside at the eucharist or anoint the sick. Otherwise, they baptize, preach, distribute communion, and preside at weddings and funerals. The Anglican/Episcopal, Lutheran, and Orthodox Churches conform to this pattern, with some curtailing of liturgical duties among the Orthodox to preaching and communing.

Presbyters in the ancient church formed a council of advisors to the bishop as well as the elders of local communities. In time, with the disappearance of the assistant bishops (*chorepiskopoi*), presbyters became the pastors of parishes, the bishop remaining the archpastor in principle, hence the local presbyter became the bishop's vicar. Presbyters or priests Doyle sees as connected to parish communities to witness to the gospel and social justice, to lead liturgies, preach, teach, counsel, and perform other pastoral acts. But as the renewed liturgies of most churches attest, both the celebration of the liturgy and the ministry are holy works shared by all according to one's place in the community, training, and gifts.

As is already the case, more and more presbyters would have a "day job" and would no longer depend on the parish for compensation or housing. An important consequence of such changes would be that the pastor would be on a more level footing with the rest of parish members. This would be a check on pastors piling services and classes and meetings on the community in the absence of a regular job. This would also dramatically change the financial obligations of the community.

Deacons are today mostly parish-based. In addition to roles in the liturgy such as leading intercessions, reading, preaching, and assisting in the distribution of communion, there are many other forms of work they can perform, again given their gifts and education as well as local need. Most deacons today have professions and jobs alongside their diaconal service, probably more so than presbyters. As with presbyters, deacons would be coordinating their work with others in and outside the parish, all kinds of outreach, as well as pastoral visiting and education.

Doyle's chief point is that clergy need to be allowed to go beyond the parish structure as we have known it for over a thousand years, since this model of parishes is disappearing, as we have seen. He also wants to see an end to the two-tiered institutional church structure of clergy and laity and the accompanying clerical caste and culture. Clergy who are members of their parish communities and less dependent on them for compensation because of a secular job would facilitate a doing away with historical clericalism.

It also goes without saying, for Doyle, that the model of a parish we have been using since the Middle Ages is disappearing, or is long gone in many places. There is nothing sacred about the arrangements that made sense in a rural, agricultural economy, in a monarchial political system, and under very different life spans and infant mortality rates, not to mention social contexts that were uniform in language, ethnicity, and religion. The diocese of Chelmsford in the Church of England looked hard at the range of practical factors bearing on parishes and clergy. The diocese, after considerable study and discussion, is cutting sixty stipendiary, that is, full-time paid, pastoral posts.[35] This is due to the shrinking financial ability to support priests. Going forward, the diocese hopes to have 215 such posts by 2021, though every one of them will be revaluated over time in view of need and sustainability. This reality of matching communities with pastors, as we have seen in variations throughout the book, has to continue.

All the ordained—bishops, presbyters, and deacons—have ministries particular to both their ordination and their specific local setting. The real changes are twofold. The parish and the church, more broadly speaking, would step away from its established, sometimes monopolistic character and again become a mission, an outpost for witness and work in the world, a home for the people of God that makes sense in the twenty-first rather than the fourth or eleventh or for that matter the nineteenth or early twentieth centuries. We no longer require a gathering place that can be gotten to by horse or wagon or on foot. Each parish is but one of several church bodies, denominations, or franchises in that area. As a number of churches in the US have declared themselves in full communion with each other, it will be sensible not to duplicate efforts and instead to begin to pray and work together. This is already happening in many places among Lutherans, Presbyterians, Episcopalians, and Reformed Church parishes.

The second principal change that Doyle hopes for is that the ordained retake their place among the whole baptized people of God. They would equip and support the mission work of the whole community. John Jillions brilliantly shows Paul's passionate concern for his "building up" the community, the body of Christ.[36] Everything done by the church—prayer, baptism, the eucharist, preaching, and service to the world—was the work of the community, of the whole people of God. This building up was Paul's principal task and it is the task of all who minister, both the ordained and the rest. If more parishes and their pastors would move in these directions, the ones Doyle points to, along with others, it would be a remarkable return to the most ancient models as well as boldly choosing new ones for our time.

Faith, Ministry, and Church in a Secular Age

Andrew Root also has provocative ideas about ministry in the twenty-first century, what he sees as a time when, increasingly, people have little or no need for God. On the faculty of Luther Seminary in St. Paul, Minnesota, Root is producing some intriguing work on faith, the pastor, and ministry

35. Williams, "Chelmsford Set to Cut 60 Stipendiary Posts."
36. Jillions, *Divine Guidance.*

in a secular age.[37] He is in the process of completing a trilogy on the matter. A constant conversation partner and, what is more, a foundation for these volumes, is Charles Taylor's magisterial work.[38]

Root aims to reflect, as his book's subtitle puts it, on "ministry to people who no longer need a God." His first volume looks at the severe challenge that the secular age—in Taylor's vision—presents to forming and living in faith. Root goes to Paul's conversion for an image of ministry, a complete transformation and dedication to a self-emptying ministry, in the likeness of the self-emptying Christ (*kenosis*). It is an echo of the Finnish Lutheran theologians' rereading of Luther in the light of what they learned from Eastern Orthodox theology and spirituality.[39] This is a perspective found in both Western and Eastern church teachers, based on union with and entering into God (*theosis* or deification). No strategies, no market-driven techniques, so often employed in faith formation and parish life, can come near to the power of encounter with the risen Lord. Paul has no choice but to model the Christ who sought him out on the Damascus road, and then ministered to his blindness and bewilderment. And not only Paul, as the apostle makes clear, there is a like pattern for each disciple, for everyone who hears Christ.

Root's look at ministry first takes us on a journey through church history. He selects some notable figures in what he calls a historical map of ministry leading up to our secular age. The pastors he selects are not presented, he admits, as exemplars of ministry. They are not necessarily the only or the best ones to model the pastoral office. The selected are Augustine, Thomas Becket, Jonathan Edwards, Henry Ward Beecher, Harry Emerson Fosdick, and Rick Warren. Root feels they embody what is distinctive in the periods in which they lived. These pastors grappled with monumental issues and events—from the ancient and medieval enchantment of the world—with devils and angels lurking everywhere. Then on to the disenchantment, the discovery of the self, and the severing of connections between faith and ordinary life. So many things packed here—the rise of nation-states, colonial expansion, revolutions for self-determination, not to mention towering issues such as civil war, slavery, industrialization, massive immigration, world war, economic depression, cultural revolution, and the hunt for authenticity. These give a sense of the sweep of history Root pursues. And to come to our own time, the loss of faith in anything beyond the empirical and experiential.

37. Root, *Faith Formation in a Secular Age*; Root, *Pastor in a Secular Age*.

38. Taylor, *Secular Age*.

39. Braaten and Jenson, *Union with Christ*.

Root employs Foucault's lectures on pastoral power in Paris in 1978 as a bridge to the second half of this volume, in which he takes us back to fundamental biblical images of God, drawing also on Robert Jenson.[40] Root is convinced that we must again see ministry as the replicating of God's own actions, not merely professional performance in a congregation of a church body by one educated and ordained to that service. Thus the God of Exodus and Resurrection is the model of ministry. In this return to the core of faith, we are no longer seeking to retain cultural, political, and social expressions of faith from historical periods now past and gone. Nor are we ignoring or trying to overcome the time and perspectives in which we live in the twenty-first century. Here, I believe, is Root's distinctive contribution. His approach is savvy to the disenchantment of mystery and the spiritual, also to the indifference as well as suspicion of religious Nones, Dones, and all those at a distance from faith and communities of faith. Where to turn?

The pastoral careers of the figures he tracks depict how previous eras confronted the tradition of faith and change. In our time, though, their encounters and their strategies cannot be simply borrowed. Nor can they be manipulated to fit the political and social conflict in which we exist. It will not do to try to become Augustine, or for that matter Becket or Edwards or any other of Root's pastors, or for that matter, other notables he does not include like John Chrysostom, Luther, or Calvin. Their efforts in ministry cannot simply be repeated in our twenty-first century's blend of sheer ignorance and sophistication.

Root takes us back to the realism of the Hebrew Bible and New Testament. Despite the distance of millennia, Root is quite right about the unremittingly concrete experience of God amid murder, all sorts of personal and political mayhem, totally corrupt and wicked rulers, warring factions within communities of faith, and the enduring hardness of the human heart. There is so much of this we seldom hear in the Scriptures.

Root invites us to dwell on the many names and images of God these writings present to us—shepherd, lover, hunter, farmer, nurturing mother, forgiving father, to mention just a few. He chooses to redirect us to God as "minister," a bit jarring at first, when we connect the divine servant and sheepherder with the all-too-human ministers/pastors/priests we know. But in the end this is a discerning theological choice on his part, echoed, to be sure, by exegetes and well supported by the texts themselves.

The other part of this equation, namely, how God as minister in turn shapes the women and men who minister, both as laity and ordained, is more challenging. Now and again, my own experience in pastoral ministry

40. Jenson, *Systematic Theology.*

made me pause and question some of his examples. Good clinical pastoral practice does demand many times simply presence, listening, silence, not the word of preaching or reading the Scriptures, the presentation of holy communion or the imposition of anointing, not to mention confession and counsel. Yet these incarnational, interactional sacramental actions, while perhaps more difficult for some to access today, remain nonetheless powerful gestures in which bread and wine and oil, touch, and words bridge between the human and the divine. These are indeed the divine actions which Root rightly says are still powerful even in a secular time, when our "immanent frame" permits no outside intervention.

Lastly, where is the church, the people of God, for Root? Thankfully, he wastes little time on the institutional apparatus. For him, it is wonderfully clear. The people of God are the household of faith because they are the household of ministry. This is in splendid symmetry with the rest of Root's vision. The household of ministry is where Christ's ministry is experienced in word, sacrament, fellowship, care, study, and then the members of this household, ordained in their baptism, become ministers to the neighborhood and the larger world around them—exactly what we have seen all through this book. Because the community has received the ministry of Jesus, the community is one of gratitude, of giving, and of rest, rest meaning not an absence of action but its goal—the justice and peace of God's kingdom. Community is church. Church is community.

Ministry as Delight

Jason Byassee, himself a UMC pastor and a seminary faculty member, is another insightful observer of pastors and parishes. We listened to his assessment of two parishes in Winnipeg earlier. With Duke University faculty member and clinical psychologist Rae Jean Preschold-Bell, he produced a study of clergy based on the biennial survey of UMC clergy in North Carolina in the Duke Clergy Health Initiative between 2016 and 2018. Their study is entitled *Faithful and Fractured*, and this reflects what the data reveal. While almost 83 percent of clergy surveyed express great delight and fulfillment in their ministry, they also suffer from obesity (41.4 percent), and older clergy are victims of diabetes, joint disease, and heart ailments, as well as depression. Other studies of clergy health reveal like patterns. However, what Preschold-Bell and Byassee emphasize in their assessment of the findings is that delight in their callings, a sense of satisfaction and fulfillment, while not preventative, is nevertheless crucial for pastors. It is not however, a guarantee of success, however one measures this. Some definitions are quite dysfunctional and destructive for pastors, like 24/7 availability, the sense they are never doing enough, or never done with any aspect of pastoral service. These are impossible demands, both by pastors themselves as well as their parish councils, members of their congregations, and regional leaders. The earlier-referred-to study by the Church of England recognized precisely this dangerous collection of impossible demands.

Delight, that is, true joy in their vocations and in their work experienced as pastors—this is a sign of health, no matter the challenges and problematic conditions that may also exist in ministry. Preschold-Bell and Byassee urge bishops and other church leaders to recognize not just how well pastors may be doing but also the real afflictions many of them experience.[41]

Recently, Byassee used a visit to Austin to highlight three pastors who, despite all the challenges we have viewed here, are doing well in their ministries.[42] Taylor Fuerst was appointed to be the pastor of a large downtown congregation, First United Methodist, close to the Texas state capitol, other government buildings, banks, and office buildings. It is a parish that has long had leading members of Austin society, business, and government among its members. But despite this solid legacy and place, First UMC became notable in declaring a moratorium on weddings until LGBTQ people could also marry there. Fuerst is under forty, a gifted preacher, and Vanderbilt trained. First UMC already was a socially engaged congregation, with its own food truck for those in need, breakfast for the homeless on site, among other outreach efforts. LGBTQ people are welcome there.

At another parish, Bee Creek UMC, Byassee found Laura Heikes as pastor. The congregation was heavily indebted when she was appointed, this the result of a costly building campaign. Not only has that debt been erased, but an entirely new recreational center has been constructed since her beginning to lead the congregation. Attendance is high, spirits as well, and Byassee attributes this to Heikes's gifts both as a preacher and leader, and to the community's rededication to their life together and outreach to the people around them. At First United Methodist Church, Taylor Fuerst was open in supporting LGBTQ people, this in the face of the recent United Methodist General Conference passage of a traditional plan for ministry and discipline, one not recognizing but rejecting LGBTQ clergy and members' need for a place in the church. She voiced opposition to this plan and argued that there must be and will be a place for equality in the church. In a very conservative community and congregation, Laura Heikes has been much less vocal, almost

41. Preschold-Bell and Byassee, *Faithful and Fractured*; Joyner, "What You Need to Know to Care for Your Clergyperson (Even If That's You)."

42. Byassee, "Three United Methodist Pastors and Their Delight in Ministry."

silent on all of this. But behind the scenes, LGBTQ people are accepted in the parish and the head of the parish council at Bee Creek noted that if one group is excluded, the whole body is weakened. In neither parish, First UMC or Bee Creek UMC, were there any unusual tactics employed, no attempt to turn back the clock nor to throw out what was traditional. There was innovation, but the core seems to be the cooperation of members of a community with a pastor flourishing in their work, all "delighting" in service.

Finally, Byassee visited Austin New Church, a recent parish plant, with Jason Morriss as pastor. The congregation was originally established by Brandon and Jen Hatmaker, well-known evangelical writers and speakers, thus a parish outside the United Methodist Church, in a separate Methodist denomination. Morriss was trained as a missionary at Chicago's Northern Seminary and first worked at a Joel Osteen plant, Lakewood Church in Houston. It was controversy that led to Austin New Church's transition from the Free Methodists to the UMC. The controversy was the Hatmakers's turn away from standard evangelical positions on LGBTQ to an inclusive, welcoming stance. Members left the parish and the Free Methodist denomination cut them off. But Jen Hatmaker's high profile as a writer drew many who were unable to continue in what they felt were homophobic evangelical settings. Bishop Robert Schnase of the Rio Texas UMC Conference gave them the buildings of Faith United Methodist, a congregation in decline. It also happened to be in the part of South Austin becoming a location for young adults, a "hipster" milieu, with all kinds of eateries and venues for music, coffee, and the like.

Morriss draws on his missionary experience in Mexico to open the congregation, which was nonliturgical and focused on preaching and praise music, to many elements of the Catholic tradition. Foremost is the weekly celebration of the eucharist, a necessity for not just members but all Christians—connection with Christ. He also has put before them the Virgin Mary and communion of saints as ways to experience the incarnational, communal vision of the faith. He also stresses the prophetic side, as echoed in Mary's song, the *Magnificat*, in which God sides with the oppressed and the helpless and the rich and powerful are overturned. Austin New Church, Byassee reports, is profoundly committed to the immigrants seeking asylum, freedom, and safety. Austin New Church members bring food, water, and funds to immigrants dumped at bus stations and other locations by INS agents. Austin may have roots in the evangelical movement, but it has become a place of prayer as well as social justice in the neighborhood.

What Byassee finds as a common trait in all these three congregations and their pastors is not just the growth of the communities at a time when many parishes are facing decline and shrinkage—something we have heard a great deal of here. For him, the crisis in parish life, as well as in the lives of pastors, is not the only reality we should see. As I have argued throughout, it is also necessary to see the examples of parishes which have experienced resurrection, revival, and reinvention, which have repurposed their buildings, replanted themselves in their neighborhoods, and have renewed their identities and missions, often by including new and different Christians into their fellowship.

There have been other experiments along these lines. We have referred to some already here. There were the itinerant Methodist preachers from the eighteenth century onward, and the inner-city mission priests in the UK in the late nineteenth and early twentieth centuries, and more recently the "worker priests" in Europe after WWII. More recently, team ministries have been covering a number of parishes in the Church of England. This has also been the case in Lutheran and Methodist and Episcopal associations of parishes in the US. Remember the circuit-riding Lutheran clergy couple in West Virginia. Most of these efforts did little to change the identity and clerical character of pastors. What was different was the nonresidential deployment of them and, in many cases, the absence of income or "benefice," that is, a "living" from a particular parish.

The principal criticism of such efforts, possibly of Bishop Doyle's as well, is that they do not essentially change the separation of the clergy from the rest of the people of God. Even if titles were eliminated along with distinctive clerical dress and other institutional requirements such as participation in church pension plans and having attended recognized seminaries and earning MDiv degrees, it would take more radical change in the culture, the structure, as well as the thinking of churches, to alter the clerical establishment.

In the wake of the revelation of massive sexual abuse by clergy, some Catholic commentators have called for both a rethinking and redefining of the clerical establishment in multiple dimensions. This is beyond the now-almost-constant calls for rehauling of the formation path for clergy, away from the professionalized three to four years to earn an MDiv degree, toward much shorter, intense programs, possibly without a formal academic degree. The previously noted experimental program at Luther Seminary in St. Paul, Minnesota by the ELCA is an example. It would dramatically reduce the length of formation from three to two years, at least half of which would be spent not in residence at a seminary campus but in an internship/apprentice-like residence in a parish, with the local pastor as mentor. It would significantly reduce more educational debt, actually coming close to not creating any more debt at all.

Given the institutionalization of seminary formation programs by all major church bodies, even such a modest change as this experiment poses would require substantial change in legislation by the church bodies beyond the experimental stage. But in light of the state of things—the recent shocking findings on lack of trust in and need for clergy, the situation of so many congregations, as described here—debate about institutional-ecclesiastical approbation of formation for ordained ministry begins to appear alarmingly out of touch with reality.

Thriving Rural Communities/Congregations and Conciliarity

Another heartening example of pastors reshaping their ministry is found in Duke Divinity School's program Thriving Rural Communities (TRC). Laura Beach Byrch was a classmate and friend of my daughter at Davidson College, and was supported in her MDiv studies at Duke as a Rural Ministry Fellow by this program and now has been serving eight years in rural ministry in North Carolina. She now serves as one of several pastors at Boone UMC. Almost sixty pastors have been trained and appointed to congregations and ministries through the state of North Carolina in the decade since TRC's implementation. In addition to Laura, others who have been reviving or continuing congregations and their presence and outreach include Rebekah Shuford Ralph at Mitchell's Chapel UMC in Boonville, Jason Villegas at Murfreesboro UMC, Sara Beth Pannell at Pittsboro UMC, and James Henderson in the Sanford Circuit. Whether more than 200 years downtown in Pittsboro, or outreach in Boone and Boonville, these are congregations that have held onto their legacy of presence but have also discovered new ways to welcome the communities around them, and offer space for service as well as outreach.

Adam De Ville argues for a somewhat more ancient change to renew the churches.[43] Consistently, from the local parish on up to the diocese and beyond to the national and international levels of the church, he calls for a return to the *synodality* or *conciliarity* of the early church in both East and West. The Eastern churches have continued the use of synods of bishops but only rarely has the conciliar representation of all the church—bishops, priests, deacons, religious, and lay people—survived in actual deliberation and decision-making. DeVille sees the recovery of the communal character

---

43. DeVille, *Every Hidden Thing Shall Be Revealed.*

of the church as a way of restoring checks and balances, especially where there has been abusive behavior and lack of oversight.

Admittedly, this is hardly an original discovery on his part, as he is quick to note, for in the past, more than a century, the rediscovery of the church as the people of God, as a community of faith, is likely the major theological insight. Of course, the communal character of church was never completely obscured. The words of hymns and liturgical texts are largely in the plural. One "cannot be a Christian by oneself," to paraphrase Tertullian, as noted elsewhere here. If community is church, then such cannot be defined principally as rules or canons, as the bishops or the rest of the ordained, but as all members praying, ministering, deciding matters together.

The return to the church's conciliar shape and function is a renewal of church as the work of the laity as well as the clergy. If the church again acted like a community at every level, it would be hard to maintain the clericalism of the past and the distance this creates and maintains from the laity. Conciliar gathering and process of course cannot eliminate human weakness. It however allows the vocations of all God's people to be recognized and put to work. DeVille focuses on how the behavior of bishops could finally be held accountable, something that even at this stage of the sexual abuse crisis does not exist. A church that operated in synodality, as an assembly of all, would first be able to elect its own bishops rather than their being appointed by other bishops. There would be more effective monitoring of the formation and activity of all clergy. This is not dismissible as sheer anti-clericalism, for in a conciliar body, all are held accountable in the positions they have.

Community and "the Other": Welcome in a Time of Division, Suspicion, and Hate

ItLittle attention has been paid, in our visits to congregations here, to what seems to be a matter of constant controversy now. I mean here the racism historically embedded in the structures of, and behavior in, the churches. There also has emerged an antagonism toward refugees, and immigrants, whether documented or not. Alongside these eruptions of racial and ethnic intolerance are hostile attitudes toward Muslims and Jews and toward LGBTQ people. It is not necessary to say where legitimation for all this resentment and hate originates. Classical voices like James Baldwin, Malcolm X, Martin Luther King Jr., and more recently Ta-Nehisi Coates and Ibram X. Kendi, have no doubt raised awareness of racism's persistence.[44] The only

---

44. Coates, *Between the World and Me*; Coates, *We Were Eight Years in Power*; Kendi, *Stamped from the Beginning*; Kendi, *How to Be an Antiracist*.

new wrinkle is the role of the chief executive in encouraging such prejudice, without using the explicit epithets, though some of his descriptions of Baltimore and countries in Africa and the Caribbean come quite close.

Identity politics are hardly the tools of persons of color and other ethnicities. Resentment of nondocumented migrants and lower-income people allegedly enjoying fraudulent use of entitlements, taking government handouts, while at the same time taking away jobs and using benefits—all these are attacks on the white working class. This was the finding of Arlie Russell Hochschild in *Strangers in Their Own Land*. The branding of Mexican immigrants as murderers and rapists, criminals and "bad hombres," the claim that there are many fine people among both white supremacist and anti-Semitic protestors and anti-racist resistance protestors, makes it clear where both the president and his party stand, and those who identify as Republicans hold the president in 90 percent approval or better.[45] No president or administration stays indefinitely. Yet the contentious, conflicted state of things in America will be with us for some time. Inequality and government policy slanted toward the banks, corporations, and the wealthy has not trickled down into better lives for many. Despite historically low unemployment numbers, many live hand-to-mouth, often having to choose between housing costs, food, and medical expenses, and not just the elderly, chronically ill, and permanently low-income segments of the population.

What one can see fairly clearly in so many of the congregations, the ones we visited here and many more, is an almost instinctive resistance to such division, suspicion, and outright hate. And it is not just in challenging inner-city congregations trying to replant themselves in neighborhoods with very different migrant communities than the ones who established the parishes long ago. One can also see this in the small-town and rural parishes too.

If church can be accurately and rightly described as community, in all the wrinkles and richness of the term, then overwhelmingly the holy communities we have visited are welcoming, open, and affirming ones. They know that those whom they welcome are angels, or better, Christ himself.

They do not make distinctions about who comes for groceries from the food bank or a meal. There is no person or group excluded because of their addiction, or sexual, racial, or ethnic identity. Health clinics for all, for mothers and babies and children, after-school and ESL programs, in some cases residential space and space for small businesses as well as nonprofit groups—the table is set and overflowing and all are welcome, as St. John Chrysostom said in the fourth century in an Easter homily that is read every

45. "Presidential Approval Ratings—Donald Trump."

Easter vigil in the Eastern churches. All are welcome to feast, receive assistance, counseling, education, and clothing because all are children of the Father, sisters and brothers in the Lord Jesus.

As a parish priest myself for decades, I have to say that this may be one of the truly revolutionary transformations going on in otherwise discouraging accounts of congregational life today. I mean here the willingness of members to get out of the comfortable box a parish can become, to be willing to venture beyond the friendship networks they come to church to sustain, and to be part of the greater community's life. The ways in which this welcoming community spirit can be enacted are numerous, and we have seen it as we visited so many different congregations here. As diverse as the repurposing of space and the reinvention of congregations may be, what is common and the real gift is the opening up to the world, the people around them, regardless of religion, ethnicity, and race, or economic and political identity.

The wind and fire of the Spirit rocked the world of the disciples still hiding in fear after the death and supposed rising of Jesus their teacher. They could not have expected or hoped for what transpired on Pentecost in Jerusalem. It was wonderful to sense the new life the wind and fire brought. But it was more than terrifying to realize this was not just for their little band but for all these others—foreigners, people of other cultures and faiths, outsiders. Yet there would never be strangers again in their community, the church.

There is great support for such an embracing attitude in the New Testament itself. The actual foundational event of the Christian community, the coming down of the Holy Spirit on the Jewish feast of Pentecost—fifty days after Passover, a feast of the giving of the Torah on Sinai to Moses, the establishment of the covenant between God and God's people. In the Torah, the story of the Tower of Babel symbolized the tragic division and suspicion that arose among human beings when their languages were no longer mutually intelligible, when they no longer could see each other as sisters and brothers, children of the Most High.

Pentecost, as described in the Acts of the Apostles, was the exact opposite, the undoing of the human tendency to suspect and mistrust "the other" who is different in language, faith, appearance, culture. In Jerusalem, where pilgrims gathered to celebrate the Jewish Pentecost, people from all over the world were present. Yet when the apostle Peter started speaking to them, though they were from varied countries and language backgrounds, everyone understood his words. The text enumerates people there from Galilee, but also

Parthians, Medes, Elamites, and residents of Mesopotamia, Judea and Cappadocia, Pontus and Asia, Phrygia and Pamphiliya, Egypt and the parts of Libya belonging to Cyrene, and visitors from Rome, both Jews and proselytes, Cretans and Arabs—in our own languages we hear them speaking about God's deeds of power. (Acts 2:1–13)

And soon, in the same Acts of the Apostles, Pentecost would spread outside the people of Israel to the gentiles, to the entire world they knew. It was as if a translation application was implanted in everyone there. They all understood what was being said and understood each other as if it was in their own language—as if they were a community. All this was after there was a violent rush of wind and fire descending upon all. This coming of the Holy Spirit, the text says, enabled those who received the spirit to speak in other languages. And everyone seemed to receive the gift of universal translation. Peter would see that "God shows no partiality, but in every nation anyone who fears him and does what is right is acceptable to him (Acts 10:34). Being able to understand, to speak the same language, means all are part of the same household, a community of the people of God.

The Acts of the Apostles is a collection of "greatest hits" of the early church, the adventures of the first Christians, many of them miraculous and extraordinary. Yet the point of this pivotal event, often called the church's birthday, could not be clearer. The community of those following Jesus knew none of the ancient Greco-Roman divisions by gender, race, class, or faith. Later the Pauline Letters would say that in Christ there was neither male nor female, master or slave, Jew or Greek. If today church offers anything to a divided society, an often suspicious and hateful world, it offers fellowship, community in the holy things, sacred as well as secular and ordinary. It is not just a "safe" place for people of differing political perspectives or social and economic backgrounds to gather. Church as community is where those who would not otherwise be together can connect, talk, pray, eat, study, and work together. "Red" and "blue" Christians put aside what divides them. What they believe erases these differences, or shows that there are other truths that unite them.

Thinking back to the many examples of parishes that have redefined themselves, repurposed their buildings, and renewed their roots and commitments to the neighborhood around them—in every case, none of this renewal could have taken place without communal deliberation, decision, and then commitment to act together. True, in many cases, a pastor may have realized holding onto expensive or decaying buildings was not possible. In so many instances, pastors inspired members to move forward—to acquire the rest of the buildings on the block, perhaps, as Redeemer Lutheran in North Minneapolis did. But I found it telling that when a pastor stepped aside to another call or retirement, or when a new pastor arrived, the parish community, having experienced its strength as a community, was able to welcome and then integrate a new pastor. Surely this was the case in those parishes looked at in detail, ones in which I knew the clergy personally. Even despite difficult transitions and conflict, I know of parishes where the durability of the community, paired with the dedication of lay leaders, enabled the parish to survive a most unsuccessful pastoral appointment and potentially damaging tension with the diocesan bishop.

Though for centuries clergy and laity have understood themselves almost as separate divisions within the church, this was not the original state of the community in its earliest days. And in the twenty-first century, where so many cultural, political, and economic institutional supports for the church have disappeared, there are striking parallels with those first years. But it is impossible to return to the past or recreate it. The situation that this new century has brought is distinctive. Not better, not far worse than the best, but simply different. As much as the church is a community over time, as much as church is rooted in the memory of those who gathered around Jesus in the beginning, all the way down the centuries to now—church is not a museum, not merely a repository of beloved practices and items from so many periods.

As I have learned myself, many times, the conditions in which parishes existed, even thrived just a couple of decades ago, are gone. The people who make up the community of faith are a mixed group. Some of us can remember a different time. Others have no memory of that whatsoever. The network of small-interest groups that wove together to create growing, vibrant parishes in the 1950s down through the 1980s have been replaced since church is no longer the principal social hub for many. Mobility means few of us have the comfort of knowing our grandparents prayed here in this sanctuary, possibly more family earlier than them too. The cohesion of coming from the same country and speaking the same language somewhere in Europe, yes, this remains in those parishes that are of one culture and language. Vietnamese and Chaldean Catholic parishes come to mind, some Ethiopian, Coptic, and Palestinian ones as well.

Time Flies

Recently, some scenes from an HBO dramatization of Wally Lamb's novel, *I Know This Much Is True,* were shot in the parish I served. In the book, a particularly intense confrontation between brothers takes place at the funeral of the child of one of them, a victim of sudden infant death syndrome. The novel's storyline required the burial service of a child in an Eastern Orthodox Church. This led one of the principal actors, Mark Ruffalo, also a producer, to select the sanctuary of the parish as well as the beautiful acapella sacred music of the Eastern church.

The novel's story at that point was set in the 1980s. Thus those who appeared as mourners, the congregation at the service, as well as those singing in the choir, all had to be costumed with the big glasses and hairstyles and the now-dated but vintage clothing of that decade. It would be one thing if the period of the piece were the 1890s or even the 1920s or 1940s. But the 1980s are almost too close for comfort for some of those participating in the shoot.

I was not there for the filming. The celebrant of this filmed bit of a child's funeral liturgy, my good friend and longtime colleague, Alexis Vinogradov, was in fact the rector of the parish at that point in time, just newly arrived. I was already ordained then too and was serving in a fairly large parish not far from my present one. I have drawn on my experience there several times. When I look at photos of myself and the parish I served in the early 1980s, I hardly recognize myself or the people in them. And when I go through notes and other documents I kept from those days, likewise. Back then, my mentor, H. Henry Maertens, the senior pastor of the parish, and I saw that that things were changing, and rapidly, right before us. I recalled this earlier. That was almost forty years ago. What was then changing or beginning to change—multigenerational families, parish as significant locus of social belonging—is long gone.

Time plays tricks with us. For many, "church" and "community" may be hard to separate from a particular parish, and the years in which one was part of its community. Yet, even the parish and community life of less than forty years ago is long gone, as are the clothing and hairdos and the American culture of that time. No cell phones, no internet, and still many ties to what now would be the more distant past of the 1950s, 1940s, and beyond.

Church, the local church of the parish, is no longer the social hub it was even as late as the 1980s and perhaps the 1990s. And yet, as we have seen over and over again in the congregations examined here, there are still strong networks of friendship and belonging in parishes. Clearly, the Sunday Church School classrooms are not as full as they once were. Neither are the pews for Sunday services. In some cases, entire congregations have ceased to exist and members merged into new ones or simply disappeared, as we all do, eventually, in transition to the kingdom of heaven.

And yet, the bread is broken, the cup is shared. There are baptisms, burials, and weddings, Christians wend their way through Advent and Lent, celebrate Easter and Christmas and the rest of the year. People pray, hear the Scriptures and sermons. Then they celebrate the "sacrament after the sacrament," the fellowship of a coffee hour. Even more, they celebrate the "sacrament of the sister/brother." From the eucharistic table to the table that is the heart of the neighbor, God Christ is received and then gifted away.

The parish buildings are no longer empty all week long. There are classes, pre- and after-school programs, clinics for mothers and children and seniors, clothing and food pantries for those in need. In some places, meals are served to anyone who is hungry. Clothes may be available too. Parish communities sponsor housing as well as space for start-up ventures and freelancers.

Everywhere, disciples go out to put the gospel into practice—at work, in school, at home, in their neighborhood. And they will be reaching out as well and keeping company (*koinonia*) with each other, next year, in five, ten, fifty, 100 years. I know that if I were around to write about it some years from now, it would be so. Over and over here, you have seen this, as we visited congregation after congregation. Death gives way to life, just as with the Lord. Fragile yet amazingly durable as an infant who will grow up, live, and move into the life without end. Every congregation is, as the Lutheran canticle based on the *Didaché* says, "a foretaste of the feast to come." Abundant life, experience of the joy and community of Jesus's kingdom will be there, shared, by community as church, church as community.

The Pandemic, the Anti-racism Movement, and After

My teacher Peter Berger told us that as sociologists we should be wary of making predictions. That, however, did not bar us from having opinions, based on what we knew. As I conclude with the briefest of epilogues, I find his wisdom enduring. Already now, there are numerous ponderings about the future, predictions too. This is some months into the pandemic of the Covid-19 virus, as well as the movement of protest and demand for social justice after the death of George Floyd and so many African Americans at the hands of the police. That it is the time before a major presidential and congressional election only intensifies frustrations and hopes going forward. I have no doubt that we will have a literature of what the society that lies ahead should and might look like. There are already appearing reflections of the post Covid-19 church. Thomas G. Bandy recently put forward some thoughtful observations.[1]

He first reminds us that the usual procedure for church people is "attractional"—to go inward, to elements and church life and structure first, rather than outward, to the community and world in which a congregation is located. We've heard a great deal about that here so no need to elaborate. But what for me is important is that Bandy has authored a number of volumes on connecting church with world, and the most recent of these, Sideline Church, was published in 2018—long before the pandemic and the current protest movement.[2] He identifies a number of real issues that churches must confront going forward. These include the rising and open prejudice toward people of color, toward LGBTQ folk, also the rage rising from economic inequality and declining income and standard of living. With the colossal

1. Bandy, "Realities and the Future of the Post-Covid-19 Church."
2. Bandy, *Sideline Church.*

layoff and furloughs of 50 million or more since the pandemic's start, the social and economic suffering has grown. Increasingly for work and connection and religious belonging, Zoom and streaming services, prayer and preaching, have kept communities of faith going when public gatherings were not possible. Quarantining and work from home or loss of work and income have contributed to increasing levels of depression and personal conflict, abusive behavior as well. And the all-too-familiar list goes on. Many of the parishes we have visited here have some sort of remote worship going on, either livestream and archived videos of services on Facebook or YouTube or live services on Zoom or like platforms.

David Gibson is one of the first to predict a "religious recession" in the aftermath of the pandemic and the movement for justice.[3] Head of The Center on Religion and Culture at Fordham, Gibson surveyed researchers on whether there will be a religious awakening or revival "after the plague." The jury seems still out. Some detect modest increases in accessing service, classes, sermons, and the like on various video communication platforms. A few note increased googling about prayer and spiritual practices. Still others hope the isolation will result in more reaching out to friends, neighbors, and families. Perhaps there will be a rebirth of local gatherings. But even with demands for reopening houses of worship, these services remain dangerous places of infection and those sixty-five and older are encouraged to stay away. Some commentators see the need for spiritual consolation and encouragement and point to upticks in religious activity after wars and destructive storms and economic depressions. Ryan Burge, from whom we heard earlier, notes that massive shifts back toward churchgoing, even after major catastrophes, seldom are longlasting. People are most likely to return to the "church" of the *New York Times*, the local coffee shop or the PGA, the NFL, or the NBA. Or the pull of the open road in their RVs.

Peter Berger was quite right about predictions. But notice that Bandy and so many others from whom we heard in this book are pointing out the challenges and issues of the church well before the pandemic and protest movement. Despite our longings, we will not be able to return to the ways things used to be, what some call "Before Time," the old "normal." It is clear that there will be changes resulting from the upheavals of the present, the turmoil produced by the present administration included. We have no idea of the scope of these changes either, it is simply too early to tell. But my sense is that we are seeing an acceleration of the changes and trends that were already present before the winter of 2020 when the number of Covid-19 cases and deaths escalated so rapidly.

3. Gibson, "Coming Religion 'Recession.'"

We can, however, see some outlines of the future. Bill Wilson summarizes these as what we will see less and more of in parishes for the rest of this decade and beyond.[4] Full-time pastors are disappearing as parishes cannot support them. Members of all varieties, from frequent to rare attendance, will continue to decline. Beyond congregations, there will be shrinkage of denominational staff and agencies, of the larger regional and national apparatus of church bodies. Again, what we once had has shown to be financially unsustainable. Buildings will show themselves to be less important, especially if used primarily or only on Sundays. And parishes that operate in inversion, that is, with no interest in or contact with the neighborhood, cultures, and society outside will become more anachronistic, and they will close. So goes "survival theology" and its practice.

But we will see more part-time pastors and pastors having a full-time profession or occupation, a financial necessity already. Much more church activity, from worship and learning to administrative/council meetings, will migrate online. Buildings likely will be repurposed, as we have seen throughout here, so that they really take a place in the service and educational work of the local community. The relationship of a congregation to the community around will no longer be intriguing innovation but necessity. Parishes will become a major location of pastoral training, with seminarians assigned to serve a congregation and to be mentored by its pastor from the start and through formation. As we have argued, it is clearly not just the death of congregations that we can expect but their resurrection, a living out of Christ's own action and the heart of the faith. And the community of the people of God will be a sacrament, just as the sacraments of the table and font that gather them. Church will endure because community will persist. God, as Eugene Peterson says in his translation, will continue to "move into the neighborhood." As some eucharistic prayers proclaim it: Christ has died, Christ is risen, Christ will come again.

4. Wilson, "What Will We See Less of and More of in America's Churches in the 2020s?"

Bibliography

Abro, James. "The Power and Purpose of Small Community Churches." *RealClearReligion*, July 23, 2018. https://www.realclearreligion.org/articles/2018/07/23/the_power_and_purpose_of_small_community_churches_110196.html.

Afanasieff, Marianne. "La genèse de 'L'Église du Saint-Esprit.'" In *L'Eglise du Saint-Esprit*, by Nicholas Afanasieff, 13–23. Paris: Cerf, 1975.

———. "Nicholas Afanasieff (1893–1966) Essai de biographie." *Contacts* 66 (1969) 99–111.

Afanasiev, Nicholas. *The Church of the Holy Spirit*. Translated by Vitaly Permiakov. Edited by Michael Plekon. Notre Dame, IN: University of Notre Dame Press, 2007.

Allchin, Donald. *N. S. F. Grundtvig: An Introduction to His Life and Work*. Aarhus, Denmark: Aarhus University Press, 2015.

Allen, Bonnie. "From Sacred to Secular: Canada to Lose 9,000 Churches, Warns National Heritage Group." *CBC online*, March 10, 2019. https://www.cbc.ca/news/canada/losing-churches-canada-1.5046812.

Alper, Becka. "Why America's 'Nones' Don't Identify with a Religion." *Pew Research Center*, August 8, 2018. http://www.pewresearch.org/fact-tank/2018/08/08/why-americas-nones-dont-identify-with-a-religion/.

Ammerman, Nancy T. *Congregation and Community*. New Brunswick, NJ: Rutgers University Press, 1997.

———. *Everyday Religion*. Oxford: Oxford University Press, 2007.

———. *Sacred Stories, Spiritual Tribes*. Oxford: Oxford University Press, 2014.

"Angie Thurston: How Secular Organizations Connect to Institutional Religion." *Faith & Leadership*, January 24, 2017. https://faithandleadership.com/angie-thurston-how-can-secular-organizations-connect-institutional-religion.

Arjakovsky, Antoine. *The Way: Religious Thinkers of the Russian Emigration in Paris and Their Journal*. Translated by Jerry Ryan. Edited by John A. Jillions and Michael Plekon. Notre Dame, IN: University of Notre Dame Press, 2013.

Ashworth, Pat. "Birmingham Diocese Seeks to Undo Parish System." *Church Times*, March 1, 2019. https://www.churchtimes.co.uk/articles/2019/1-march/news/uk/birmingham-diocese-seeks-to-undo-parish-system.

Bailey, Sarah Pulliam. "A Church Allegedly Asked Older Members to Leave. Leaders Say That It Didn't Actually Happen." *Washington Post*, January 22, 2020. https://www.washingtonpost.com/religion/2020/01/22/church-allegedly-asked-older-members-leave-leaders-say-that-didnt-actually-happen/.

Ballmer, Randall. *Mine Eyes Have Seen the Glory: A Journey into the Evangelical Subculture in America*. Oxford: Oxford University Press, 1989.

Balthasar, Hans Urs von. *Dare We Hope That "All Men Be Saved"? With a Short Discourse on Hell*. 2nd ed. San Francisco: Ignatius, 2014.

Bandy, Thomas G. "Realities and the Future of the Post-Covid-19 Church." *Ministry Matters*, April 28, 2020. https://www.ministrymatters.com/all/entry/10304/positive -trends-social-realities-and-the-future-of-the-post-covid-19-church.

———. *Sideline Church: Bridging the Chasm Between Churches and Cultures*. Nashville: Abingdon, 2018.

Banister, Jon. "Dupont Circle Church Redevelopment Opens with Corporate Housing Units." *Bisnow*, April 18, 2019. https://www.bisnow.com/washington-dc/news/ multifamily/contentious-dupont-circle-church-redevelopment-pivots-to- corporate-housing-model-98548.

Banks, Adele. "Americans Have Limited Knowledge about World Religions, Including Their Own." *Religion News Service*, July 24, 2019. https://www.americamagazine. org/faith/2019/07/24/new-survey-americans-have-limited-knowledge-world- religions-including-their-own.

Barnhart, Dave. "Methodist House Churches." *Ministry Matters*, June 8, 2018. https:// www.ministrymatters.com/all/topic/Methodist+house+churches.

Barr, Cameron. "The Pastor as Convener." *Faith & Leadership*, May 30, 2017. https:// faithandleadership.com/cameron-barr-pastor-churchs-principal-convener.

Barron, James. "The Bells of St. Martin's Fall Silent as Churches in Harlem Struggle." *New York Times*, September 30, 2018. https://www.nytimes.com/2018/09/30/ nyregion/harlem-church-nyc-.html.

Bass, Diana Butler. *Christianity for the Rest of Us: How the Neighborhood Church Is Transforming the Faith*. New York: HarperOne, 2006.

Becket, Adam. "Change Is Worse Than a Rest, Say Stressed Clergy." *Church Times*, October 18, 2018. https://www.churchtimes.co.uk/articles/2018/19-october/ news/uk/change-is-worse-than-a-rest-say-stressed-clergy.

Beinhart, Peter. "Breaking Faith: The Culture War over Religious Morality Has Faded; in Its Place Is Something Much Worse." *The Atlantic*, April 2017. https://www. theatlantic.com/magazine/archive/2017/04/breaking-faith/517785/.

Bender, Jonathan. "A Priest, a Chef, and a Hunger to Feed Kansas City." *Flatland*, February 6, 2019. https://www.flatlandkc.org/eats-drinks/priest-chef-hunger- kansas-city-thelmas-kitchen-troost/.

Berg, Elizabeth. *Open House: A Novel*. New York: Ballantine, 2000.

Berger, Peter L. *The Desecularization of the World: Resurgent Religion and World Politics*. Grand Rapids: Ethics and Policy Center, 1999.

———. "The Good of Religious Pluralism." *First Things*, April 2016. https://www. firstthings.com/article/2016/04/the-good-of-religious-pluralism.

———, ed. *How My Mind Has Changed*. Grand Rapids: Eerdmans, 1991.

———. *The Many Altars of Modernity: Toward a Paradigm for Religion in a Pluralistic Age*. Berlin: De Gruyter, 2014.

Bilefsky, Dan. "Where Churches Have Become Temples of Cheese, Fitness and Eroticism." *New York Times*, July 30, 2018. https://www.nytimes.com/2018/07/30/ world/canada/quebec-churches.html.

Bloom, Mina. "Historic Logan Square Church Now Luxury Housing Complex." *Block Club Chicago*, January 31, 2019. https://blockclubchicago.org/2019/01/31/logan-square-church-apartments-renting-for-up-to-4000/.

Bonfiglio, Ryan P. "It's Time to Rethink Our Assumptions about Where Theological Education Happens." *Christian Century*, January 31, 2019. https://www.christiancentury.org/article/opinion/it-s-time-rethink-our-assumptions-about-where-theological-education-happens.

———. "Let's Make the Church a Center of Theological Education Again." *Faith & Leadership*, August 21, 2018. https://faithandleadership.com/ryan-p-bonfiglio-lets-make-church-center-theological-education-again.

Braaten, Carl, and Robert Jenson, eds. *Union with Christ: The New Finnish Interpretation of Luther*. Grand Rapids: Eerdmans, 1998.

Brekke, Greg. "Houses of Worship Are Not Just for Worship Anymore." *Religion News Service*, March 8, 2019. https://religionnews.com/2019/03/08/houses-of-worship-are-not-just-for-worship-anymore/.

Brinius, Harry. "Why These Americans Are 'Done' with Church, But Not with God." *The Christian Science Monitor*, December 19, 2015. https://www.csmonitor.com/USA/Society/2015/1219/Why-these-Americans-are-done-with-church-but-not-with-God.

"Broad-based Declines in Share of Americans Who Say They Are Christian." *Pew Research Center*, October 16, 2019. https://www.pewforum.org/2019/10/17/in-u-s-decline-of-christianity-continues-at-rapid-pace/pf_10-17-19_rdd_update-00-017/.

Brooks, David. "Your Loyalties Are Your Life." *New York Times*, January 25, 2019. https://www.nytimes.com/2019/01/24/opinion/josiah-royce-loyalty.html.

Brooks, Jonathan. *Church Forsaken: Practicing Presence in Neglected Neighborhoods*. Downers Grove, IL: InterVarsity, 2018.

Brown, Raymond. *The Churches the Apostles Left Behind*. New York: Paulist, 1984.

Bulgakov, Sergius. *Apocatastasis and Transfiguration*. Translated by Boris Jakim. New Haven, CT: Variable, 1995.

———. *The Bride of the Lamb*. Translated by Boris Jakim. Grand Rapids: Eerdmans, 2001.

Bullivant, Stephen. *Mass Exodus: Catholic Disaffiliation in Britain and America Since Vatican II*. Oxford: Oxford University Press, 2019.

Burge, Ryan. "The Age of Nones May Favor Churches Who Welcome Doubters." *Religion New Service*, January 14, 2020. https://religionnews.com/2020/01/14/the-age-of-nones-may-favor-churches-who-welcome-doubters/.

———. *The Nones: Where They Came From, Who They Are, and Where They Are Going*. Minneapolis: Fortress Press, 2021.

Burton, Tara Isabella. "Christianity Gets Weird." *New York Times*, May, 8, 2020. https://www.nytimes.com/2020/05/08/opinion/sunday/weird-christians.html.

———. *Strange Rites: New Religions for a Godless World*. New York: Hachette, 2020.

Butler, Jason. "Disruption Is Often the Key to Renewal." *Faith & Leadership*, July 23, 2019. https://www.faithandleadership.com/jason-butler-disruption-often-key-renewal.

Byassee, Jason. "The Richness of the Faith: Two Vibrant Anglican Churches in Winnipeg." *Christian Century*, December 19, 2018. https://www.christiancentury.org/article/features/two-vibrant-anglican-congregations-winnipeg.

———. "Three United Methodist Pastors and Their Delight in Ministry." *The Christian Century*, May 29, 2019. https://www.christiancentury.org/article/features/three-united-methodist-pastors-and-their-delight-ministry.

Cabasilas, Nicolas. *The Life in Christ.* Translated by Carmino J. De Cantazaro. Crestwood, NY: St. Vladimir's Seminary Press, 1997.

Cafferata, Gail. *The Last Pastor: Faithfully Steering a Closing Church.* Louisville: Westminster John Knox, 2020.

Caimano, Catherine. "Free Range Priests Solve Traditional Church Problems." *Faith & Leadership*, March 19, 2019. https://www.faithandleadership.com/catherine-caimano-free-range-priests-solve-traditional-church-problems.

Case, Anne, and Angus Deaton. "Mortality and Morbidity in the 21st Century." *Brookings*, March 23, 2017. https://www.brookings.edu/bpea-articles/mortality-and-morbidity-in-the-21st-century/.

Chaves, Mark. *American Religion: Contemporary Trends.* 2nd ed. Princeton: Princeton University Press, 2017.

———. "The Decline of American Religion?" *The Association of Religion Data Archives.* http://www.thearda.com/rrh/papers/guidingpapers/Chaves.pdf.

———, dir. *Religious Congregations in 21st Century America.* Durham, NC: National Congregations Study, 2015.

———. "A Sociologist Looks at the Church in America." *Duke Divinity Magazine* 13.1 (2013) 10–11.

Chu, Jeff. "Rebranded ELCA Church Is a Place of Welcome for Believers and Nonbelievers Alike." *Faith & Leadership*, May 30, 2017. https://www.faithandleadership.com/rebranded-elca-church-place-welcome-believers-and-nonbelievers-alike.

"Church Has No Walls but Many Doors, Accessible to Seekers and Skeptics." *Faith & Leadership*, May 2, 2017. https://www.faithandleadership.com/church-has-no-walls-many-doors-accessible-seekers-and-skeptics.

Coates, Ta-Nehisi. *Between the World and Me.* New York: Spiegel & Grau, 2015.

———. *We Were Eight Years in Power: An American Tragedy.* New York: One World, 2018.

Colby, Sandra L., and Jennifer M. Ortman. "Projections of the Size and Composition of the U.S. Population: 2014 to 2060." *United States Census Bureau*, March 3, 2015. https://www.census.gov/content/dam/Census/library/publications/2015/demo/p25-1143.pdf.

Comacho, David José. "The Racial Aesthetics of Burton's 'Weird Christians.'" *Sojourners*, May 15, 2020. https://sojo.net/articles/racial-aesthetics-burtons-weird-christians.

Congar, Yves. *Église Catholique et France moderne.* Paris: Hachette, 1978.

———. *True and False Reform in the Church.* Translated by Paul Philbert. Collegeville, MN: Liturgical, 2011.

Corrigan, Patricia. "A Tiny Congregation with a Big Building Is Resurrected as a Center of Peace." *Faith & Leadership*, March 20, 2018. https://www.faithandleadership.com/tiny-congregation-big-building-resurrected-center-peace.

Cruz, Christopher De La. "A Light to the City." *The Thread.* https://thethread.ptsem.edu/leadership/a-light-to-the-city.

Cunningham, Caroline. "Philadelphia Episcopalians Explore What Happens When Church Is Separated from Sunday." *Religion News Service*, June 21, 2019. https://religionnews.com/2019/06/20/philadelphia-episcopalians-explore-what-happens-when-church-is-separated-from-sunday/.

———. "Redesigning Sacred Spaces to Serve Their Communities and Save Their Congregations." *Religion News Service*, January 2, 2019. https://religionnews.com/2019/01/02/redesigning-sacred-spaces-to-serve-their-communities-and-save-their-congregations/.

Curry, Michael. "Video & Text: Presiding Bishop's royal wedding sermon." *Episcopal News Service*, May 19, 2018. https://www.episcopalnewsservice.org/2018/05/19/video-text-presiding-bishops-royal-wedding-sermon/.

Daley, Brian. *The Hope of the Early Church: A Handbook of Patristic Eschatology*. 2nd ed. Grand Rapids: Baker Academic, 2002.

Dallas, Kelsey. "Can a Good Meal Bring People Back to Church? A Growing Number of Congregations Think So." *Deseret News*, March 5, 2019. https://www.deseretnews.com/article/900058881/can-a-good-meal-bring-people-back-to-church-lent-ash-wednesday-fat-tuesday.html.

Davies, Madeline. "Clergy Burdened by Unrealistic Job Specs, C of E Told." *Church Times*, October 5, 2018. https://www.churchtimes.co.uk/articles/2018/5-october/news/uk/clergy-burdened-by-unrealistic-job-specs-c-of-e-told.

———. "Clergy Living Comfortably, Long Term Study Suggests." *Church Times*, September 14, 2017. https://www.churchtimes.co.uk/articles/2017/15-september/news/uk/clergy-living-comfortably-long-term-study-suggests.

———. "Mission—But at What Cost?" *Church Times*, November 22, 2019. https://www.churchtimes.co.uk/media/5664134/8175_22-november-2019_tgffy.pdf.

———. "Not Doing Too Badly, Clergy Tell Survey." *Church Times*, December 13, 2019. https://www.churchtimes.co.uk/articles/2019/13-december/news/uk/clergy-positive-about-ministry-in-ten-year-study.

———. "Number of Ordinands in Contextual Training Increases by 142 per cent." *Church Times*, December 6, 2019. https://www.churchtimes.co.uk/articles/2019/6-december/news/uk/number-of-ordinands-in-contextual-training-increases-by-142-per-cent.

Denysenko, Nicholas E. *The People's Faith: The Liturgy of the Faithful in Orthodoxy*. Lanham, MD: Lexington, 2018.

DeVille, Adam. *Every Hidden Thing Shall Be Revealed: Ridding the Church of the Abuses of Sex and Power*. Brooklyn: Angelico, 2019.

DeYmaz, Mark. *Disruption: Repurposing the Church to Redeem the Community*. Nashville: Nelson, 2017.

Dionne, E. J. "No Wonder There's an Exodus from Religion." *Washington Post*, May 6, 2018. https://www.washingtonpost.com/opinions/no-wonder-theres-an-exodus-from-religion/2018/05/06/4ad8c33a-4feb-11e8-84a0-458a1aa9ac0a_story.html.

Douthat, Ross. *To Change the Church: Pope Francis and the Future of Catholicism*. New York: Simon & Schuster, 2018.

Doyle, C. Andrew. *Church: A Generous Community Amplified for the Future*. Alexandria, VA: Virginia Theological Seminary Press, 2015.

———. *Vocātiō: Imaging a Visible Church*. New York: Church, 2018.

Dreher, Rod. *The Benedict Option: A Strategy for Christians in a Post-Christian Nation*. New York: Penguin, 2017.

———. "Fundamentalism and 'Dialogue.'" *The American Conservative*, April 13, 2018. http://www.theamericanconservative.com/dreher/fundamentalism-dialogue-orthodoxy/.

Durkheim, Emile. *The Elementary Forms of the Religious Life.* New York: Free Press, 1965.

Earls, Aaron. "The Church Growth Gap: The Big Gets Bigger while the Small Gets Smaller." *Christianity Today,* March 6, 2019. https://www.christianitytoday.com/news/2019/march/lifeway-research-church-growth-attendance-size.html.

Ellis, Sarah. "Losing Faith: Why South Carolina Is Abandoning Its Churches." *The State,* August 9, 2018. https://www.thestate.com/news/local/article215014375.html.

Ellis, Sarah, et al. "Church in a Bar? SC Churches Are Thinking Outside the Steeple to Reach New Members." *The State,* August 9, 2018. https://www.thestate.com/news/local/article215389120.html.

Émile of Taizé. *Faithful to the Future: Listening to Yves Congar.* London: Bloomsbury, 2013.

Escobedo-Frank, Dottie. *ReStart Your Church.* Nashville: Abingdon, 2012.

Evans, Rachel Held. *Searching for Sunday.* Nashville: Nelson, 2015.

Evdokimov, Paul. *In the World, of the Church: A Paul Evdokimov Reader.* Edited and translated by Michael Plekon and Alexis Vinogradov. Crestwood, NY: St. Vladimir's Seminary Press, 2000.

Faggioli, Massimo. *A Council for the Global Church: Receiving Vatican II in History.* Philadelphia: Fortress, 2015.

———. *Vatican II: The Battle for Meaning.* Ramsey, NJ: Paulist, 2012.

Feuerhard, Peter. "Methodist Experiences in Closing Congregations Offers Lessons to Catholics." *National Catholic Reporter,* October 19, 2017. https://www.ncronline.org/news/parish/methodist-experience-closing-congregations-offers-lessons-catholics.

———. "Road to the True Vatican II Parish Is Downward Mobility." *National Catholic Reporter,* February 21, 2019. https://www.ncronline.org/news/parish/road-true-vatican-ii-parish-downward-mobility.

Finke, Roger, and Rodney Stark. *The Churching of America, 1776–2005: Winners and Losers in Our Religious Economy.* New Brunswick, NJ: Rutgers University Press, 2005.

Fishbeck, Lisa G. "The Strength and Beauty of Small Churches." *Faith & Leadership,* July 15, 2013. https://www.faithandleadership.com/lisa-g-fischbeck-strength-and-beauty-small-churches.

Flanigan, Robin L. "City's PCUSA Churches Band Together to Face Ongoing Decline." *Faith & Leadership,* February 20, 2018. https://www.faithandleadership.com/citys-pcusa-churches-band-together-face-ongoing-decline.

Fletcher, Jeannine Hill. *The Sin of White Supremacy: Christianity, Racism, and Religious Diversity in America.* Maryknoll, NY: Orbis, 2018.

Florer-Bixler, Melissa. "Capitalism Is Killing the Small Church." *Faith & Leadership,* April 30, 2019. https://www.faithandleadership.com/melissa-florer-bixler-capitalism-killing-small-church.

Flynn, Eileen E. "Dying Texas Church Gives Life to a New Congregation." *Faith & Leadership,* April 4, 2017. https://www.faithandleadership.com/dying-texas-church-gives-life-new-congregation.

———. "In Booming Austin TX, Churches Struggle to Keep Pace." *Faith & Leadership,* March 19, 2019. https://faithandleadership.com/booming-austin-texas-churches-struggle-keep-pace-citys-growth.

Ford, Ann. "A Church and Community Partnership Helps Bring Fresh Groceries to a Food Desert." *Faith & Leadership*, February 19, 2019. https://www.faithandleadership.com/church-and-community-partnership-helps-bring-fresh-groceries-chicago-food-desert.

Forrest, Andrew. "Every Dying Church in America Has a Community Garden." *Faith & Leadership*, April 18, 2017. https://www.faithandleadership.com/andrew-forrest-every-dying-church-america-has-community-garden.

Frances, Hillary. "They Sold First UMC and Put Up a Tent in the Parking Lot." *Christian Century*, August 8, 2018. https://www.christiancentury.org/article/interview/they-sold-first-umc-and-put-tent-parking-lot.

Friedman, Zach. "78% Live Paycheck to Paycheck." *Forbes*, January 11, 2019. https://www.forbes.com/sites/zackfriedman/2019/01/11/live-paycheck-to-paycheck-government-shutdown/#2991d5c74f10.

Fuggi, Robert. *A New Model of the Authentic Church*. Scotts Valley, CA: CreateSpace, 2017.

Gallagher, Sally K. *Getting to Church: Narratives of Gender and Joining*. Oxford: Oxford University Press, 2017.

Galli, Mark. "Trump Should Be Removed From Office." *Christianity Today*, December 19, 2019. https://www.christianitytoday.com/ct/2019/december-web-only/trump-should-be-removed-from-office.html.

Garrison, Elaine. "Orthodox-affiliated Nonprofit Helps Neighborhood Heal a Legacy of Trauma." *Faith & Leadership*, February 5, 2019. https://www.faithandleadership.com/orthodox-affiliated-nonprofit-helps-neighborhood-heal-legacy-trauma.

Gibson, David. "The Coming Religion 'Recession.'" *Religion & Politics*, June 23, 2020. https://religionandpolitics.org/2020/06/23/the-coming-religion-recession/.

Gilbert, Kathy L. "Panel Offers Peek behind Scenes of Separation Plan." *UM News*, January 10, 2020. https://www.umnews.org/en/news/panel-offers-peek-behind-scenes-of-separation-plan.

Graham, Ruth. "What's Really Going On Inside the Minnesota Church Accused of Trying to Expel Its Aging Members?" *Slate*, January 23, 2020. https://slate.com/human-interest/2020/01/inside-minnesotas-grove-united-methodist-church-accused-of-trying-to-kick-out-elderly-members.html.

Grant, Tobin. "The Great Decline: 61 Years of Religiosity in One Graph, 2013 Hits a New Low." *Religion News Service*, August 5, 2014. https://religionnews.com/2014/08/05/the-great-decline-61-years-of-religion-religiosity-in-one-graph-2013-hits-a-new-low/.

Graveling, Liz. *Negotiating Wellbeing: Experiences of Ordinands and Clergy in the Church of England*. London: Church of England Ministry Division, 2018.

Gray, Lisa. "St. Peter Reborn: A Gay Black Preacher and His Diverse Congregation Merge with One of Houston's Oldest White Churches." *Houston Chronicle*, April 17, 2019. https://www.houstonchronicle.com/life/houston-belief/article/St-Peter-reborn-A-gay-black-preacher-and-his-13774744.php.

Green, Emma. "Convert Nation." *The Atlantic*, August 12, 2017. https://www.theatlantic.com/politics/archive/2017/08/conversions-lincoln-mullen/536151/.

———. "The Secret Christians of Brooklyn." *The Atlantic*, September 8, 2015. https://www.theatlantic.com/politics/archive/2015/09/st-lydias-microchurch-brooklyn-secret-christians/404119/.

Green, Peter S. "Houses of Worship Grappling with Harlem's Development Boom." *Crain's New York Business,* March 18, 2019. https://www.crainsnewyork.com/features/houses-worship-grappling-harlems-development-boom.

Gushee, David. *A Letter to My Anxious Christian Friends.* Louisville: Westminster John Knox, 2016.

———. "Seven Follow-Ups on Ten Reasons for Christian Decline." *Religion New Service,* September 12, 2016. http://religionnews.com/2016/09/12/seven-follow-ups-on-ten-reasons-for-christian-decline/.

———. *Still Christian.* Louisville: Westminster John Knox, 2017.

———. "Why Is Christianity Declining?" *Religion News Service,* September 6, 2016. http://religionnews.com/2016/09/06/why-is-christianity-declining/.

Hackel, Sergei. *Pearl of Great Price: The Life of Mother Maria Skobtsova 1891–1945.* Crestwood, NY: St. Vladimir's Seminary Press, 1981.

Harrington, Michael. *The Other America: Poverty in the United States.* New York: Simon & Schuster, 1962.

Hart, David Bentley. *The New Testament: A Translation.* New Haven: Yale University Press, 2017.

———. *That All Shall Be Saved.* New Haven: Yale University Press, 2019.

Heath, Elaine. "Breathe: Our Identity Is Found in God's Love during Times of Anxiety and Change." *Divinity Magazine* 17.1 (Fall 2017) 5–9.

Hochschild, Arlie Russell. *Strangers in Their Own Land: Anger and Mourning on the American Right.* New York: New Press, 2016.

Hodges, Sam. "Diverse Leaders' Group Offers Separation Plan." *UM News,* January 3, 2020. https://www.umnews.org/en/news/diverse-leaders-group-offers-separation-plan.

Holloway, Richard. *Leaving Alexandria: A Memoir of Faith and Doubt.* Edinburgh: Canongate, 2012.

Holmes, Kirsten E. "From Backyard Baptism to Potluck Bible Study, Church Starts at Home." *The Inquirer,* September 5, 2017. http://www.philly.com/philly/news/house-church-meeting-organic-simple-backyard-baptism-religion-home-20170905.html.

Hoover, Brett. *The Shared Parish: Latinos, Anglos, and the Future of U.S. Catholicism.* New York: New York University Press, 2014.

Hopfensperger, Jean. "As Churches Close, a Way of Life Fades." *Minneapolis Star Tribune,* July 8, 2018. http://www.startribune.com/as-minnesota-churches-close-a-way-of-life-fades/486037461/.

———. "Fastest Growing Religion Is None." *Minneapolis Star Tribune,* November 11, 2018. http://www.startribune.com/fastest-growing-religion-in-minnesota-the-nation-is-none/498664191/.

———. "Study Shows Why Young Catholics Leave the Church." *Minneapolis Star Tribune,* March 2, 2018. http://www.startribune.com/study-shows-why-young-catholics-leave-the-church/475709783/.

———. "Test of Faith: The Unchurching of America: Fewer Ministers, Heavier Burdens." *Minneapolis Star Tribune,* August 18, 2018. http://www.startribune.com/fewer-men-and-women-are-entering-the-seminary/490381681/.

———. "What's in a Name? Churches Trade Old Names for New, Younger Members." *Minneapolis Star Tribune,* April 15, 2017. http://www.startribune.com/what-s-in-a-name-churches-trade-old-names-for-new-younger-members/419529003/#1.

Hovorun, Cyril. *Meta-Ecclesiology: Chronicles on Church Awareness.* London: Palgrave Macmillan, 2015.

————. *Political Orthodoxies: The Unorthodoxies of the Church Coerced.* Minneapolis: Fortress, 2018.

————. *Scaffolds of the Church: Towards Poststructural Ecclesiology.* Eugene, OR: Cascade, 2017.

"How Many Quit? Estimating the Clergy Attrition Rate." *Into Action.* http://into-action. net/research/many-quit-estimating-clergy-attrition-rate/.

Hughes, C. J. "Church Turned Club Is Now a Market." *New York Times,* March 16, 2010. https://www.nytimes.com/2010/03/17/realestate/commercial/17limelight.html.

————. "For Churches, a Temptation to Sell." *New York Times,* October 4, 2019. https:// www.nytimes.com/2019/10/04/realestate/for-churches-a-temptation-to-sell. html.

Iati, Marisa. "A Liberal Baptist Church Will Close Its Doors and Give $1 Million to Non-profits." *Washington Post,* August 4, 2019. https://www.washingtonpost. com/religion/2019/08/04/progressive-baptist-church-will-close-its-doors-give-million-nonprofits/.

"In U.S., Decline of Christianity Continues at Rapid Pace." *Pew Research Center,* October 17, 2019. https://www.pewforum.org/2019/10/17/in-u-s-decline-of-christianity-continues-at-rapid-pace/.

Irenaeus of Lyons. *Against Heresies. Ante-Nicene Fathers* 1. Translated by Alexander Roberts and William Rambaut. Edited by Alexander Roberts, et al. Buffalo: Christian Literature, 1885.

Jenkins, Jack. "Nones Now as Big as Evangelicals and Catholics in the US." *Religion News Service,* March 21, 2019. https://religionnews.com/2019/03/21/nones-now-as-big-as-evangelicals-catholics-in-the-us/.

Jenson, Robert W. *Systematic Theology.* 2 vols. New York: Oxford University Press, 2001.

Jillions, John A. *Divine Guidance: Lesson for Today from the World of Early Christianity.* New York: Oxford University Press, 2020.

Johnson, Stephen. "The US Is Losing Its Religion Faster than You Think." *Big Think,* November 6, 2017. http://bigthink.com/stephen-johnson/the-us-is-losing-its-religion-and-faster-than-you-may-think.

Jones, Jeffrey M. "U.S. Church Membership Down Sharply in Past Two Decades." *Gallup,* April 18, 2019. https://news.gallup.com/poll/248837/church-membership-down-sharply-past-two-decades.aspx.

————. "US Church Membership Falls Below Majority for First Time." *Gallup,* March 29, 2021. https://news.gallup.com/poll/341963/church-membership-falls-below-majority-first-time.aspx.

Joyner, Alex. "What You Need to Know to Care for Your Clergyperson (Even If That's You)." *Heartlands,* March 19, 2019. https://alexjoyner.com/2019/03/19/what-you-need-to-know-to-care-for-your-clergyperson-even-if-thats-you/.

Judis, John B. *The Nationalist Revival: Trade, Immigration, and the Revolt Against Globalization.* New York: Columbia Global Reports, 2018.

————. *The Populist Explosion: How the Great Recession Transformed American and European Politics.* New York: Columbia Global Reports, 2016.

Karoub, Jeff. "AP-NORC Poll: Americans Rarely Seek Guidance from Clergy." *Religion News Service,* July 9, 2019. https://religionnews.com/2019/07/08/ap-norc-poll-americans-rarely-seek-guidance-from-clergy/

Kavanagh, Aidan. *On Liturgical Theology.* New York: Pueblo, 1984.

Kawamoto, Janet. "St. Barnabas Church Concludes Parish Ministry after 104 Years in Eagle Rock." *Episcopal News*, June 27, 2018. https://episcopalnews.ladiocese.org/dfc/newsdetail_2/3193071.

Kellner, Mark A. "Shuttered Houses of Worship Get a Reboot and Find New Life." *Religion News Service*, September 10, 2018. https://religionnews.com/2018/09/10/shuttered-houses-of-worship-get-a-reboot-find-new-life/.

Kendi, Ibram X. *How to Be an Antiracist*. New York: One World, 2019.

———. *Stamped from the Beginning: The Definitive History of Racist Ideas in America*. New York: Bold Type, 2016.

King, Robert. "Death and Resurrection in an Urban Church." *Faith & Leadership*, March 24, 2015. https://www.faithandleadership.com/death-and-resurrection-urban-church.

Kirchengessner, Pius. "Christus und Abt Menas." *Exerzitien mit P. Pius*, August 2014. https://www.pius-kirchgessner.de/07_Bildmeditationen/4_Christus/Menas.htm.

Kirkpatrick. Nathan. "Adjusting to the New Normal." *Faith & Leadership*, July 22, 2014. https://www.faithandleadership.com/adjusting-new-normal.

———. "Are Churches Counting What Counts?" *Faith & Leadership*, January 20, 2020. https://faithandleadership.com/nathan-kirkpatrick-are-churches-counting-what-counts.

Kling, Garret. "The Origin Story of St. Lydia's #Brooklyn." *A Journey through NYC Religions*, July 9, 2014. http://www.nycreligion.info/origin-story-st-lydias-brooklyn/.

Kountz, Peter. "New Life in Old Space." *Christian Century*, December 9, 2019. https://www.christiancentury.org/article/first-person/new-life-old-space-st-stephen-s-philadelphia.

Krishna, Priya. "From House of Worship to House of Sin: The History of Chelsea's Limelight Building." *Curbed New York*, November 30, 2016. https://ny.curbed.com/2016/11/30/13769350/limelight-building-chelsea-nyc-history.

Krugman, Paul. "Armpits, White Ghettos and Contempt." *New York Times*, April 25, 2019. https://www.nytimes.com/2019/04/25/opinion/midwest-economy.html.

Kruse, Kevin M., and Julian E. Zelitzer. *Fault Lines: A History of the US since 1971*. New York: Norton, 2019.

Kurutz, Steven. "The Many Lives of Limelight." *New York Times*, January 20, 2016. https://www.nytimes.com/2016/01/21/fashion/the-many-lives-of-limelight.html.

Kwon, Duke. "The Tragedy to Communities When Church Buildings Are Demolished to Make Condos." *Washington Post*, March 28, 2018. https://www.washingtonpost.com/news/acts-of-faith/wp/2018/03/28/the-tragedy-to-communities-when-church-buildings-are-demolished-to-make-condos/.

Lawrence, Cheryl M. "A Good Death." *Faith & Leadership*, April 21, 2014. https://www.faithandleadership.com/cheryl-m-lawrence-good-death.

Liptak, Adam. "In Narrow Decision, Supreme Court Decides with Baker Who Turned Away Gay Couple." *New York Times*, April 6, 2018. https://www.nytimes.com/2018/06/04/us/politics/supreme-court-sides-with-baker-who-turned-away-gay-couple.html.

Longhurst, John. "Anglican Church in Canada May Disappear by 2040, Report Says." *Religion News Service*, November 18, 2019. https://religionnews.com/2019/11/18/church-of-canada-may-disappear-by-2040-says-new-report/.

"Loren B. Mead: The Last Interview." *Alban Weekly*, May 7, 2018. https://alban.org/2018/05/07/loren-b-mead-the-last-interview/.

Lubac, Henri de. *The Splendor of the Church*. San Francisco: Ignatius, 1999.

Lurie, Joshua. "LA Church Cafes Provide a Fresh Blend of Jesus, Community and Coffee." *LA Eater*, May 24, 2017. http://la.eater.com/2017/3/24/15015852/coffee-jesus-collaborate-community-charity-church-cafes.

MacCulloch, Diarmaid. *Christianity, the First Three Thousand Years*. New York: Viking, 2009.

MacDonald, G. Jeffrey. "A Move to Part-time Clergy Sparks Innovation in Congregations." *Faith & Leadership*, March 21, 2017. https://www.faithandleadership.com/move-part-time-clergy-sparks-innovation-congregations.

———. "Pay for a Priest or a Building." *Living Church*, May 19, 2017. http://livingchurch.org/2017/05/19/pay-priest-or-building/.

———. "Retooling for Ministry." *Living Church*, April 18, 2017. http://livingchurch.org/2017/04/18/retooling-ministry/.

———. "Small Rural Church Is Bringing Together People Affected by the Opioid Epidemic." *Faith & Leadership*, November 14, 2017. https://www.faithandleadership.com/small-rural-church-bringing-together-people-affected-opioid-epidemic.

Mander, Brigid. "Small Church Upholds History of Outreach to Make Big Impact on Frontier Town." *Faith & Leadership*, June 27, 2017. https://www.faithandleadership.com/small-church-upholds-history-outreach-make-big-impact-frontier-town.

Manolo, Ricky. *The Liturgy of Life: The Interrelationship of Sunday Eucharist and Everyday Worship Practices*. Collegeville, MN: Liturgical, 2014.

Manson, Jamie. "As US Nones Increase We Must Start Asking Different Questions." *NCRonline*, October 19, 2019. https://www.ncronline.org/news/opinion/grace-margins/us-nones-increase-we-must-start-asking-different-questions.

Mariani, Mike. "The New Generation of Self-Created Communities." *New York Times T-Style Magazine*, January 19, 2020. https://www.nytimes.com/2020/01/16/t-magazine/intentional-communities.html.

Martin, Jessica, and Sarah Coakley, eds. *For God's Sake: Reimagining Priesthood and Prayer in a Changing Church*. Norwich: Canterbury, 2017.

Martos, Joseph. "Can Laypeople Lead a Parish? Look to Louisville for a Thriving Example." *NCRonline*, July 11, 2019. https://www.ncronline.org/news/parish/can-laypeople-lead-parish-look-louisville-thriving-example.

Marty, Martin E. "Malls, Small-Town Stores Are Closing All Across America. And Churches?" *Religion News Service*, August 1, 2017. http://religionnews.com/2017/08/01/malls-small-town-stores-are-closing-all-across-america-and-churches/.

McCann, Adam. "Fastest Growing Cities." *WalletHub*, October 14, 2019. https://wallethub.com/edu/fastest-growing-cities/7010/.

McCarthy, Robert J., and John M. Vitek. *Going, Going, Gone: The Dynamics of Disaffiliation in Young Catholics*. Winona, MN: St. Mary's Press, 2018.

McCaughan, Pat. "Diocese of Los Angeles Heralds Birth of Closed Church as New 'Exploratory Community.'" *Episcopal News Service*, September 5, 2019. https://www.episcopalnewsservice.org/2019/09/05/diocese-of-los-angeles-heralds-rebirth-of-closed-church-as-new-exploratory-community/.

———. "Revival or Resurrection: Eagle Rock Church is Coming Back as 'St. Be's.'" *Episcopal Diocese of Los Angeles*, September 4, 2019. https://diocesela.org/uncategorized/st_bes_eagle_rock_new_opening/.

McClymond, Michael J. *The Devil's Redemption: A New Interpretation of Christian Universalism*. Grand Rapids: Baker Academic, 2018.

McConnell, Jason R. "Pulpits in the Public Square?" *Faith & Leadership*, May 16, 2017. https://www.faithandleadership.com/jason-r-mcconnell-pulpits-public-square.

McDonald, G. Jeffrey. "Simple Church Blends Dinner, Worship and Enterprise to Create a New Model." *Faith & Leadership*, June 13, 2017. https://www.faithandleadership.com/simple-church-blends-dinner-worship-and-enterprise-create-new-model.

———. "Steps for Flourishing in Ministry." *Living Church*, July 8, 2019. https://livingchurch.org/2019/07/08/steps-for-flourishing-in-ministry/.

McGrath, Maggie. "63% of Americans Don't Have Savings Enough to Cover a $500 Emergency." *Forbes*, January 6, 2016. https://www.forbes.com/sites/maggiemcgrath/2016/01/06/63-of-americans-dont-have-enough-savings-to-cover-a-500-emergency/#6d2e13dc4e0d.

McKenna, Kate. "Montreal Church Partners with Circus Company to Help Pay the Bills." *CBC*, February 17, 2017. https://www.cbc.ca/news/canada/montreal/montreal-church-circus-1.5022352.

McLoughlin, William G. *Revivals, Awakenings, and Reform*. Chicago: University of Chicago Press, 1978.

McPartlan, Paul. *The Eucharist Makes the Church*. Edinburgh: T. & T. Clark, 1993.

Mead, Loren B. *More Than Numbers: The Ways Churches Grow*. Lanham, MD: Rowman & Littlefield, 1993.

———. *The Once and Future Church: Reinventing the Church for a New Mission Frontier*. Lanham, MD: Rowman & Littlefield, 1991.

Melosh, Barbara. *Loving and Leaving a Church*. Louisville: Westminster John Knox, 2018.

Mercadante, Linda. *Belief without Borders: Inside the Minds of the Spiritual but Not Religious*. Oxford: Oxford University Press, 2014.

———. "Start by Listening: How Christians Can Find Common Ground with SBNR." *Collegeville Institute*, November 9, 2017. https://collegevilleinstitute.org/bearings/start-listening-sbnr/.

Merritt, Jonatha. "America's Epidemic of Empty Churches." *The Atlantic*, November 28, 2018. https://www.theatlantic.com/ideas/archive/2018/11/what-should-america-do-its-empty-church-buildings/576592/.

Meyer, Holly. "Houses of Worship Do Some Soul-Searching as Their Neighborhoods Change." *Religion News Service*, July 23, 2017. http://religionnews.com/2017/07/23/houses-of-worship-do-some-soul-searching-as-their-neighborhoods-change/.

Michael, Mark. "Review Could Lead to 'Massive Shrinkage' of England's Dioceses." *The Living Church*, May 25, 2020. https://livingchurch.org/2020/05/25/review-could-lead-to-massive-shrinkage-of-english-dioceses/.

Miles, Sara. *City of God*. New York: Jericho, 2014.

———. *Jesus Freak*. San Francisco: Jossey-Bass, 2010.

———. *Take This Bread*. New York: Ballantine, 2007.

Miller, Emily McFarlan. "Minnesota Methodists Say Rebooting Churches Can Be Helpful but Comes with Peril." *Religion News Service*, January 31, 2020. https://

religionnews.com/2020/01/31/lets-try-this-again-minnesota-church-at-center-of-controversy-is-one-of-many-attempting-a-restart/.

Mills, William C. *Losing My Religion: A Memoir of Faith and Finding.* Eugene, OR: Resource, 2019.

Molina, Alejandra. "'Yes in God's Backyard' to Use Church Land for Affordable Housing." *Religion News Service,* November 12, 2019. https://religionnews.com/2019/11/12/yes-in-gods-backyard-to-use-church-land-for-affordable-housing/.

Mork, Joely Johnson. "How Serving Its Community Transformed a Dwindling Church." *Faith & Leadership,* July 11, 2017. https://www.faithandleadership.com/how-serving-its-community-transformed-dwindling-church.

Moskowitz, P. E. *How to Kill a City: Gentrification, Inequality, and the Fight for the Neighborhood.* New York: Nation, 2017.

Mullen, Lincoln. *The Chance of Salvation: A History of Conversion in America.* Cambridge: Harvard University Press, 2017.

Murray, Charles. *Coming Apart: The State of White America.* New York: Crown Forum, 2012.

Nash, Dennison. "'A Little Child Shall Lead Them': A Statistical Test of a Hypothesis that Children Were the Sources of the 'American Religious Revival.'" *Journal for the Scientific Study of Religion* 7.2 (1968) 239–40.

Nash, Dennison, and Peter L. Berger. "Church Commitment in an American Suburb." *Archives de sociologie des religions* 7 (1962) 105–20.

Noem, Stacey. "We Need to Stop Separating Seminarians from Lay Ministers in Formation." *America Magazine,* November 20, 2019. https://www.americamagazine.org/faith/2019/11/20/we-need-stop-separating-seminarians-lay-ministers-formation.

Noll, Mark, et al. *Evangelicals: Who They Have Been, Are Now, and Could Be.* Grand Rapids: Eerdmans, 2020.

Oakes, Kaya. *The Nones Are Alright.* Maryknoll, NY: Orbis, 2015,

———. "An Unlikely Alliance: What Can Nuns and 'Nones' Learn from One Another?" *America,* September 17, 2018. https://www.americamagazine.org/faith/2018/09/04/what-can-nuns-and-nones-learn-one-another.

———. "When Americans Say They Believe in God, What Do They Mean?" *Pew Research Center,* April 25, 2018. http://www.pewforum.org/2018/04/25/when-americans-say-they-believe-in-god-what-do-they-mean/.

Odum, David L. "Reclaiming the Distinctive Gifts of the Small Church." *Faith & Leadership,* May 31, 2016. https://www.faithandleadership.com/dave-odom-reclaiming-distinctive-gifts-small-church.

———. "RIP, Average Attendance." *Faith & Leadership,* August 21, 2014. https://faithandleadership.com/rip-average-attendance.

Olsen, Charles M. "A Resurrection Story." *Alban Weekly,* April 19, 2011. https://alban.org/archive/a-resurrection-story/.

O'Malley, John W. *What Happened at Vatican II.* Cambridge: Belknap, 2010.

Ospino, Hosffman. *Cultural Diversity and Paradigm Shifts in Latino Congregations.* New York: Fordham University Press, 2018.

Owens, L. Roger. "Seminary Students and Their Professor Benefit from the Wisdom of a Local Pastor." *Faith & Leadership,* April 18, 2017. https://www.faithandleadership.com/seminary-students-and-their-professor-benefit-wisdom-local-pastor.

Pappas, Anthony G. *Entering the World of the Small Church*. Landham, MD: Rowman & Littlefield, 2000.

Pascal, Blaise. *Pensées*. New York: Dutton, 1958.

"Patrice L. Fowler-Searcy: You Have to Listen to the Community." *Faith & Leadership*, April 18, 2017. https://www.faithandleadership.com/patrice-l-fowler-searcy-you-have-listen-community.

Pavlovitz, John. "Dear Church, Here's Why People Are Leaving." *John Pavlovitz* (blog), May 14, 2019. https://johnpavlovitz.com/2019/05/14/dear-church-heres-why-people-are-leaving/.

Plekon, Michael. "Before the Storm: Kierkegaard's Theological Experimentation and Preparation before the Attack on the Church." *Faith and Philosophy* 21.1 (January 2004) 45–64.

———. *The Church Has Left the Building*. Eugene, OR: Cascade, 2017.

———. *Hidden Holiness*. Notre Dame, IN: University of Notre Dame Press, 2009.

———. "Kierkegaard at the End: His 'Last' Sermon, Eschatology and the Attack on the Church." *Faith and Philosophy* 17.1 (January 2000) 68–86.

———. *Living Icons: Persons of Faith in the Eastern Church*. Notre Dame, IN: University of Notre Dame Press, 2002.

———. *Saints as They Really Are: Voices of Holiness in Our Time*. Notre Dame, IN: University of Notre Dame Press, 2012.

———. *Uncommon Prayer: Prayer in Everyday Experience*. Notre Dame, IN: University of Notre Dame Press, 2016.

———. *The World as Sacrament: An Ecumenical Path Toward a Worldly Spirituality*, Collegeville, MN: Liturgical, 2017.

Plekon, Michael, et al., eds. *The Church Has Left the Building: Faith, Parish, and Ministry in the Twenty-First Century*. Eugene, OR: Cascade, 2016.

Pound, Jesse. "These 91 Companies Paid No Federal Tax in 2018." *CNBC*, December 17, 2019. https://www.cnbc.com/2019/12/16/these-91-fortune-500-companies-didnt-pay-federal-taxes-in-2018.html.

Preschold-Bell, Rae Jean, and Jason Byassee. *Faithful and Fractured: Responding to the Clergy Health Crisis*. Grand Rapids: Baker Academic, 2018.

"Presidential Approval Ratings—Donald Trump." https://news.gallup.com/poll/203198/presidential-approval-ratings-donald-trump.aspx

Putnam, Robert. *Better Together: Restoring the American Community*. New York: Simon & Schuster, 2004.

———. *Bowling Alone: The Collapse and Revival of American Community*. New York: Simon & Schuster, 2001.

———. *Our Kids: The American Dream in Crisis*. New York: Simon & Schuster, 2016.

Putnam, Robert D., and David E. Campbell. *American Grace*. New York: Simon & Schuster, 2010.

Quinn, Christopher. "Church's Radical Act: Sell Building and Use Money for Outreach." *Atlanta Journal-Constitution*, July 28, 2009. https://www.ajc.com/news/local/church-radical-act-sell-building-use-money-for-outreach/frI9bWnXNopwFmjCOMZX6M/.

Rah, Soong-Chan. *Many Colors: Cultural Intelligence for a Changing Church*. Chicago: Moody, 2010.

———. *The Next Evangelicalism: Freeing the Church from Western Cultural Captivity*. Westmont, IL: InterVarsity, 2009.

Raines, Thom S. "Hope for Dying Churches." *Facts & Trends Newsletter*, January 16, 2018. https://factsandtrends.net/2018/01/16/hope-for-dying-churches/.

"Religious Belief and National Belonging in Central and Eastern Europe." *Pew Research Center*, May 10, 2017. https://www.pewforum.org/2017/05/10/religious-commitment-and-practices/.

"The Religious Typology." *Pew Research Center*, August 29, 2018. http://www.pewforum.org/2018/08/29/the-religious-typology/.

Rendell, Mark. "United Church of Canada Embraces Startups as It Updates Its Social Mission to Engage Millennials." *Globe and Mail*, July 3, 2017. https://beta.theglobeandmail.com/report-on-business/small-business/startups/united-church-of-canada-fostering-startups-amid-shifting-role-of-religion/article35512698/.

"Reported Cull of Bishops, Cathedrals, and Dioceses Is Misleading, Says Cottrell." *Church Times*, May 29, 2020. https://www.churchtimes.co.uk/articles/2020/29-may/news/uk/reported-cull-of-bishops-and-dioceses-is-misleading-says-cottrell.

Rice, R. Alan. "The Demise of Haystacks and the Future of the Rural Church." *Alban Weekly*, June 22, 2017. https://alban.org/2017/06/22/r-alan-rice-the-demise-of-haystacks-and-the-future-of-the-rural-church/.

Riebe, Angie. "Old Church Demolition Saddens and Improves Catholic Community." *AP News*, February 4, 2019. https://www.apnews.com/369c7f07ffcd4322a04945df782b1fb5.

Riess, Jana. "New Study of Millenials and GenZ Points to a 'Massive Realignment.'" *Religion News Service*, January 29, 2018. https://religionnews.com/2018/01/29/new-study-of-millennials-and-genz-points-to-a-massive-religious-realignment-in-america/.

———. "Religious 'Nones' Are Gaining Ground in America and They're Worried about the Economy, Says New Study." *Religion News Service*, November 16, 2017. https://religionnews.com/2017/11/16/religious-nones-are-gaining-ground-in-america-and-theyre-worried-about-the-economy-says-new-study/.

Robinson, Marilynne. *Gilead*. New York: Picador, 2004.

———. *Home*. New York: Picador, 2008.

———. *Lila*. New York: Picador, 2014.

Robinson, Sean. "Megachurch Meeting Reveals that Fired Pastor Faced Two Separate Investigations for Sexual Misconduct." *News Tribune*, September 21, 2018. https://www.thenewstribune.com/news/local/article218827470.html.

Rohr, Richard. *Falling Upwards*. San Francisco: Jossey-Bass, 2011.

———. *Immortal Diamond*. San Francisco: Jossey-Bass, 2013.

Root, Andrew. *Faith Formation in a Secular Age*. Grand Rapids: Baker Academic, 2017.

———. *The Pastor in a Secular Age*. Grand Rapids: Baker Academic, 2019.

Ross, Taylor. "The Severity of Universal Salvation." *Church Life Journal*, June 4, 2019. https://churchlifejournal.nd.edu/articles/the-severity-of-universal-salvation/.

Roxburgh, Alan J. "Attend to What's Happening on the Ground." *Faith & Leadership*, November 27, 2018. https://www.faithandleadership.com/alan-j-roxburgh-attend-whats-happening-ground.

Rumsey, Andrew. *Parish: An Anglican Theology of Place*. London: SCM, 2017.

Ryder, Gina. "Faith and Freelancers: Why Churches Are Turning into Co-working Spaces." *Guardian*, August 28, 2019. https://www.theguardian.com/cities/2019/aug/28/faith-and-freelancers-why-churches-are-turning-into-co-working-spaces.

Sager, Rebecca. *Faith, Politics and Power*. Oxford: Oxford University Press, 2010.

Schaper, Donna. "Remove the Pews and Let Sacred Sites Evolve." *NCRonline*, May 26, 2017. https://www.ncronline.org/blogs/eco-catholic/remove-pews-and-let-sacred-sites-evolve.

Schenk, Christine. "A Parish Is the Body of Christ—Not a Starbucks Franchise." *National Catholic Reporter*, September 15, 2017. https://www.ncronline.org/news/opinion/parish-body-christ-not-starbucks-franchise.

Schjonberg, Mary Frances. "Coffee on the Corner Helps Fort Worth Episcopalians Get to Know, Serve Their Neighbors." *Episcopal News Service*, February 6, 2019. https://www.episcopalnewsservice.org/2019/02/06/coffee-on-the-corner-helps-fort-worth-episcopalians-get-to-know-serve-their-neighbors/.

Schnabel, Landon, and Sean Bock. "The Persistent and Exceptional Intensity of American Religion: A Response to Recent Research." *Sociological Science*, November 27, 2017. https://www.sociologicalscience.com/articles-v4-28-686/.

Schneider, Renee Jones. "Lutherans Work to Shed Stuffy Images and Kick-start Change." *Minneapolis Star Tribune*, July 3, 2017. http://www.startribune.com/lutherans-work-to-shed-stuffy-image-and-kick-start-change/432012663/#1.

Shapiro, Tim, and Kara Faris. *Divergent Church: The Bright Promise of Alternative Faith Communities*. Nashville: Abingdon, 2017.

Shaw, Bob. "Best Path to a Younger Flock? Church Asks Older Members to Worship Elsewhere." *St. Paul Pioneer Press*, January 18, 2020. https://www.duluthnewstribune.com/lifestyle/faith/4871798-Best-path-to-a-younger-flock-Church-asks-older-members-to-worship-elsewhere.

Shellnut, Kate. "#ChurchToo: Andy Savage Resigns from Megachurch Over Past Abuse." *Christianity Today*, March 20, 2018. https://www.christianitytoday.com/news/2018/march/andy-savage-resigns-abuse-megachurch-standing-ovation.html.

———. "James MacDonald Fired from Harvest." *Christianity Today*, February 13, 2019. https://www.christianitytoday.com/news/2019/february/james-macdonald-fired-harvest-bible-chapel.html.

———. "Just Give Me Jesus: A Closer Look at Christians Who Don't Go to Church." *Christianity Today*, April 7, 2017. http://www.christianitytoday.com/gleanings/2017/april/love-jesus-not-church-barna-spiritual-but-not-religious.html.

Shimron, Yonat. "Amid Decline, One Lutheran Church Strives to Live Up to Its Namesake's Spirit." *Religion News Service*, October 16, 2017. http://religionnews.com/2017/10/16/amid-decline-one-lutheran-church-strives-to-live-up-to-its-namesakes-spirit/.

———. "A Church Reborn." *Faith & Leadership*, April 21, 2014. https://www.faithandleadership.com/church-reborn.

———. "Downtown Church Forges New Path When It Decides to Tear Down Two Decaying Buildings." *Faith & Leadership*, December 12, 2017. https://www.faithandleadership.com/downtown-church-forges-new-path-when-it-decides-tear-down-two-decaying-buildings.

———. "Is American Religion Exceptional? Maybe, Maybe Not." *Religion News Service*, November 19, 2018. https://religionnews.com/2018/11/19/is-american-religion-exceptional-maybe-maybe-not/.

———. "Legacy Ministries to Dying Churches Give Congregations a Way to End Well." *Faith & Leadership*, September 5, 2017. https://www.faithandleadership.com/legacy-ministries-dying-churches-give-congregations-way-end-well.

———. "New Poll Shows Growing View That Clergy Are Irrelevant." *Religion News Service*, July 16, 2019. https://religionnews.com/2019/07/16/new-poll-shows-growing-view-that-clergy-are-irrelevant/.

———. "North Carolina Nonprofit Helps Churches Convert Property from Liabilities to Assets." *Faith & Leadership*, February 4, 2020. https://faithandleadership.com/north-carolina-nonprofit-helps-churches-convert-property-liabilities-assets.

———. "PCUSA Faith Community Takes Flight Celebrating Appalachian Music and Culture." *Faith & Leadership*, May 15, 2018. https://www.faithandleadership.com/pcusa-faith-community-takes-flight-celebrating-appalachian-music-and-culture.

———. "Pew Report: Older US Christians Being Quickly Replaced by Young Nones." *Religion News Service*, October 17, 2019. https://religionnews.com/2019/10/17/pew-report-older-u-s-christians-being-quickly-replaced-by-young-nones/.

———. "A Small NC Church Reaches Out in Big Ways." *Faith & Leadership*, December 1, 2014. https://www.faithandleadership.com/small-nc-church-reaches-out-big-ways.

Sierra, Jeremiah. "A Dinner Church Finds a Home in Brooklyn." *On Faith*, July 14, 2014. https://www.faithstreet.com/onfaith/2014/07/14/a-dinner-church-finds-a-home-in-brooklyn/33042.

Simon, Mashaun D. "Church without Walls Offers Unconditional Acceptance to People Who Are Homeless." *Faith & Leadership*, June 25, 2019. https://www.faithandleadership.com/church-without-walls-offers-unconditional-acceptance-people-who-are-homeless.

Sink, Susan. "Loving and Leaving a Church: An Interview with Barbara Melosh." *Bearings Online*, January 17, 2019. https://collegevilleinstitute.org/bearings/loving-and-leaving-a-church/.

Skobtsova, Maria. *Mother Maria Skobtsova: Essential Writings*. Translated by Richard Pevear and Larissa Volokhonsky. Maryknoll, NY: Orbis, 2002.

Smith, C. Christopher. "Cultivating Cultural Proximity." *Christian Century*, May 8, 2019. https://www.christiancentury.org/article/critical-essay/becoming-neighborhood-church.

Smith, Peter. "Bishop Zubik Unveils Parish Reorganization Plans for Pittsburgh Diocese." *Pittsburgh Gazette*, April 28, 2018. http://www.post-gazette.com/local/region/2018/04/28/Roman-Catholic-parishes-mergers-Bishop-Zubik/stories/201804280011.

Sokol, Donna Claycomb, and L. Roger Owens. *A New Day in the City*. Nashville: Abingdon, 2017.

Solomon, Serena. "Fighting Gentrification with the Holy Spirit." *Pacific Standard*, January 1, 2018. https://psmag.com/social-justice/the-holy-ghost-hates-gentrification.

Solzhenitsyn, Alexander. *The Gulag Archipelago*. London: Collins, 1974.

"Soong-Chan Rah: Freeing the Captive Church," *Faith & Leadership*, September 12, 2011. https://www.faithandleadership.com/soong-chan-rah-freeing-captive-church.

Stanton, Allen T. "Are Aging Churches a Bad Thing?" *Ministry Matters*, December 11, 2019. https://www.ministrymatters.com/all/entry/9989/are-aging-churches-a-bad-thing.

———. "The Gifts of a Small Church in a Pandemic." *Faith & Leadership*, May 5, 2020. https://faithandleadership.com/allen-t-stanton-gifts-small-church-pandemic.

———. "Misunderstanding the Small Church." *Ministry Matters*, January 29, 2020. https://www.ministrymatters.com/all/entry/10105/misunderstanding-the-small-church.

———. "OK, Boomer and the Church." *Ministry Matters*, November 26, 2019. https://www.ministrymatters.com/all/entry/9964/ok-boomer-and-the-church.

———. "Rural Congregations Can Thrive beyond Numbers." *Faith & Leadership*, February 19, 2019. https://www.faithandleadership.com/allen-t-stanton-rural-churches-can-thrive-beyond-numbers.

———. "What Can the Rural Church Offer a Declining Community? Hope." *Faith & Leadership*, May 30, 2017. https://www.faithandleadership.com/allen-t-stanton-what-can-rural-church-offer-declining-community-hope.

Steinke, Darcey. *Easter Everywhere*. New York: Bloomsbury, 2007.

Stewart, Ryan. "Is It Good or Bad When Churches Shrink?" *Sojourners*, May 5, 2015. https://sojo.net/articles/it-good-or-bad-when-churches-shrink.

Stiglitz, Joseph. *The Price of Inequality*. New York: Norton, 2012.

Stone, Zara. "How a Spirituality Startup Is Solving Silicon Valley's Religious Apathy." *Forbes*, April 26, 2018. https://www.forbes.com/sites/zarastone/2018/04/26/how-a-spirituality-startups-solving-silicon-valleys-religious-apathy/2/#144ee7cf1ada.

Strickler, Jeff. "Church Finds New Life, Focusing on the 'Congregation' Outside Its Walls." *Faith & Leadership*, October 2, 2018. https://www.faithandleadership.com/church-finds-new-life-focusing-congregation-outside-its-walls.

———. "Minneapolis Congregation Finds New Life through Ancient Practice of Keeping Sabbath." *Faith & Leadership*, March 22, 2016. https://www.faithandleadership.com/minneapolis-congregation-finds-new-life-through-ancient-practice-keeping-sabbath.

Tabor, Nick. "The Evangelist: Can Shane Claiborne's Progressive Version of Evangelical Christianity Catch On With a New Generation?" *Washington Post*, January 6, 2020, https://www.washingtonpost.com/magazine/2020/01/06/can-this-preachers-progressive-version-evangelical-christianity-catch-with-new-generation/.

Taft, Robert F. "Mrs. Murphy Goes to Moscow: Kavanagh, Schmemann, and 'The Byzantine Synthesis.'" *Worship* 85.5 (2011) 386–407.

Taylor, Barbara Brown. *An Altar in the World*. New York: HarperOne, 2008.

———. *Holy Envy*. New York: HarperOne, 2019.

———. *Leaving Church*. New York: HarperOne, 2006.

———. *Walking in the Darkness*. New York: HarperOne, 2012.

Taylor, Charles. *A Secular Age*. Cambridge: Belknap, 2007.

"Theological Education Rebounds, but Fewer Students Enroll." *Insights into Religion*. https://web.archive.org/web/20190331193004/http://www.religioninsights.org/articles/theological-education-rebounds-fewer-students-enroll.

Thornton, Ed. "What Future Does the Parish Have in the 21st Century?" *Church Times*, October 13, 2017. https://www.churchtimes.co.uk/articles/2017/13-october/news/uk/what-future-does-the-parish-have-in-the-21st-century.

Tillard, J. M. R. *Church of Churches*. Collegeville, MN: Liturgical, 1992.

———. *Flesh of Christ, Flesh of the Church.* Collegeville, MN: Liturgical, 2001.

Townsend, Matthew. "Lessons in Humility for a Downtown Parish." *Living Church,* February 20, 2018. https://livingchurch.org/2018/02/20/lessons-in-humility-for-a-downtown-parish/.

"Two Religious Censuses." St. George-in-the-East Church. http://www.stgitehistory.org.uk/media/census.html.

Vance, J. D. *Hillbilly Elegy.* New York: Harper Collins, 2016.

Vanderslice, Kendall. *We Will Feast: Rethinking Dinner, Worship, and the Community of God.* Grand Rapids: Eerdmans, 2019.

Virtue, David W. "Anglican Church in Canada Faces Extinction by 2040, a New Report Reveals." *Virtue Online,* October 5, 2019. https://virtueonline.org/anglican-church-canada-faces-extinction-2040-new-report-reveals.

Voas, David, and Mark Chaves. "Even Intense Religiosity Is Declining in the United States: Comment." *Sociological Science,* November 15, 2018. https://www.sociologicalscience.com/articles-v5-29-694/.

Warren, Tish Harrison. "Willow Creek's Crash Shows Why Denominations Still Matter." *Religion News Service,* March 25, 2019. https://religionnews.com/2019/03/25/willow-creeks-crash-shows-why-denominations-still-matter/.

Wells, Sam. "At the Heart, on the Edge." *Alban Weekly,* November 15, 2019. https://alban.org/2019/11/15/sam-wells-at-the-heart-on-the-edge/.

———. *Face to Face: Meeting Christ in Friend and Stranger.* Nashville: Abingdon, 2020.

———. *A Future That's Bigger Than the Past: Towards the Renewal of the Church.* Norwich, UK: Canterbury, 2019.

———. *Incarnational Ministry.* Grand Rapids: Eerdmans, 2017.

———. *Incarnational Mission.* Grand Rapids: Eerdmans, 2018.

———. "It's About Abundant Life, not Hell-avoidance." *Church Times,* October 6, 2017. https://www.churchtimes.co.uk/articles/2017/6-october/comment/opinion/it-s-about-abundant-life-not-hell-avoidance.

———. *A Nazareth Manifesto.* Oxford: Wiley, 2015.

Wells, Sam, and Sarah Coakley. *Praying for England: Priestly Presence in Contemporary Culture.* London: Continuum, 2008.

"What Are We Paying You For? Shifting the Way We Ask Lay Leadership to Run the Church." *Alban Weekly,* January 13, 2009. https://alban.org/archive/what-are-we-paying-you-for-shifting-the-way-we-ask-lay-leaders-to-run-the-church/.

Wheeler, Barbara G., and Arthur T. Ruger. "Sobering Figures Point to Overall Enrollment Decline." *In Trust* (Spring 2013) 5–11.

Whitehead, Alfred North. *Religion in the Making.* New York: Fordham University Press, 1996.

"Why Americans Go (and Don't Go) to Religious Services." *Pew Forum,* August 1, 2018. http://www.pewforum.org/2018/08/01/why-americans-go-to-religious-services/

"Why America's 'Nones' Left Religion Behind." *Pew Research Center,* August 24, 2016. http://www.pewresearch.org/fact-tank/2016/08/24/why-americas-nones-left-religion-behind/.

Williams, Hattie. "Chelmsford Set to Cut 60 Stipendiary Posts." *Church Times,* June 12, 2020. https://www.churchtimes.co.uk/media/5669489/8204_12-june-2020_nvrte.pdf.

Williams, Rowan. *Christ the Heart of Creation.* London: Bloomsbury, 2018.

Williamson, Kevin D. "The White Ghetto." *National Review*, January 9, 2014. https://www.nationalreview.com/2014/01/white-ghetto-kevin-d-williamson/.

Wilson, Bill. "What Will We See Less of and More of in America's Churches in the 2020s?" *Baptist News Global*, June 29, 2020. https://baptistnews.com/article/what-will-we-see-less-of-and-more-of-in-americas-churches-in-the-2020s/#.XvoM9yhKg2x.

Wooden, Anastacia. "Eucharistic Ecclesiology of Nicolas Afanasiev and Its Ecumenical Significance: A New Perspective." *Journal of Ecumenical Studies* 45 (2010) 543–60.

———. "The Limits of the Church: The Ecclesiological Project of Nicolas Afanasiev." PhD diss., Catholic University of America, 2018.

Worthy, Ariel. "Pastor David Barnhart on What Love Looks Like in Public." *Birmingham Times*, October 11, 2018. https://www.birminghamtimes.com/2018/10/pastor-david-barnhart-on-what-love-looks-like-in-public/.

Wuthnow, Robert. *American Misfits and the Making of Middle-Class Respectability.* Princeton: Princeton University Press, 2017.

———. *The Left Behind: Decline and Rage in Rural America.* Princeton: Princeton University Press, 2018.

———. *Remaking the Heartland: Middle America since the 1950s.* Princeton: Princeton University Press, 2013.

———. *Small-Town America: Finding Community, Shaping the Future.* Princeton: Princeton University Press, 2015.

Wyatt, Tim. "How Rural Churches Are Fighting Stereotypes of Neglect and Decline." *The Church Times*, March 29, 2018. https://www.churchtimes.co.uk/articles/2018/29-march/features/features/how-rural-churches-fighting-stereotypes-neglect-and-decline.

Zauzmer, Julie. "The Circuit Preacher Was an Idea of the Frontier Past. Now It's the Cutting-edge Response to Shrinking Churches." *Washington Post*, September 23, 2019. https://www.washingtonpost.com/religion/the-circuit-preacher-was-an-idea-of-the-frontier-past-now-its-the-cutting-edge-response-to-shrinking-churches/2019/09/23/e3cced32-d348-11e9-9343-40db57cf6abd_story.html.

Zizioulas, John. *Being as Communion: Studies in Personhood and the Church.* Crestwood, NY: St. Vladimir's Seminary Press, 1985.

———. *Eucharist, Bishop, Church: The Unity of the Church in the Divine Eucharist and the Bishop during the First Three Centuries.* Brookline, MA: Holy Cross Orthodox Press, 2001.

Printed in Great Britain
by Amazon